D0778546

# ACES AND AIRCRAFT OF WORLD WAR I

## Christopher Campbell

Illustrated by the author
and John W Wood

TREASURE PRESS

*Title Page:* Manfred *Freiherr* von Richthofen

*Below:* RFC pilots drawn up in front of a DH2 at the Fourth Army Aircraft Park, Beauval, France, 1916

**For Clare**

First published in Great Britain in 1981 by Blandford Press Ltd

This edition published in 1984 by Treasure Press
59 Grosvenor Street
London W1

© 1981 Christopher Campbell

ISBN 0 907812 62 7

All rights reserved. No part of this book may be reproduced or transmitted in any form or by any means, electronic or mechanical, including photocopying, recording or any information storage and retrieval system, without permission in writing from the Publisher.

Printed in Hong Kong

Designed by Roger Hammond

Photographs reproduced by kind permission of the following sources:
Fleet Air Arm Museum: 13, 54, 75—Imperial War Museum: 4/5, 8/9, 10/11, 14, 18/19, 23, 26, 29, 31, 32, 33, 44/45, 49, 52, 56/57, 61, 68, 76/77, 78, 81, 100, 101, 104/5, 106, 113, 114, 117, 123, 124, 125, 128, 129, 132, 133, 136/7, 140, 141—Smithsonian Institution: 15—Musée de l'Air: 24/25, 37, 65, 69, 92/93, 96, 97, 135—J W R Taylor: 43—Thijs Postma: 65, 68, 90, 91—Canadian Armed Forces Museum: 77, 78—E G Gee: 85, 88, 140—Musée Royale de l'Armée Belge: 112—Science Museum (photos by Simon Dunstan): 118, 119—Royal Air Force Museum: 143—Topham: 6/7.

# Contents

Ground crew attend a
French Morane Parasol
two-seater, 1916

# Prologue

In June 1914 the entire Military Wing of Britain's Royal Flying Corps gathered at Netheravon on Salisbury Plain to assess the efficiency of its seven hundred officers and men, thirty-one aircraft and six squadrons. The star was the latest Blériot Experimental 2 from the Royal Aircraft Factory, the BE2c with a 70-hp engine, new wings introducing ailerons and dihedral, and modified tail surfaces. The first example was flown in from Farnborough by Major Sefton Brancker. He had climbed to 2000 feet and, without touching the controls again until his landing approach, wrote a reconnaissance report along the way, so great was the new machine's inherent stability. The primary military function of aircraft was then reconnaissance, requiring stability, not manouevrability.

On 28 June the Austro-Hungarian Empire's Crown Prince was assassinated in Sarajevo, Serbia by Bosnian nationalists. On 2 July the Netheravon camp broke up and the pilots returned to their squadrons. At the end of the month the sixth instruction course at the Central Flying School, Upavon was approaching written examinations; the pupils had over twenty-four flying hours each and were anticipating the award of the Military Wing's pilot's badge, the RFC crest held in the outstretched wings of a swift.

On 28 July Austria-Hungary declared war on Serbia: the allies of both took arms. On 3 August German troops crossed into Belgium. All the pupil pilots at Upavon were summoned to the lecture room and told by the Commandant, Capt G M Paine RN, that all men considered sufficiently advanced would be posted immediately to active service squadrons.

A day later Britain was at war. In France, Germany, Austria and Russia pilots were flying off on reconnaissance missions as the great armies manoeuvred and clashed below them: the first war in the air had begun. The value of the aircraft as a weapon of war was still hardly appreciated; but within little over a year it would introduce a revolutionary aspect to machine warfare—the struggle for air superiority.

# Introduction

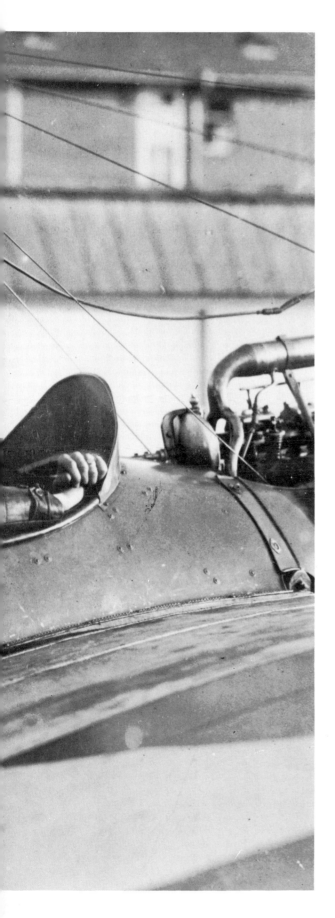

HIGH up in the attics of the Imperial War Museum in London, preserved in mothballs as part of the reserve uniform collection, there is a unique piece of military tailoring. It is a tailor's trial for the dress uniform of an officer of the Military Wing, Royal Flying Corps, dated 1912. There is no evidence that it was ever officially worn or indeed approved, but simply as a fashionable military tailor's exercise it presents a fascinating piece of historical evidence.

The tunic is cut from blue-grey material with a black 'plastron' front in the manner of a lancer regiment. The tailor offered a choice of headgear, a conventional forage cap and more significantly a red *képi*, piped in gold for officers and black for other ranks.

The *képi* had gone out of fashion very suddenly indeed in 1870 when even the British and American Armies went into Prussian-style spiked helmets in the time-worn tradition of adopting the uniform of the last victorious nation. The *képi* was all things French but in 1912 France really did lead the world in this one respect—in the air.

The achievements of the Wright brothers had been recognized first in France and ignored in the United States. In 1909 Louis Blériot flew the English Channel and the same year his triumph, the first great flying event which really marked the arrival of the aircraft as a practical machine was held at Reims and dominated by French machines. 1909 was the year that 'Aileron', 'Fuselage' and 'Nacelle' were admitted to the Oxford Dictionary—all words of French origin.

In the decade before World War 1 British and American newspaper proprietors repeatedly reached into their pockets to pay a Frenchman for some new prize or a new record broken. Paris was ringed with small workshops turning out airframes and aero-engines. If you wanted to learn to fly, if you wanted to learn how to build an airframe or learn the mysteries of the rotary engine—you went to France.

In the skies at least, 1913 was France's *Glorieuse Année*. In August Adolphe Pégoud made the first parachute jump from an aircraft in Europe and in September he made the first intentional aerobatics, which a year later would become translated into the necessary manoeuvres for wartime flying. In 1913 Frenchmen were making world-beating long distance international flights in French machines, including non-stop across the Mediterranean. The world records for 1913 tell their own story. Speed: 126.67 mph by M Prévost of France on a Deperdussin at Reims. Distance: 634.54 miles for distance over a closed circuit by A Seguin of France on a Henri Farman at Buc. Height: 20,079 feet by G Legagneux of France on a Nieuport at St Raphael.

No wonder that unknown Savile Row tailor ordered a *képi* to crown his creation.

The tunic of the mysterious RFC uniform borrows two images from central Europe, the 'Austrian knot' of a hussar on each cuff and the

Weeks before the outbreak of war, men of the fledgeling German *Fliegertruppe* prepare for a flight in a *Taube* monoplane

*Right:* Proposal for a full dress uniform for the Royal Flying Corps Military Wing, 1913. The cut of the tunic was a clear reference to cavalry tradition and the fact that the tailor proposed a *képi* was an act of deference to French predominance in the air, although a forage cap was also offered. The uniform was not adopted and the eventual RFC full-dress uniform was a much simpler affair. The original is in the Imperial War Museum in London.
*Far right:* Wiltshire rustics seem undisturbed by the arrival of two Blériot Type XIs of the RFC Military Wing during 1913 manoeuvres on Salisbury Plain

plastron front to the tunic made popular first in Western Europe by Napoleon's Polish lancers and adopted by Britain's first lancer regiment in 1816. Both were instantly recognizable in 1912 as pertaining to cavalry. The RFC, in spite of their noisy, smelly aeroplanes, could be as dashing and fashionable as any other regiment in the British Army. Here were the new cavalry of the air.

In the end it was different. The bizarre uniform was consigned to the mothballs and the RFC went into a simple blue tunic and forage cap for full dress. The famous 'maternity jacket' service dress formalized in 1913 kept the lancer image but was cut in the drab serge cloth of modern warfare.*

### Great Britain

Military flying in Great Britain began in 1878 with the construction of a balloon at Woolwich Arsenal. In 1880 a balloon section of the Royal Engineers took part in the Aldershot manoeuvres and during the next twenty years balloons accompanied several expeditions to the outposts of Empire. In 1890 the Balloon Section was formally established as a unit of the Royal Engineers and a factory was set up at South Farnborough in 1894. Four sections operated with some success in South Africa during the war of 1899-1901. The factory grew steadily in size becoming HM Balloon Factory in 1908, the Army Aircraft Factory in 1911 and 'Royal Aircraft Factory' in 1912.

Army experiments with dirigible airships began as early as 1902 but it was not until 1907 that the first named *Nulli Secundus* made a successful sustained flight. Meanwhile between 1906-09 a trickle of funds sponsored the heavier-than-air experiments of S F Cody and J W Dunne in their efforts to produce practical powered aircraft. In October 1908 Cody's enormous 'British Army Aeroplane No 1' droned 1390 feet across Laffan's Plain at Farnborough but the War Office cut off funds after a grand total of £2500 had been spent.

Then in October 1910 the Balloon Section of the Royal Engineers was allotted funds to 'afford opportunities for aeroplaning'.

---

*The phrase was based on the style of then fashionable 'Maternity Suits' for women which buttoned under the arm.

On 28 February 1911 came the Army Order which brought into existence the Royal Engineer Air Battalion with No 1 (Airship) Company commanded by Captain E M Maitland and No 2 (Aeroplane) Company at Larkhill on Salisbury Plain commanded by Captain J D B Fulton.

Volunteers had to learn to fly at their own expense —if they were successful the government would repay them £75—and one of the first pilots, Lt B A Cammell, even brought his own Blériot XI to join the six Bristol Boxkites, a Henri Farman and an old reconstructed Howard Wright biplane that formed the equipment of Britain's first air force.

On 18 December 1911 the Committee of Imperial Defence established an eight man technical sub-committee to examine the prospects of establishing an efficient aerial service. Their recommendations published at the end of February 1912 were the formation of a 'Flying Corps' with separate Military and Naval Wings, a reserve of trained pilots, retention of the Royal Aircraft Factory and the setting up of a Central Flying School with an Air Committee to hold the ring between War Office and Admiralty.

The opening words of the committee report read 'The British Aeronautical Service should be regarded as one and should be designated "The Flying Corps" '. From the start however this admirable unity proved as fragile as a contemporary aeroplane.

The 'Royal Flying Corps' was constituted by a Royal Warrant on 13 April 1912 with a 'Military Wing' and a 'Naval Wing'. A month later it absorbed the old Air Battalion and its reserve with £308,000 voted by Parliament for its establishment. The problems of the fledgeling air force were already considerable but a major new stumbling block lay in old and irreconcilable jealousies between the War Office and Admiralty.

The Royal Navy already had some years of experience in the air. In 1908 Captain Murray Sueter, a torpedo expert, was appointed to be the first Inspector of Airships on the Admiralty Staff. In 1909, £35,000 was allocated for the construction of a naval airship but its début was disastrous. The Vickers-built rigid, named ominously *Mayfly*, broke its back before even taking off for its first flight. One old Admiral took one look and called it 'the work of a lunatic'. The beginning of heavier than air flying in the Royal Navy was somewhat more successful.

In February 1911 Francis McClean offered the Admiralty two Short biplanes for volunteer officers to learn to fly at his flying school at Eastchurch in Kent. Four officers graduated in six winter weeks and by the beginning of the year Eastchurch had become the Admiralty's own *de facto* flying school. The 'Naval Wing, Royal Flying Corps' came into existence on 13 April 1912 formally recognized by Admiralty Circular Letter 22 on 11 July 1912 but from the outset the regulations tended to be treated by the Navy with a Nelsonian blind eye. Eastchurch under the command of C R Samson was an Admiralty private preserve and Sueter, now Director of the Admiralty Air Department, jealously guarded naval interests with the encouragement of the First Lord of the Admiralty Winston Churchill. The Navy also set the pace in using aircraft for fighting, experimenting with machine-guns, bomb and torpedo dropping while the Army stuck rigidly to reconnaissance. The Admiralty also tended to patronize British independent manufacturers such as Shorts and Sopwith and energetically buy aircraft from France and even Germany for comparison while the War Office favoured the docile products of the Royal Aircraft Factory.

The only real common ground was the Central Flying School at Upavon in Wiltshire commanded by a naval officer, Capt G M Paine, assisted by a Major of the Royal Scots Fusiliers named Hugh Montague Trenchard, and here the pilot training for each Wing was the same, with each expected to act as a reserve for the other in the event of war.

The uneasy marriage was sundered on 1 July 1914. The Military Wing of the RFC kept the title Royal Flying Corps and the Naval Wing formally adopted the name that had been in unofficial use since the beginning—Royal Naval Air Service.

As the official historian said . . . 'the national air force was broken in two. The Army and the Navy had been willing enough to co-operate but the habits of life and thought of a soldier and a sailor are incurably different.' Nowhere perhaps were these differences so marked and passions more easily roused than in the question of uniforms.

A notable social historian of costume* has divided the function of any military uniform into three basic principles—Hierarchy, Seduction and Utility. From 1900 onwards 'Utility' came out on top in the uniforms of most European metropolitan armies as tradition collided with machine warfare, as it had long since done in their colonies, spurred by the development of machine-guns and quick firing artillery.

Utility had certainly triumphed in the uniform of a British naval officer and Hierarchy reduced to a simple and elegant pattern of rank cuff-rings. Very largely this pattern was copied around the world. Arguably, the stylish double-breasted eight-buttoned 'Monkey Jacket' remained seductive. The British Army incorporated the lessons of colonial wars and South Africa in the highly utilitarian 1902 pattern of khaki service dress with its 'forage-cap', patch pockets and puttees. 'Hierarchy' in the Edwardian Army still pertained very much to the horse—the officers' service dress of 1902 featured breeches in Bedford Cord, riding boots and a khaki tunic flared at the skirts with massively capacious pockets, plus the Sam Browne belt with its vestigial sword slings. A system of lace cuff rings, pips and crowns indicated rank with a different pattern for Scottish regiments. In 1913 a lapel tunic with collar and tie was introduced for commissioned officers much to the consternation of the traditionalists, but the effect was still one of horsey squirearchical elegance and again this officer's uniform was eventually copied around the world.

The quest for a distinctive uniform for a British air service began with the Air Battalion of the Royal Engineers. They wore RE service dress with no official distinctive badges but in 1911 began an urgent search for a form of working clothing which would allow the wearer to be recognized as an aviator and officer. The three traditional principles of uniform development came under considerable strain in the new airborne environment—'Utility' triumphed in a leather motoring coat worn in flight but a faint aroma of burnt castor-oil rotary engine lubricant did little for 'Seduction'. 'Hierarchy' too was under pressure as flying skill or lack of it was a great leveller, and rank badges did not last long stitched to a leather jacket. Although no patterns of special working clothing for the Air Battalion were officially sealed, a uniform of fur cap with ear flaps, gauntlets and leggings was proposed with a double breasted leather jacket with rank badges on the shoulder. This is sometimes taken as the basis for the distinctive RFC Military Wing tunic of 1913.

Title page of the RFC Military Wing's first training manual, issued in June 1914

The képied-lancer tunic is another source for the 'special pattern' tunic. A journalist calling himself 'Union Jack' visited the Central Flying School at Upavon a few days before the official opening on 19 June 1912 and reported:

'The uniform of the Flying Corps has not yet been issued, but I learn it is to be French-grey in colour and that the tunic will be of the lancer shape, but with no buttons. Knee breeches with leggings, and an ordinary military cap with the aeroplane as a badge complete the outfit.'†

The aeroplane badge never appeared—the RFC, Military Wing, badge was a development of the Royal Engineer's with a monogram inside a laurel wreath. The colour 'French grey' is highly significant as this blue-grey shade re-emerged in 1919 as the colour of the Royal Air Force service dress and again became a world wide air force trademark even adopted by the German Luftwaffe of World War II.

The lancer cut of the tunic was perpetuated in the double-breasted plain-fronted jacket of the RFC Military Wing authorized in Army Order 378 of November 1913. The cut of the tunic was basically the same for officers and other ranks although with a variation in the quality of cloth and tailoring. Cuffs for other ranks, were plain, with a special fastening tab for officers, later pointed. Other ranks wore a dark blue shoulder title with ROYAL FLYING CORPS embroidered in white and officers wore the letters R.F.C. in gilt metal on a curved bar on the shoulder straps below the embroidered rank badges. No collar badges were authorized although officers frequently transferred their full dress badges to the collar of the service dress.

This jacket caused quite a stir at the time of its introduction yet it made remarkably practical concessions to utility. The *Tailor and Cutter* in a retrospective look at flying clothing could say in 1940 'Why did the RAF decide to scrap the old RFC uniform? We can forgive their choice of blue in place of khaki. Yet there is a lack of imagination in allowing a uniform, original and distinctive to be superseded by a copy of the military style. It was liked by those who wore it and is remembered with a certain sentiment. No superfluous pockets plaster the façade, nothing is caught up on the plain surface. The overlapping front affords protection and no tie need be worn.' Working around aircraft these were matters of prime consideration although officers perpetuated wearing Sam Brownes with their slings and hooks until the introduction of the Royal Air Force uniform in 1918 with its integral belt.

The 1913 service dress was completed for officers by 'Austrian pattern' cap with bronze RFC badge, Bedford cord breeches, drab putties and brown ankle boots. Officers seconded for duty with the

---

*James Laver, *British Military Uniforms*, Penguin, 1948.

†Quoted in J W R Taylor, *C.F.S. Birthplace of Air Power*, Putnam, 1958.

Royal Naval Air Service
(Nº 2 Squadron)

Royal Flying Corps wore the full dress, undress and mess dress of their permanent unit.

The CID's Aerial Navigation Committee's report of February 1912 recommended in two clauses:

**158:** The sub-committee recommend that officers of the Royal Navy and the Army should wear their naval or military uniform with the addition of the flying badge.

**161:** The Flying Badge should consist of a brooch or embroidered pattern about three inches long of the design of a pair of wings (or similar design). It should be worn on all occasions in uniform on the left breast—above medals or ribbons embroidered in the case of service dress, metal brooch in other orders of dress.

After King George V had given his consent in June 1912, Army Order 40 of February 1913 authorized a flying badge for qualified Military Wing pilots in gilt metal for full dress and embroidered on blue cloth for service dress. The design was the RFC cap badge mounted between two outspread wings, based on those of a swift.*

The Admiralty reacted indignantly, piqued that they were not consulted before the RFC Military Wing badge was submitted to the King. Typically Murray Sueter began a search for a quite distinct flying badge for qualified pilots of the Naval Wing, and the search was made more urgent by the fact that Military Wing pilots would be sporting their flying badge to a levée at Upavon on 13 February 1913. The naval pilots had to attend without such distinctions—the first embroidered badge, an anchor between wings, commissioned from the famous typographer and graphic designer Eric Gill, was rejected in October 1913. The commission (worth 25 guineas) went out again to an artist named

* Following the formation of the RFC, maintaining the flow of 'suitable candidates for commissions' was something of a problem. It was recalled by Air Chief Marshal Hugh Dowding, in 1915 a Lieutenant Colonel in charge of recruitment, 'The only impression that remained in his mind of that time was his failure to get from the headmasters of the better known public schools the response he hoped for. . . . even his own school was not at all helpful. "The fact was that, in modern argot" he ruefully recalled "the Royal Flying Corps was distinctly non-U".' (*Dowding and the Battle of Britain*, Robert Wright, Macdonald, 1969.)

Petty Officers and Officers of No 2 Squadron RNAS, France, 1915, wearing a mixture of navy-blue and khaki

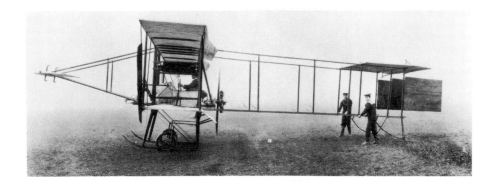

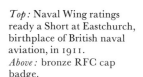

*Top:* Naval Wing ratings ready a Short at Eastchurch, birthplace of British naval aviation, in 1911.
*Above:* bronze RFC cap badge.
*Above right:* RFC Military Wing breast badge authorised in February 1913. A smaller gilt metal version was worn on the dark-blue full dress uniform.
*Right:* Cloth breast badge designed for the RFC Naval Wing by Eric Gill in 1912. The Public Records Office, London has the original sample and a die for striking a metal version.
*Below:* Claude Grahame-White joined the RNAS in 1914 as a Flight-Commander. Note eagle on cap and sleeve

Alexander Fisher, who produced a bird badge. It 'looked like a goose' according to Sueter's autobiography and Fisher's badge was rejected in favour of a Napoleonic gold eagle based on a brooch bought by Sueter's wife in Paris. In December Sueter 'took this eagle brooch to the Admiralty to show to Mr Churchill and Admiral Prince Louis of Battenberg. They much preferred it to the goose design of the artist and adopted it for the badge of the Royal Naval Air Service.* Only with difficulty was the First Sea Lord dissuaded from paying Fisher 5 guineas.

In May 1914 Sueter set out in an Admiralty minute the basis of a uniform for the Royal Naval Air Service:

**Working dress for officers:**
Naval Monkey Jacket,
Blue Breeches,
Uniform black lace boots,
Blue putties,
White flannel shirt,
Soft white linen collar and black tie, the collar to be fastened by a gold pin passed under the tie.

---

*Murray Sueter, *Noahs and Airmen*, Sir Issaac Pitman and Sons, 1928.

**Flying Uniform:**
Brown leather cap or helmet,
White sweater and scarf,
Leather overcoat with sleeves,
Blue overcoat,
Fur or leather gloves,
Brown leather trousers (optional).

Ratings were to be dressed in the naval uniform of their rating with special badges based on the eagle in cloth to be worn on the left arm. A rating's cap band emblazoned with the words ROYAL FLYING CORPS has survived but there is no evidence it was ever issued.

At this stage the Naval Wing was not ranked with the 'executive' or fighting branch of the Navy and officers were not entitled to wear the executive curl on their cuff rings until July 1914. By then at last, on 1 July, the Royal Flying Corps and the Royal Naval Air Service were officially established as separate entities. At the same time on 26 June Admiralty Orders authorized dress regulations for the RNAS.

The dress proposals in Sueter's minute of May were adopted with the addition of the eagle in gilt on the left sleeve. The anchor on cap badge, buttons, epaulette and sword belt was replaced by the eagle. Working clothing at this stage, as in the RFC, was still largely a matter of improvization and private purchase. (For British flying services uniforms see pages 30, 52, 54, 58, 62, 63, 75, 114, 138, 142.)

**France**
As Britain was the greatest naval power on the eve of war, France was the centre of world aviation. The first flying instruction under military auspices took place in March 1910 and a certain *Lieutenant* Camerman was the first soldier to qualify for the brevet of the Aéro-Club de France. The first military brevet proper was awarded to *Capitaine* Tricornot de Rose in March 1911. By then military pilots were taking active part in all the important flying displays and their participation in the *Grandes Manoeuvres* of September 1910 had been a great success. Useful loads had been taken aloft including still and movie cameras and some intrepid pilots were taking pistols and carbines up with them. Until October 1910 military aviation had been split between the balloon section or *Corps d'Aérostation* of the Engineers and the Artillery but on 22 October the service was granted a degree of autonomy within the War Ministry with the creation of the *Inspection Permanente de l'Aéronautique* with *Général* Roques as its first head. In October/November 1911 the first *Concours Militaire* was held and the competition was won by a Nieuport flown by the American Charles Weymann. Orders for ten Nieuports followed and the robust French aero industry got into its stride meanwhile amply supplying the Army's needs. In 1913 not a single airframe or engine was imported into France. The same year France sold overseas 285 aircraft and over a hundred tons of spares. The

*Service des Fabrications de l'Aéronautique* was set up to control technical development and purchasing policy. The first five *escadrilles* formed early in 1912 had grown to twenty one *escadrilles* and two *escadrilles de cavalerie* on the outbreak of war, with a nominal strength of six aircraft each.

The French Navy had also been following aviation developments with interest. On 12 March 1912 a *Commandement Supérieur de l'Aviation* was established within the Admiralty with a tiny naval *Service Aéronautique* under its command equipped mainly with single-seat flying boats. On the outbreak of war the French Army's *Service d'Aviation Militaire* could muster some 138 front-line aircraft and the naval *Service Aéronautique* 14 seaplanes, although France's aero-industrial base gave adequate room for an immediate expansion.

The first French pilots of 1910 wore the uniforms of their various original units—then with the establishment of the Inspectorate of Military Aeronautics at the end of the year, a uniform was authorized based directly on that of the engineers. Balloon personnel wore dark blue *groupe* numbers on scarlet collar patches and on the *képi* and for flying personnel the colours were reversed.

In 1914 special insignia were introduced for qualified pilots—a winged five-pointed star collar flash and a winged propeller to be worn on a brassard on the left sleeve. These were gold for officers and in a combination of red and white cloth for other ranks (pages 38, 66, 70, 94, 98).

## Germany

Military aeronautics began in Germany when the Prussian Army established a balloon detachment in 1884, initially attached to the railway troops. By 1901 it had grown into a fully-fledged *Luftschiffer Bataillon* with two companies. On 2 July 1900 *Graf* Zeppelin's first rigid airship *LZ1* emerged from its floating hangar on the Bodensee and made a controlled flight lasting 17 minutes. *LZ1* was broken up in 1901 and it was not until 1905 that Zeppelin began construction of *LZ2*. His second airship was destroyed on her second flight but undeterred the Count put the last of his private fortune into *LZ3* which achieved a record flight of eight hours. The German Army was sufficiently impressed to agree to purchase a Zeppelin if it could pass certain tests. *LZ4* was completed in June 1908 but during its Army trials it was wrecked in a storm. At last in March 1909 the earlier *LZ3* was accepted by the Army and commissioned as *Zeppelin Luftschiff I*, the first of many more.

The commercial success of Zeppelin's airships meanwhile attracted the interest of the German Navy, who trained their first crews aboard ships of DELAG, the airship transport company set up in 1909. The first Navy airship was ordered on 24 April 1912.

In spite of several disasters, Zeppelin's extraordinary aircraft had caught the imagination of the German public and General Staff alike and overshadowed heavier than air flying. Nevertheless in

During the manoeuvres of 1912, the traditional reconnaissance arm of the French army meets the new: Hussars clatter through a northern French town while a Lebaudy dirigible drones above. France meanwhile was the world centre of heavier than air aviation

The Bavarian army operated several pusher types built before the war by the Munich concern of Otto. Here an example takes off from a rain-soaked wooden runway soon after the outbreak of war

autumn 1909 the first German flying meeting took place at the new airfield of Johannistal bei Berlin. Names such as Euler, Rumpler, Albatros and DFW sprung up on the wooden hangars, and while France monopolized the technology of the lightweight rotary engine, Mercedes were building excellent water-cooled in-line aero engines in some quantity. The Mercedes-powered bird-like *Taube* tractor monoplanes, with their strong echoes of Otto Lilienthal's gliders represented the first German type to go into large scale production between 1910 and 1913. The *Taube* in fact originated in Austria, but they were built in quantity by Rumpler, Albatros, DFW, Aviatik and Jeannin for private customers and later for the Army itself.

The training of volunteer officer pilots began in July 1910 at Döberitz and, a few months later, the purchase of seven aeroplanes for the Army was

officially sanctioned including *Taube*s and some French types. On 1 April 1911 an *Inspektion des Militar Luft und Kraftfahrwesens* was established and more aircraft were purchased while the debate continued within the War Ministry on the allocation of resources. The supremacy of the expanding *Luftschiffertruppe* and their Zeppelins was now questioned by the obvious potential of heavier than air machines. On 1 April a training and experimental establishment for military aviation (*Lehr und Versuchsaustalt für das Militärflugwesen*) was formed and disbanded again on 29 June with orders to form 'Flying Troops' with a total strength of 332 men including Saxon and Würtemberg units.

In 1912 plans for small battlefield reconnaissance airships were dropped in favour of aeroplanes. On 1 October 1912 the Döbertiz establishment was expanded into a *Fliegertruppe* attached to the

*Pionier Gardekorps* and on 1 October 1913, *Oberst* von Eberhardt became the first *Inspecteur der Fliegertruppe* when *Idflieg* was established and four *Flieger Bataillone* of three Companies each were formed (*Nr1* to *Nr4*) based on garrison towns across the *Reich*. A Saxon unit formed the 3rd Company of *Flieger Bataillone Nr1*.

The Bavarian Army formed a two-company-strong *Flieger Kompanie* at the same time. In the event of war a number of mobile *Feldflieger Abteilung* would be formed from these garrison units to serve with the Army in the field. Such service was almost completely envisaged to be Army and Corps HQ reconnaissance with some artillery co-operation by unarmed aircraft although some experiments had been made taking machine-guns aloft by 1914. On mobilization they could call on 246 aircraft, half of these *Taube* types, and 254 pilots and 271 observers.

The German Navy was also committed to big airships before the war and in 1913 began a large-scale airship expansion programme but it did not entirely neglect the heavier than air side. On 10 March 1911 *Marine Oberinginieur* Carl Loew gained a Flying Certificate having trained at the Albatros *Fliegerschule*. He was soon followed by five other officers to be the first naval flying centre established at Putzig near Danzig, on the Baltic. In June 1913 the *Marine Luftschiffabteilung* and *Marine Fliegerabteilung* were formally separated controlling airships and aeroplanes respectively. Experiments were conducted with seaplanes and several British and American types were bought for comparative trials. By 1914 flying stations were established at Kiel, Heligoland, Putzig and Warnemunde. A volunteer Naval Flying Corps was based on Johannistal bei Berlin—and in the Far East at Kiauo-Chow there

*Above far left:* Field-grey M.1910 tunic and shako in cloth cover of an *Unteroffizier* of *Flieger Bataillon Nr 2* of 1914.
*Left:* From left: *Luftschiffer* shoulder strap 1887; *Fliegertruppe* shoulder strap 1915; Officer's shoulder strap 1914 on blue base colour of *Bataillon Nr 4*; Prussian pilot's badge and Bavarian Observer's badge.
*Above:* Officers and men of *Flieger Bataillon Nr 2* pose proudly in front of a *Taube* at Königsberg, summer 1913

was a biplane with a naval officer to fly it. On mobilization the *Marine Fl Abt* had only twenty aircraft and a handful of trained pilots and no trained observers.

The development of German flying uniforms went back to the establishment of the original *Luftschiffer Abteilung* in 1887 out of the balloon detachment of the railway troops. They wore the uniform of *Pionier Gardekorps*, Guard Engineers, with a yellow 'L' on red shoulder flaps and from 1895 onwards the *Jäger* shako as headgear. In 1911 the shoulder strap became light grey and the letter 'L' with a battalion number (1 to 5) inscribed in red.

At first officers attached to the Experimental Flying Troop establishment kept the uniforms of their former unit. NCOs and other ranks were issued with *Luftschiffer-Abt* light-grey shoulder tabs. Then from 1 October 1912 officers were instructed to wear *Luftschiffer* uniform without shoulder strap insignia.

At the beginning of October 1913 the four Prussian *Flieger* battalions were formed and for other ranks a red winged propeller was added above the battalion number on the shoulder straps. For officers these were edged in white, red, yellow and blue for Battalions 1–4 respectively on the base colour of mouse grey. Officers wore the winged propeller badge in gilt and later grey metal on the straps as did officers attached to the *Fliegertruppe* who retained their original regimental uniforms.

The M.1910 Field Uniform featured scarlet piping on the field-grey tunic front and trouser seams, black piping around collar and cuffs. The field cap and officer's peaked cap had a black band piped with scarlet around the crown, with Reich and Prussian state cockades. The Saxon company wore a similar uniform to the Prussian, but with Saxon national insignia and a Saxon star on the shako.

The shako had a cloth cover. Officers wore a single silver *litzen* (lace braid) on a black velvet collar patch edged in scarlet and two *litzen* on the 'Swedish-pattern' cuffs. For other ranks these were in white embroidery. The Bavarian *Fliegerkompanie* wore a similar uniform but with their own state cockade and two collar *litzen*. On 21 January 1913 the Prussian breast badge for qualified pilots was introduced showing in relief a *Taube* monoplane flying over a landscape contained in a laurel and oak leaf wreath with the Prussian royal crown at the top. The Bavarian badge was similar but surmounted by the Bavarian crown. Observers were granted a badge on 21 January 1914 with a black and white chequer on a red square in enamel mounted in the same wreath with the Prussian and Bavarian distinctions. Naval pilots were granted a gold badge in June 1913 with an eagle in flat relief flying over a seascape (pages 43, 46, 50, 102, 110, 123, 126, 130).

**Austria-Hungary**

The *Taube* types which dominated German pre-war flying originated in Austria. Dr Igo Etrich had begun his experiments in 1904 in Bohemia and his

Army and Navy officers gather for the first Austro-Hungarian military flying course held at Wiener Neustadt in April 1911. The aircraft is an Etrich *Taube*

first *Taube* proper flew at Wiener Neustadt in November 1909 with an Austro-Daimler engine. The sprawling multi-national Hapsburg Empire had only a small industrial base, but had by 1914 several airframe and aero-engine manufacturers within its boundaries and licence tie-ups with German manufacturers. In June 1912 a central aeronautical committee was formed under the presidency of Prince Furstenburg. On their recommendation an engineer officer was promoted to *Oberstleutnant* and appointed to command the *K u K Luftfahrtruppen*. He was a Croat named Emil Uzelac and at the age of 45 he learned to fly and with the slenderest of resources began to organize an air force. In February 1914, his command was formed into a battalion of four companies stationed at Vienna, Cracow, Sarajevo and Goerz. On mobilization their total strength was 36 machines, mostly Etrich *Tauben* and Lohner-Daimler *Pfielflieger*.

Several officers of the *K u K Kriegsmarine* learned to fly in Britain and France in 1909 including *Linienschiffleutnant* Viktor Klobucar. He set up an experimental station near Pola which transferred to the island of Santa Catarina in Pola harbour itself in 1911. A naval technical committee under his presidency tested several seaplanes either built in the Pola naval arsenal or bought from Austria, French and American manufacturers. By January 1913 the Pola station had four French Donnet-Levêques, two Curtiss flying boats and four Lohners. During that year the Donnet-Levêques flew operationally with the 1st Battleship Division off Albania. Meanwhile a temporary base was established in Cattaro Bay to support them and a training station established on the island of Cosada, outside Pola. On 1 June 1914 the Pola station abandoned its experimental role and became directly operational under the command of the base commander. The total number of naval aircraft on 1 August 1914 was twenty two (see pages 34, 86).

## Italy

Facing the Austro-Hungarian Empire uneasily across the Adriatic in 1914 was her nominal ally Italy. The comparatively new nation had come very early to military aeronautics and remained consistently in the vanguard. In 1884 an Army Aeronautical Section had been formed and their reconnaissance balloons were used in the Eritrea campaigns of 1887. Five aeroplanes and two small airships took part in army manoeuvres of 1911 in Libya. The same year *Capitaine* Carlo Piazza grandly styled 'Commander of the Air Fleet' made the first ever operational war flight on 22 October 1911 when he flew a Blériot XI from Tripoli to Azazia spotting Turkish positions. Within days the Italians were dropping bombs. By 1913 there were thirteen military airfields in Italy and industrial concerns such as Savoia and Macchi were building French types under licence. The same year the foundations of a naval air force were laid with two small airships and a handful of small flying-boats.

During Italy's nine months of neutrality the *Aeronautica del Regio Escercito* and *della Regia Marina* were expanded. When war came on 25 May 1915 they were in an unusually reasonable state of readiness to face Austria (see page 107).

## Belgium

In May 1908 Henri Farman made the first heavier than air flight in Belgium before a large crowd and the small country caught the flying mania that so infected France. In July 1910 an Aeroplane Section was established within the Engineer Balloon Section —the *Compagnie des Ouvriers et Aérostatiers*—with the stricture that all future pilots should be volunteer engineer officers. Meanwhile young men from cavalry and artillery regiments were enthusiastically taking flying lessons at their own expense. At last the Belgian Military Aviation School was opened on 1 March 1915 on the artillery range at Brasschaet near Antwerp, commanded by *Commandant* Mathieu and made open to the whole army. By summer it had two Farmans and more on order from Bollekens in Antwerp building the French type under licence. It was here in September 1912 in a Belgian-built Farman that the first European air-firing trials were conducted with a Lewis machine-gun.

On 16 April 1913 by Royal Decree the *Compagnie des Aviateurs* was formally established with Mathieu in command, distinct from the Aerostatiers and their balloons—with a winged 'A' in silver to be worn on the upper left sleeve as their distinction. On mobilization on 1 August 1914 the *Compagnie* could put two operational Farman *escadrilles* into the field with two more forming.

## United States

The United States was the cradle of powered flight but France was its nursery. The Wright brothers were met with scepticism and official obfuscation in their country while they were fêted in Europe. At last in 1907 the US War Department opened discussions with the Wrights and on 2 August 1908, after acceptance trials at Fort Meyer in Virginia, a Wright Flyer became US Army Aeroplane No 1. America's air arm consisted of this single aircraft until March 1911 when further funds were released to buy more aircraft.

In 1892 a balloon section had been established within the Army Signal Corps. A single balloon was used in Cuba during the war against Spain in 1898 but, after its destruction, the section was disbanded.

In August 1908, as the Wright Flyer was finishing its trials, an Aeronautical Division was established within the Signal Corps responsible for 'balloons, air machines and kindred subjects'—at first the single Flyer and a small dirigible. An Aviation school was set up at North Island San Diego in 1913, and the same year the US Navy created an office of Naval Aeronautics and established a base and its own school at Pensacola, Florida.

On 18 July 1914 Army aviation was recognized by an Act of Congress and the Aviation Section of the Signal Corps was officially authorized with a strength of sixty officers and 260 enlisted men, and established the rank of Military Aviator. On the outbreak of the European war, the Aviation Section had twenty aircraft available, and the US Navy twelve (pages 131, 132, 134).

### Russia

Whether it was Krupp cannon, Maxim machine-guns or French warship designs, Imperial Russia had to import weapons technology wholesale from the West at the beginning of the twentieth century to stand a chance of remaining a first class military power. After the shock of defeat by Japan, the modernization of Russia's ramshackle armed forces stumbled onwards—but there was already a Russian tradition of military flying. In 1869 General Mikulin established a 'Commission for the Utilization of Aeronautics for Military Purposes' and in 1885 Volkov outside St Petersburg had been established as a balloon training centre. In the war of 1904-05 a balloon section had operated successfully from besieged Port Arthur.

Dirigible airships were bought from France and Germany by the Army in 1909-10 but the Navy took the lead with heavier than air flying. Admiral the Grand Duke Alexander dipped into funds allocated for torpedo boats and diverted them to his 'Committee for Strengthening the Air Fleet'. Sevastopol became a naval training station in 1910 and in 1911 Gatchina/Volkov became an Army School. Meanwhile naval and military officers were sent to France and Britain to learn to fly. In 1912 a large aircraft meeting at Gatchina and participation by aircraft in the annual manoeuvres in the Ukraine proved the point and, with the active support of the Tsar, on 30 July 1912 an aviation section of *Stavka* was instigated commanded by Gen. Shishkevich. Its equipment grew rapidly, Nieuports and Farmans built under licence by Dux, plus some of the native designs of Sikorsky, and they were organizationally grouped in units of six, later ten, called an *otryed*, one attached to each army Corps.

On the outbreak of war Russian air strength was 244 aeroplanes and twelve airships. There was also a sizeable number of trained pilots and an outline aero-industrial base. There were however few aero-engines and fewer manufacturing facilities and most technicians were French (page 90).

Thus, on the eve of World War I, the armed forces of the major powers all possessed a vestigial air force. No formation was independent but controlled directly either by an Admiralty or General Staff. In most cases however they possessed a training organization, military airfields and a technical and experimental department, indeed some had a government aircraft factory building airframes and aero-engines. The men in charge, from Johannistal to San Diego, were nearly all senior military officers, often from a technical branch, with long professional careers behind them, aided and advised by a smattering of actual pioneer aviators and a very few scientists. They all concurred however as to how their fragile charges should be used in war.

The military aircraft of 1913-14 were seen as vehicles of reconnaissance, a way of getting the binocular-enhanced eyes of an officer over enemy territory or a manoeuvring enemy formation and back again to report.

Such aircraft as the *Taube* and BE2c were deliberately developed for military use because of their 'inherent stability'—the steadiest observation platform being the aim and the very antithesis of combat manoeuvrability being the result. The General Staffs of 1914 were obsessed with complex and enormous plans of manoeuvre, convinced they could move whole armies along railways and detrain them into action as simply as they could move troops in a war game, and win this steam-powered war within weeks. In such circumstances, the advantages of strategic reconnaissance were apparently absolute. German Army rigid airships operating at an invulnerable ceiling were envisaged commanding vast military amphitheatres through Zeiss lenses and in pre-war planning they were reserved as the long arm of the *Obersten Heeresleitung*, the Army High Command, with an *OHL* staff-officer in nominal command of each battle flight.

The same German organizational planning attached the *Feldflieger Abteilung* and their short range aeroplanes rigidly to Army and Corps HQs for tactical reconnaissance. Artillery co-operation had been considered by several countries but experiments had been unsuccessful, due to the problem of communicating to batteries on the ground in time.

Britain, France and Germany conducted several experiments with airborne wireless and aerial cameras before the outbreak of war but the technical limitations of the pre-war generation of aircraft made lifting the crew an effort, let alone carrying a wireless-set, machine-gun or a camera bigger than a Kodak.

# 1914

ON 28 July 1914, one month after their crown prince had been shot dead by Slav nationalists at Sarajevo, the government of Austria-Hungary declared war on Serbia. Two days later Russia ordered general mobilization. At noon on Saturday, 1 August a German ultimatum to St Petersburg expired and four hours later the *Fliegertruppe*, along with the rest of the German Army, received orders by telegraph for full mobilization.

At 4.00 pm on the afternoon of 1 August mobilization orders went out by telegraph across France. On the 3rd, Germany declared war, on the unfounded pretext that French aircraft had bombed Nuremberg and the first German units crossed into Luxembourg on their way, it was planned, to Paris and victory within six weeks, wheeling in a great right hook through Belgium. By midnight Britain was at war with Germany. The German General Staff in their planning predicted that the main British Expeditionary Force would land in France two weeks after mobilization and they were almost exactly right.

The first Royal Flying Corps personnel embarked at Southampton for France on 11 August. A day later they had reached Amiens by road—in time to meet Lt H D Harvey-Kelly's BE2a flying in from Dover, the first RFC aircraft on French soil, landing at 8.20 am on 11 August. In the next few days a total of 63 further machines arrived, some flew, others came by road, until on the 17th the RFC's HQ moved forward to Maubeuge 11 miles south west of Mons in commandeered furniture waggons. On the 27th Sqdn Cdr C R Samson's Eastchurch wing of the RNAS arrived at Ostend, but by then the RFC had fallen back with the BEF in its great retreat beginning on the morning of 25 August, occupying sixteen airfields on the way, to arrive battered but intact at St Omer on 12 October in time for the first Battle of Ypres.

The *Fliegertruppe* completed mobilization within five days as planned and 33 *Feldflieger Abteilungen* equipped with six aircraft each were incorporated into the command of their allotted armies and army corps advancing in the field. The début of the Army airships on low level tactical reconnaissance was near disastrous. *Z6* was lost on its first operation on 6 August, *Z7* and *Z8* on the 22nd in the Argonne and *Z5* fell ignominiously to ground fire in Russia on the 28th and its crew of thirty were captured. None brought back any useful operational intelligence about the unfolding battles and within a month half the fleet had been lost and the remainder were switched to night operations or bombing.

The heavier-than-air efforts of the *Feldflieger Abteilungen* were much more successful. The Army HQs, Corps HQs and the Army High Command (*OHL*) were fed with a stream of accurate reports about the swiftly changing disposition of the enemy both in the west and with spectacular success in East Prussia covering the Russian advance.

The French took two weeks to mobilize their air forces and once in action they were hampered at first by the great diversity of equipment and the operational clumsiness of the system of forwarding all Army HQ reconnaissance reports to the *Deuxième Bureau* or Military Intelligence for analysis. Nevertheless it was an aerial report on 3 September which alerted the French to the opportunity opened by von Kluck on the Marne and some pugnacious bombing hampered the German advance. On 5 October pilot *Sergent* Frantz and his mechanic *Sapeur* Quénault shot down an Aviatik B-type, Quénault wielding a Hotchkiss machine-gun from the cockpit of a pusher Voisin, to score France's very first aerial victory.

Already *Commandant* Barès appointed by Joffre on 25 September as *Chef du Service Aéronautique aux Armées* was striving to simplify the *Aviation Militaire's* widely diversified equipment and poor organization. By 8 October Barès had initiated an expansion programme in which three main branches emerged —Reconnaissance (*Corps d'Armée*), Bombing (*Bombardement*) and fighting (*Aviation de Chasse*). Barès chose the two-seater Morane-Saulnier Type L

which was grandly designated the *Morane de Chasse* when armed with a rifle, carbine and sometimes a Lewis or Hotchkiss, for specific fighting duties. It was still very much a paper designation and encounters between armed aircraft in the first months of the war were comparatively rare. The killing in the great battles of the frontiers was done on the ground by high explosive shells and machine-gun fire—while reconnaissance aircraft blithely droned above, their crews armed only with duck guns or cavalry carbines with which unsportingly to take pot-shots at each other.

In November 1914 a famous pre-war aviator named Roland Garros was posted to *Escadrille MS 26* based at Le Bourget defending the 'entrenched camp' of Paris. With his mechanic Jules Hué, he was seconded to the Morane-Saulnier field at Villacoublay to assist the experiments of Raymond Saulnier who had been unsuccessfully testing a synchronization device for a machine-gun armed tractor aircraft since April 1914. Saulnier's experiments were hampered by variations in the Hotch-

kiss machine-gun's ammunition and its rate of fire and the device eventually included metal deflectors to minimize the effect of irregular firing and neutralize the bullets which would strike the rotating two bladed propeller when the synchronization broke down. Garros discarded Saulnier's attempts at proper synchronization and commissioned Panhard to make much heavier armoured deflectors mounted on a specially designed Chauvière airscrew waisted at its inner ends. After many mishaps and shattered airscrews Hué devised a bracing system for the deflectors and made their inner faces channel shaped efficiently to clear 8-mm solid copper bullets that did not fragment on impact. At last at the beginning of the new year Garros was able to make a completely successful air firing demonstration. After some weeks pilot, mechanic and the Hotchkiss-armed Morane Type L parasol monoplane were sent north to Dunkirk to rejoin *MS 26*. It was a fragile two-seat reconnaissance aircraft with a crude lash-up of an armament system—but a fighter aircraft had arrived at the front.

*Far left: Sergent* Frantz and *Sapeur* Quénault by the tail of their Voisin, victors of the first aerial fire-fight.
*Above:* Lt Harvey-Kelly's BE2a No 347, the first British aircraft to land in France following the outbreak of war.
*Left:* An unarmed Albatros B-type runs up its engine

# 1915

IN 1915 Europe's war spilled out into a truly world conflict fought on many fronts from German East Africa to the North Sea. Everywhere the aeroplane went with it as a weapon of war. In January the first Zeppelin raids were made on Great Britain. In February 1915 an Allied fleet arrived off the Dardanelles in the hope of knocking Turkey out of the war in one blow. With the battleships sailed a warship with an ancient name but with a new role, the seaplane carrier *Ark Royal*, and more were to follow.

On 24 May 1915 Italy declared war and the air force of Austria-Hungary turned west to face a new enemy in the south. Throughout 1915 from the Rufiji river to the Sinai peninsula aircraft were engaged in the 'side-show' operations. It was on the Western Front however that the contest was being decided and it was here in this year that air fighting really began.

On 5 February 1915 the intensive efforts of Roland Garros, Jules Hué and Raymond Saulnier at Villacoublay were rewarded by French Patent No 477.530 given to the *Société des Aéroplanes Morane-Saulnier* for the design of an armoured airscrew for use on aircraft fitted with a firearm. Bad weather and bad luck had bought Garros no reward in action and meanwhile the French authorities cancelled an order for ten armed Morane Type Ls.

On 1 April Garros set out with two 155-mm bombs aboard the armed Morane to drop on a German railway station. On the way he emptied three Hotchkiss strip magazines into a German two-seater and drove it down in flames. Two weeks later he scored a second victory and on the 18th an unwary Albatros fell over Langemarck. That same afternoon Garros set off on a bombing attack on Courtrai railway station when a bullet from the ground struck and stopped the Parasol's engine.

Garros glided down to land near Ingelmunster and frantically tried to set fire to the aircraft and destroy its secret but the Morane stubbornly just smoked and smouldered. After some hours he was taken prisoner and the Morane with its mechanics intact was shipped off to Iseghem to await the detailed scrutiny of German technical officers.

The idea of the deflectors was so simple that the officers of *Idflieg* were not unduly alarmed by the French 'secret weapon' but the tactical advantage of an aircraft that could fire along its own line of flight was made clear. In tests German chrome-steel 7.92-mm ammunition fired continuously soon shattered the propeller and its deflectors but top priority was now given to the perfection of the cam-operated synchronizing gear already under development at the Fokker Aeroplanbau GmbH at Schwerin. By May Fokker was able to give a demonstration before *Idflieg* officers, but the *Feldflugchef, Major* Thomsen, was not over impressed. He promised Fokker the Iron Cross if his device could bring down an enemy aircraft in combat. In late May 1915,. Anthony Fokker arrived at an airfield in the German V Army area opposite Verdun accompanied by the veteran

In 1915 aircraft became machine-gun armed weapons—
*Above:* French ace Jean Navarre in the cockpit of his Morane Type N. The Garros-Hué armoured propeller system, with grooved wedges mounted in the 8-mm Hotchkiss's line of fire, is clearly shown.
*Far left:* The 1914 Fokker M5K two-seat unarmed reconnaissance machine was developed into the Fokker E-type fighter of 1915.
*Left:* A Nieuport XI, the famous *Bébé* which, armed with an overwing mounted Hotchkiss or Lewis machine-gun, went some way to eroding the Fokker E-type's predominance

A young British pilot gets his training on a Bristol Boxkite early in the war at the Grahame-White flying school, Hendon. The photograph is from the Hendon studio of F N Birkett who, like W Sanke of Berlin, also based near a large training airfield, made a career out of taking aviators' graduation pictures. When his sitters became famous, they sold in thousands as postcards.

By 1914 many well-trained pilots had been turned out by British flying schools but the progressive demands of the war meant that training standards fell, and the 'Fokker Scourge' of 1915-16 pointed out bloodily that training for flying and training for air fighting were different things. The result was a disastrous period for the RFC

demonstration pilot *Leutnant* Otto Parschau and a frail underpowered scouting monoplane of pre-war design—the Fokker M5K/MG *Eindecker* (or *Eendekker* in Fokker's native Dutch). In late 1913 Fokker had acquired a well-worn Morane-Saulnier Type H and his M5 monoplane of 1914 was a pretty straight copy. Now here it was at the front after an intense period of experimentation with a lightened Parabellum lMG '14 mounted below the king post, pistol grip and clumsy shoulder stock protruding well back into the cockpit. It looked impossible—the gun was mounted to fire through the propeller arc. The secret was a cam operated interrupter-gear hidden beneath the turned aluminium cowling of the Oberursel rotary. For all its seemingly crude improvization this aircraft presaged principles of air warfare that a fighter pilot would recognize today.

For some days Fokker's search for a live target went unrewarded. In June the demonstration flight went north to Douai, home of *Fl Abt 62*, but again Fokker himself had no success. There Parschau demonstrated the machine to Oswald Boelcke, already a victor in aerial combat and an experienced pilot of rotary-engined aircraft. On 31 July Boelcke

flight tested the armed *Eindecker* E3/15 and the next day engaged RFC aircraft over Douai. *Fähnrich* Max Immelman accompanied him flying the totally unfamiliar Fokker EI3/15 for the first time but he forced down a BE2c to gain his and the Fokker's first victory. In the subsequent weeks the reports of BE2 pilots were alarming in the extreme. They were engaged by an aircraft which could fire a machinegun along its own line of flight, riddling a BE2c from behind before the hapless Lewis gunner could offer a defence from the *front* seat. Thus was opened the period of Germany supremacy over the Western Front later known in Britain as the 'Fokker Scourge'. Boelcke and Immelmann's reputation grew with a stream of victories at the front, and their fame was fanned by the press at home. The fighter aircraft and the fighter ace came of age at the same time.

The RFC was saved from being driven from the skies altogether largely because the Germans themselves failed to recognize the full potential of this new weapon. *Eindecker* pilots were forbidden to fly offensive patrols over enemy lines for the fear of delivering the synchronizing gear and its secrets into enemy hands, and the aircraft themselves were allocated singly to two-seater units for flying close

escorts and spread thinly along the line. On 31 October 1915 there were only 55 *Eindecker* types at the front and 86 Fokker E-types at the end of the year. Poor supply of Oberursel rotaries slowed down the Schwerin line and the few monoplane types from Pfalz equipped only Bavarian *Fl Abt* units.

In spite of all this, the Fokkers' grip on the western front skies tightened through the autumn. Tactics improved as pilots became more skilful and organization improved with the grouping of up to four single-seaters within the *Feldflieger Abteilungen*. These so-called *Kampfeinsitzer Kommandos* were the nursery of the fledgeling aces like Boelcke, Immelmann, Mulzer and Lörzer and were the organizational nuclei of the permanent German fighter units of a year later—the *Jagdstaffeln*.

Initially *Eindecker* pilots flew 'barrage patrols' engaging any target that came along, but, as the endurance of the EIII for example was only 1½ hours at speeds under 80 mph, the results were not outstanding. The *KEK*s were soon put under the operational orders of the *Stabsoffizier der Flieger* on the staff of their particular Army's sector of front. With a reasonably effective reporting system based on forward *Flak* units they could be vectored towards incoming enemy with a good chance of making an interception. This tight organization more than made up for lack of numbers and by the end of 1915 the Allied armies were close to be being blinded—their photographic and gunnery directing eyes put out by the Fokker monoplane barring German airspace to all but the bravest and luckiest Allied pilot.

Two Fokkers went to the Eastern Front, one flown by *Leutnant* Kurt Student, and the effect of these two fragile aircraft on the Imperial Russian Air Force was immediate. By September 1915 they had driven any opposition from their area.

The Royal Flying Corps had had a 'fighting' aircraft in France, the Vickers FB5 (Fighting Biplane) since February 1915. Its ancestry went back to November 1912 when the British Admiralty placed a contract for a fighting aeroplane armed with a machine-gun and the two-seat pusher layout was Vicker's solution. The fast tractor single-seaters available since 1913-14 such as the Bristol Scout and Sopwith Tabloid offered a much more manoeuvrable gun platform, but without an effective synchronizing-gear the earliest method of arming these single seaters tried throughout 1915 was to mount a Lewis gun on the fuselage side firing obliquely to miss the propeller and the device proved almost impossible to aim. A Martinsyde SI had been adapted with an overwing Lewis fired by a flexible Bowden cable as early as May 1915 but the device encountered the consistent problem of the high-viscosity oil freezing and jamming the weapon. Thus fighting duties devolved largely on slow pushers—the few FB5 'gun-buses' and the Royal Aircraft Factory's Fighting Experimental FE2a available from May 1915 and the improved FE2b from January 1916.

Organizationally the RFC was in fact a little ahead of the Germans. The RFC's commander in

This postcard of a Hotchkiss-armed Deperdussin was sold widely in Britain and France in 1914

the field Major-General Sir David Henderson sought to group what fighting aircraft there were in special squadrons but this was resisted at Wing level and the fighting types were distributed amongst the two-seater squadrons. Nevertheless in July 1915 the first squadron in any air force equipped with a single type of fighting aircraft, No 11 Squadron RFC flying FB5s, arrived in France. On 19 August 1915, on the eve of the Battle of Loos, Colonel Hugh Trenchard took over from Henderson and insisted on a new offensive spirit to take British aircraft into the Fokker dominated skies. What was needed were new tactics and organization but above all new aircraft to match the German's technical advance.

In spite of the blow to morale caused by the capture of Roland Garros in April the French *escadrilles de chasse* continued to score throughout 1915 and Eugene Gilbert scored five victories in his deflector equipped Morane N aptly named *Le Vengeur* before being killed. On 11 July Adolph Pégoud scored his sixth victory only to be killed himself at the end of August. Just as the Fokker E-types seemed indomitable, the Nieuport 11 with its overwing mounted Lewis or Hotchkiss and its exceptional manoeuvrability appeared in the late summer to offer a real challenge but only in small numbers. With the organizational groupings of *escadrilles de chasse* and more Nieuport 11s the French were well placed to meet the great German offensive about to break at Verdun in February 1916.

On 12 January 1916 the brilliant exponents of the Fokker *Eindecker*, Boelcke and Immelmann were both awarded the *Pour le Mérite*. Two days later Royal Flying Corps HQ issued an order urging formation flying by the RFC to combat the Fokker menace and on 27 February 1916 No 24 Squadron RFC arrived in France equipped with the first British purpose-designed single-seat fighter, the DH2. One week earlier the German offensive had broken on the fortifications around Verdun. The great war on the ground and in the air was entering a terrifying new phase and within twelve months most of the aces of 1915 would be dead.

# Charles Rumney Samson

THIS book is first of all about fighter pilots. Charles Rumney Samson rarely flew a fighter aircraft proper nor did he shoot down an enemy aircraft, although he made several attempts. Samson was however one of the truly great pioneers of military aviation. He had a uniquely adventurous wartime career which itself tells so much about the early development of air power, and particularly the development of air power at sea.

On 1 March 1911, Lt C R Samson, late of HMS *Foresight*, arrived at F K McClean's flying school at Eastchurch in Kent. He was one of the four Royal Navy and Marine officers the Admiralty had selected out of 500 applicants to learn to fly. Their Lordships had chosen well. Samson was born in Manchester in 1883, the second son of a solicitor. He entered the Navy at the age of fifteen and after a cadetship at the Royal Naval College, Greenwich, he was commissioned as a Lieutenant in 1904. The calls of gunboat diplomacy took him to Somaliland aboard HMS *Pomone* during operations in Somaliland and the Persian Gulf in 1909–10. The adventurous Samson took to flying with enthusiasm and daring and gained his Royal Aero Club Certificate No 71 on 4 April, less than two months after his arrival at Eastchurch. In June he made a three-day cross country round flight to Brooklands with a Short Biplane in company with Lt A M Longmore RN but a much more spectacular and indeed significant event came on 10 January 1912. Samson took off in a Short S27 biplane, from a sloping platform erected over the forward gun turret of the cruiser HMS *Africa* anchored off Sheerness. On 9 May the newly promoted acting commander of Eastchurch took off from a similar ramp aboard HMS *Hibernia* during a Royal Review while the old battleship was making 15 knots in Weymouth Bay. It was the first take-off in the world from a ship under way.

Equally portentous of things to come were experiments Samson conducted in the summer of 1912 at Harwich into the potential of aircraft for spotting submarines, airborne wireless telegraphy, and even dropping 100 lb bombs from his frail Short floatplane. By now the Admiralty was waking up to the potential of this new dimension to war at sea. In May 1913 the old cruiser HMS *Hermes* was converted to a rudimentary seaplane carrier and in the Naval Manoeuvres of that year Samson flew one of two Short Folders from *Hermes* equipped with wireless—until he had engine failure and had to ditch only to be picked up ignominiously by a German collier. In April 1914 Samson put up an airborne escort for the Royal Yacht *Victoria and Albert* bearing King George V to France with Samson himself leading in a BE2. These dashing assertions of naval independence in the air paid off when in June 1914 the Admiralty formally extracted the Naval Wing from the control of the RFC to form the Royal Naval Air Service. The outbreak of war was only a matter of weeks away.

When the German invasion of Belgium brought Britain's declaration of war and the British Expeditionary Force to France, the main thrust of the German armies through Belgium and France left the Flanders coast still open. The pugnacious First Lord of the Admiralty, Winston Churchill, saw the opportunity for the Royal Navy to get in on the great land battle being fought on the frontiers to the south, if only on the coastal fringe, and to take some preventative measures against Zeppelins. On 27 August therefore Samson was ordered to take his Eastchurch wing, all ten aircraft, and fly to Ostend. A motley collection of aircraft, Farmans, Blériots, Sopwiths and BE2s flew safely across the Channel with every pilot equipped with inflated bicycle tyres as a lifebelt and armed with a .45 pistol. As they came into land at Ostend racecourse they were fired on by Royal Marines. After that Samson's aircraft sported Union Jacks. On 30 August 1914, with the fate of the BEF to the south at Mons hanging in the balance, Samson's No 1 Wing RNAS was ordered back to England, but they got lost in a Channel fog and flew back to Dunkirk instead with new orders to carry out reconnaissance as directed by the French General there.

This period of World War I, the so-called 'race to the sea', was one of the few periods when a war of movement was fought on the Western Front. With the range and reliability of his 1913-vintage aircraft highly limited, Samson found another way of waging mechanized war. In Ostend his brother Felix Samson had inherited eight B-type buses still bearing the red paint of the London General Omnibus Company and the peace-time advertisements of the London music-halls. These unwarlike machines were joined in Dunkirk by a Mercedes 50-hp truck and a Rolls-Royce, and Felix Samson, with the assistance of the 'Forges et Chantiers de France' and a lot of boiler plate, began to assemble the first mechanized 'armoured' force in history. They were extraordinary vehicles, as primitive fighting machines as the Eastchurch aircraft themselves. Indeed a member of Samson's force, Lord Annesley, contributed his personal Rolls-Royce crudely armoured in mild steel. It shook to pieces after only a few days pounding the Belgian *pavé*. In England meanwhile Winston Churchill and Commodore Murray Sueter, head of the Admiralty Air Department, were eagerly studying Samson's reports and ordering new armoured cars. But Samson was to lead this improvised armoured force in an extraordinary mobile campaign that lasted some months. With neither side able to win the Battle of the Aisne, Germans, French and British turned north in an effort to reach the Channel ports first. Large and often detached formations leap-frogged each other with no real front-line. Into this war of movement Samson pitched his armoured cars and aircraft against German cavalry and managed to convince the German High Command that a large mobile force was screening their advance—and he did it all with his hastily improvized Maxim gun-armed ex-buses and the aircraft of the Eastchurch flying school.

Two famous members of Samson's original No 1 Wing RNAS of 1914: *Top*: Lieutenant R Marix who destroyed Zeppelin *LZ IX* in its shed at Dusseldorf with 20-lb Hales bombs. *Lower*: Flight Lieutenant Sidney V Sippe who flew one of the three Avro 504s which bombed the airship sheds at Friedrichshafen—ineffectively—on 21 November 1914, winning the Distinguished Service Order

On 5 September, Samson occupied Lille, already evacuated by the French, only to have to withdraw when no French troops showed up in support. A week later he was put in charge of a Marine detachment and some Belgian gendarmes had moved to a new base just south of Hazebrouck where new armoured cars from England were waiting. Of the Rolls-Royce, Talbot and Wolseleys, only the 'Rolls was any good', he wrote.

Samson's column of airborne armoured sailors now inherited a troop of French *Goumiers* (colonial cavalry) and a train of 75s. At Aniches they fought a pitched battle with German cavalry, with a Belgian steam-tram driver incredibly running his schedule while bullets flew around him, bringing Samson intelligence, between Aniches and Lewarcke!

Other major engagements followed at Cassel, Douai and Orchies with startled German cavalrymen and cyclists going down in droves when Samson's men suddenly appeared opening up with Maxims from behind armour plate.

At the end of September Samson was ordered to escort 70 London buses from Dunkirk to Antwerp. With the German armies advancing in to the south, the strange convoy rumbled along the refugee-clogged black puddled *pavé* roads of the narrowing coastal strip at 10 mph with ten Marines in every sixth bus—their posters still announcing the latest offerings of the Gaiety Theatre and the restorative powers of Iron Jelloids to wondering Belgian peasants —civilian LGOC drivers at their wheels, and Samson at the front in a Rolls-Royce.

The great Belgian port was already doomed. The Germans were bringing up their super-heavy artillery to crack open Antwerp's fortresses one by one. The Royal Marine Brigade had got there by train on 4 October and two Naval Brigades soon afterwards and Churchill himself had arrived on 3 October to stiffen the defenders' resolve. Instead of

evacuation he immediately proposed that Samson's aviators should actually attack targets in Germany.

Thus on 7 October, setting out from Antwerp with the field under German shellfire, Fl-Cdr Spenser Grey and Fl-Lt Marix in two Sopwith Tabloids attacked the railway station at Cologne with 20-lb bombs and Marix managed to destroy Zeppelin *LZIX* in its shed at Düsseldorf.

On 7 October Samson had got the order to pull out of the virtually encircled city. He managed to commandeer two trains to get his men out through the shrinking coastal corridor and extricated the armoured cars by road to Ostend on the 8th. On the evening of the 9th, the last RNAS personnel left Antwerp in two tenders, and the unserviceable aircraft were destroyed. On 12 October the whole British IV Corps under Sir Henry Rawlinson fell back, and Samson had to retreat with it from Ostend towards Ypres.

Through the rest of October, with the BEF fighting for its life at the First Battle of Ypres, the RNAS armoured cars were heavily embattled, falling back through Belgian villages with new and unpronounceable names like Passchendaele and Poperinghe, covering the retreat of the 3rd Cavalry Division. But by the end of the month, with the first trenches being hastily dug, Samson himself was admitting that 'armoured cars were of little use'. Nevertheless Sir John French still thought enough of them for Samson's force to be put under his command rather than the Admiralty's. General Sir Henry Rawlinson could write, 'I must write a line to express my very sincere thanks for your kindness in allowing me to keep the armoured motors and aeroplanes under Samson. They have done excellent work. The armoured cars pick up half a dozen prisoners a day, and have instilled a holy terror into our opponents.

Samson could see the way things were going and

*Above left:* the battleship HMS *Hibernia* with the launching platform and trackway erected over her forward turret and bow and the Short S38 in place.
*Top right:* view of the ramp for *Hibernia*'s bow.
*Above:* Samson in S38 successfully rises from *Hibernia* while she was underway at 15 knots in Weymouth Bay on 9 May 1912. He landed at Lodmoor. Over the next two years Samson conducted a wide variety of trials and experiments, including night flying and aerial wireless

**Flight Commander
C R Samson RNAS,
Tenedos, 1915**
Naval officers in hot climates
took to wearing khaki at sea
early in the war to ease
laundry problems. The
usual practise was to have
tunics made of khaki drill on
the pattern of the official
white tunic but some officers
obtained army jackets and
wore them with naval
shoulder straps. Wearing of
khaki was regularised in
1916, but before that the
RNAS in the Mediterranean
improvised unofficially.
Samson tacked his shoulder
strap insignia to his khaki
jacket and pinned the RNAS
eagle to the left breast.
Flying helmet and goggles
were private purchase. The
pistol was the RNAS issue
Webley .445

on 13 October he was in London, arguing the need
for more aircraft with Winston Churchill. Back at
Dunkirk he received a new wave of RNAS rein-
forcements, aircraft and pilots, and immediately
drew up operational plans for attacking U-Boat and
Zeppelin targets along the occupied coast. In
November three ex-Samson men, Lts Babington,
Briggs and Sippe, attacked the Zeppelin sheds at
Friedrichshafen from a base in the Vosges. Inspired
by their success, Samson attacked Bruges with 16-lb
bombs on 14 December and on 21 December he
made the first night flight of the war in a Maurice
Farman in a bombing raid on Ostend. On Christmas
Day 1914, a comparatively large force of RNAS
aircraft set out to attack Zeppelin sheds at Cux-
haven, but got lost in fog and struck Wilhelmshaven
instead.

Much bigger things came in February 1915
when RNAS aircraft, including seaplanes from
HMS *Empress*, made raids all along the coast from
Zeebrugge to Ostend. Commodore Murray Sueter,
who had already requested Frederick Handley-
Page to build him a 'bloody paralyser' of a bombing
aircraft, controlled the operation from Dover. The
Royal Naval Air Service went on flying from Dunkirk throughout the war laying the foundations of
strategic bombing. In 1915, however, flying 80 mph
aircraft armed with 20-lb bombs, Samson's raiders
were like gnats stinging a rhino.

At the end of February, however, Samson was
recalled to Britain to reform his squadron for
another Churchill-inspired venture. He came back
from France as a Commander, with the DSO, the
*Croix de Guerre* and the rosette of a *Chevalier de la
Légion d'Honneur*.

In March 1915 the Eastchurch Squadron, now
No 3 (Aeroplane) Sqn, RNAS, embarked for the
Dardanelles. Samson took a motley collection of
aircraft with him, a BE2a (No 50, the only survivor
from the Dunkirk days), two BE2cs, two Sopwith
Tabloids and a Breguet. At Imbros he reported to
Admiral Sir John de Robeck commanding the
naval forces which would attempt to force the
narrows of the Gallipoli peninsula fifteen miles to
the east of the island. Samson was ordered south to
the tiny island of Tenedos where ancient vines were
cleared by Turkish prisoners for an airstrip and huts
were improvized out of aircraft packing cases.
During the naval bombardment Samson regularly
flew the BE2 spotting for the guns of HMS *London*.
When the landing went in at Cape Helles on 25
April, Samson flew low over the beaches reporting
the dreadful sight of the sea stained red with blood
for fifty yards out from the beach.

In spite of their allotted role of reconnaissance,
Samson's wing flew armed whenever possible with
the Commander setting the example. He attacked
the German HQ with 20-lb bombs, raided Turkish
transports and shipping, and even persuaded a
Henri Farman to lumber into the air with a 500-lb
bomb. In September a Nieuport scout arrived at
Tenedos which when compared with his elderly

## BE2a

BE2a No 50 was somewhat unusual in being a product of the Royal Aircraft Factory in naval hands. Before and during the war the Admiralty did not feel the same constraints as the RFC in buying only RAF aircraft and encouraged private firms such as Shorts and Sopwith with their purchasing policies. Nevertheless BE2a No 50 built by Hewlett and Blondeau was delivered to the RNAS at Eastchurch in January 1914 and was later demonstrated at the naval review at Spithead. Samson flew it to Ostend on 27 August 1914 and it was with him throughout the campaign in France and Belgium. Sq Cdr Gerrard took No 50 to bomb Düsseldorf in September 1914 and Samson used her for bombing Ostend and Zeebrugge. Thence it went to Tenedos and the Dardenelles —an old war horse which undertook many reconnaissance and bombing missions, long after it was woefully obsolete. In January 1916 she was broken up on Tenedos. 'At the last', wrote Samson, 'I must say I only flew her occasionally simply for old acquaintance sake.'

The Farnborough designed BE2 (Blériot Experimental 2) piloted by its chief designer Geoffrey de Havilland scored the highest marks at the first Military Aeroplane Contest held in Britain, at Larkhill in August 1912. With Major Sykes, RFC, as passenger in the front seat, de Havilland took the British Altitude Record at 10,560 ft with 450 lb of useful load and went on to beat the foremost French designs. The performance was entirely unofficial as a Royal factory product was ineligible and the Farnborough Superintendent, Mervyn O'Gorman, was one of the judges. The BE2a appeared in 1913 and differed in having a more powerful 70-hp Renault engine and an aircraft of this type, No 347 piloted by Lt H D Harvey-Kelly, was the first aircraft of the RFC to land in France on 13 August 1914. The BE2b appeared in 1914 and featured built up cockpit coamings.

The BE2 was further extensively modified in 1914 according to the 'automatic stability' ideas of Edward Busk. The BE2c had differing wings and tail assembly to its predecessors and was designed as a stable reconnaissance vehicle rather than a fighting machine. As such the BE2c-equipped squadrons of the RFC were to suffer disastrously when air fighting began in earnest in 1915.

| | |
|---|---|
| Manufacturer: Royal Aircraft Factory and sub-contractors | |
| Power plant: Renault V-8, 70-hp | |
| Span: 35 ft 2 in (10.68 m) | |
| Length: 29 ft 6 in (9 m) | |
| Max. take-off weight: 1600 lb (726 kg) | |
| Max. speed: 80 mph (112 kmh) | |
| Ceiling: 11,600 ft (3048 m) | |
| Armament: — | |

*Above:* Samson prepares for take-off in his personal Nieuport X on Tenedos, the eastern Aegean island used as a base of operations by No 3 (Naval) Squadron commanded by Samson during the Gallipoli campaign, late 1915. The Nieuport is armed with a .303-in Lewis machine-gun firing obliquely over the propeller arc. The Wing received six such Nieuports in July 1915. Samson later wrote of his machine: 'it climbed like a witch'

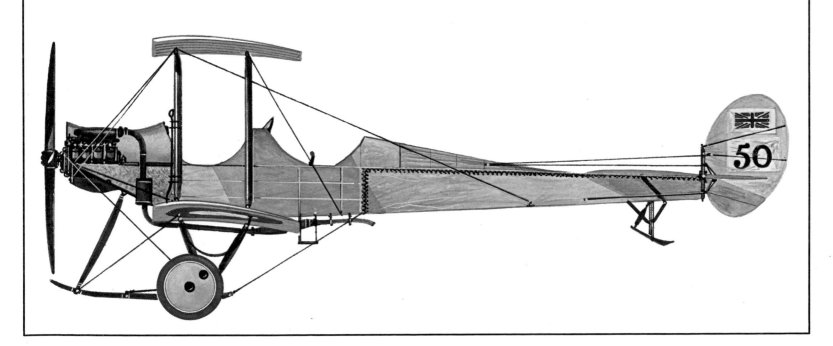

BE No 50 could as he said 'climb like a witch'. On 7 November he attacked the vital rail bridge over the river Maritza dropping two 112-lb bombs from the Farman and halting rail traffic for two days. When the submarine *U-21* sank the battleships *Triumph* and *Majestic*, Samson attempted to relieve the battle-fleet now bottled up in Mudros harbour screened by torpedo nets but in spite of sightings and an attack, his Wing was unable to despatch the German submarine.

The Gallipoli landings, which it was hoped would knock Turkey out of the war, had stalled in bitter trench warfare. By 9 January 1916 the last Allied boats slipped away from the tip of Cape Helles in the glare of blazing ammunition dumps. Churchill was swept out of the Admiralty, as was Murray Sueter from the Admiralty Air Department in the wake of the Dardanelles fiasco. A lesser casualty was Samson who came home suffering from jaundice and took some months to recover.

Charles Samson could not be kept out of the fighting for long. On 14 May 1916 he took command of the East Indies and Egypt Seaplane Squadron, embarked aboard the converted ex-Isle of Man steamer HMS *Ben-my-Chree*, cruising in the Eastern Mediterranean. Throughout 1916 the seaplane carrier was to see action in short periods of activity, punctuated by a lot of inconsequential steaming around. Samson had frequently in his words 'to proffer schemes for our employment' to his commander Rear-Admiral Rosslyn Wemyss. The French commander in the Eastern Mediterranean *Contre-Admiral* de Spitz was more amenable to Samson's pugnacious ideas however.

Samson, who had already pioneered armoured mobile warfare and strategic bombing, now had command of one of the very first aircraft carriers. Floatplanes from *Ben-my-Chree* already made successful torpedo attacks. Now Samson set about tightening up operational procedures such as aircraft launch and retrieval. With practice his crew were able to hoist out a seaplane and recover another within 45 seconds. *Ben-my-Chree*'s aircraft were still seen very much as extensions of the big-gun ship. Samson was determined however to take the war to the enemy whenever possible.

At the end of May Samson's aircraft were engaged spotting for the bombardment by monitors *M15* and *M26* of El Arish on the Mediterranean shore of Sinai. On 27 May, Samson and his observer Capt. J Wedgwood-Benn attacked Jaffa with 65-lb bombs and while the two pilots were on this mission *Ben-my-Chree* itself was attacked by a German aircraft which straddled it with four bombs. This 1916 shadow play of the great carrier battles of World War II was to be repeated again, and Samson took steps to improve the ships' anti-aircraft armament, even mounting the same 3-pdr Quick-Firer he had used from the back of a truck during his armoured car days to flush *Uhlans* out of Belgian farmhouses. When the Turkish drive on the Suez Canal was successfully held, Samson proposed to Rear-Admiral Wemyss that he should take his ship through the Suez Canal and into the Red Sea, to assist operations to the Hedjaz and Aden. On 8 June *Ben-my-Chree*'s aircraft—Sopwith Schneiders, a Sopwith Baby and Short 184s—began four days of attacks on the detached Turkish force encamped behind Aden. The water-cooled Shorts in particular suffered in the heat, and on 9 June Samson had to return early from the morning attack with a completely dry radiator. A week later the Shorts were again in action attacking Turkish shore batteries at Sheikh Said.

Meanwhile in the Hedjaz, on 5 June, Feisal's Arab Revolt had flamed into life at Medina. At Jeddah on the coast, Arab forces were besieging the Turkish garrison and on the 15th *Ben-my-Chree* steamed into harbour to lend her assistance. Samson and Wedgwood-Benn flew a Short over the town taking photographs and dropped a 112-lb bomb. Samson had a narrow escape when ground fire shot away the heel of his right shoe. The Turkish garrison surrendered at dawn the next day and the Senior Naval Officer signalled to Samson '... probably the seaplane decided the matter ...'. Meanwhile the insurgent Arabs were suitably impressed.

By the end of July the seaplane carrier was back in the Eastern Mediterranean, steaming up the coast of Palestine. On 26 July, Samson and his redoubtable observer attacked a troop train at El Afuleh to the south of Nazareth, setting it on fire. After a brief interlude at Port Said for boiler cleaning, Samson now planned a large scale attack on the important rail junction of El Afuleh. *Ben-my-Chree* and its auxiliary vessels gathered off Haifa at dawn on 25 August 1916. Six Shorts and four Sopwith Schneiders were swung out and launched, the ten aircraft forming up on Samson's Short with a red painted fin. The attack went in in three waves and the rail installations were effectively plastered.

HMS *Ben-my-Chree* and its pugnacious commander were now a real threat to Turkish-German communications. In the air Samson's aircraft however were no match for landplane opposition but nevertheless Samson armed the smaller faster Sopwiths with two Lewis guns arranged to fire at an angle and miss the propeller arc to provide 'fighter'

Samson's skid-equipped Camel 2F1 on its thirty foot lighter at Harwich in May 1918 before the first test take-off being towed at sea —a near disaster when the Camel plunged over the lighter's bows at full power

cover. On one occasion a lumbering Short drove off a German scout with fire from the observer's Lewis gun, and Samson instigated air to air gunnery practice with towed targets. Meanwhile the ship's cruise continued through the Autumn with Port Said as its base with Samson leading raids on rail targets and spotting for shore bombardments while German aircraft made several further unsuccessful attempts to bomb the seaplane carrier.

On 27 December Samson's aircraft attacked the rail bridge at Chicaldere at the tip of the Gulf of Alexandretta. This choke point on the *Bagdadbahn* and Turkish rail communications with Palestine was put out of action for a week. It was to be the last offensive action of this extraordinary warship's career.

On 5 January, HMS *Ben-my-Chree* arrived back at Port Said. On the 8th Samson sailed to aid the French naval forces at Castelorizo easternmost of the Italian Dodecanese. Almost as soon as the carrier had anchored, shells from a Turkish battery on the mainland began to strike her. When a fire in the hangar reached the petrol store, Samson ordered abandon ship. Sunk in shallow water, *Ben-my-Chree* continued to burn for five days.

At the subsequent inquiry Samson and crew were acquitted of all responsibility. Instead he was awarded a Bar to his DSO in recognition of 'his continued gallantry and distinguished service as a flying officer', and he continued to command his Seaplane Squadron now in the Indian Ocean flying from two converted ex-German merchantmen, HMS *Anne* and HMS *Raven II* until he was ordered back to England in May 1917 to take command of Great Yarmouth Air Station.

Samson's career began all over again. The North Sea Air Stations, British and German, were fighting an increasingly bitter three dimensional war for control of the North Sea—either under it in U-Boats, on it in warships or high above it in Zeppelins. With the new RAF rank of Colonel and in command of No 4 Group, Samson instigated and flew anti-submarine patrols in DH4s and long reconnaissance patrols in the big Felixstowe F2A flying boats. The major problem was getting fast fighter aircraft to sea to combat the excellent German floatplane fighters based on the Flanders coast and to establish a forward line of Zeppelin defence before they reached the East Coast. Sqdn Cdr Porte who was already a brilliant exponent of marine aircraft design, came up with specially adapted lighters to be towed behind warships from which modified Sopwith 2F1 Camels could be flown into a ready made headwind. Typically Samson conducted the first experiments himself but he insisted that his Camel should be equipped with Pup 9901a-type skids rather than wheels. On 30 May 1918 the Camel was hoisted on to the barge and its skids dropped into the troughed guide rails. Samson opened the engine and the Camel shot forward. Then disaster—the skids jumped their guides, fouled the supporting trestles and the Camel plunged at full

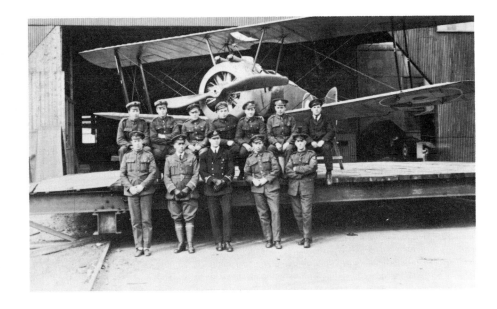

power over the bows. Samson was plucked out of the water miraculously unhurt.

On 10 August, Admiral Sir Reginald Tyrwhitt, who actively encouraged Samson's experiments, put to sea with his Harwich force of destroyers and cruisers. With them was the destroyer HMS *Redoubt* and at the end of a long hawser behind her was a lighter on which was precariously perched the Sopwith 2F1 Camel (with a wheeled under-carriage) of Lt S D Culley. The force was shadowed by the German Naval airship *L53* flying with apparent complete immunity at 19,000 feet. With *Redoubt* steaming at full speed into the wind, Culley's Camel took off from its tiny lighter and began a half-hour climb. At altitude the Camel's engine puffed and rattled in the thin air. The controls became progressively more sluggish as the huge airship manoeuvred ponderously above. Flying at the airship head on, and at some 300 feet below, Culley managed to fire a long burst into *L53*'s belly from his twin Lewis guns on the top wing.

At last Culley's Camel N6812 stalled and fell away, but it was enough. The Zeppelin was aflame and a huge blackened alloy skeleton plunged into the North Sea minutes later, along with five May-bach engines, and thirty two crew falling over three and a half miles.

C R Samson finished the war with the RAF rank of Lieut-Colonel. He had been a professional Navy Officer since 1898. He was now a professional part of Britain's peacetime air force. In 1919 he received the new RAF rank of Group Captain and in 1922 was promoted to Air Commodore in Command of No 6 Fighter Group in the Mediterranean. In the early twenties he made several epic route-proving flights over Africa and the Middle East and later was Chief of Staff in Iraq and Palestine. At last, after one of the most extraordinary fighting careers on land, sea and in the air, he retired at 46. Two years later, C R Samson was dead.

Lt S D Culley (centre, front row) destroyer of Zeppelin *L53* and his Camel 2F1, N6812, before transfer to its lighter. Culley made a successful take-off from a lighter on 31 July 1918. His handling crew wear a motley collection of Army, Navy and RAF uniform

# Gottfried Banfield

**Linienschiffsleutnant
Gottfried Banfield, 1915.**
Banfield was awarded the
*Ritterkreuz* of the *Militär
Maria-Theresien-Orderns* in
August 1917 making him
von Banfield.

The first distinction for
members of the naval flying
services of Austria-Hungary
came in 1913 with a *K u K
MARINE FLUGSTATION*
cap band for ratings at the
Pola air station and a system
of sleeve badges for NCOs.
These showed a winged
propeller under a ribboned
Kaiser's crown in gold on a
dark blue background for
*Oberstabsfliegermeister*,
*Fliegermeister* and *Flieger-
untermeister* and in yellow
wool for *Fliegerquartier-
meister* and *Fliegermaate*.
*Fliegermatrosen* (ratings)
wore the badge without the
crown. These badges were
worn halfway up the left
sleeve.

A breast badge for
qualified naval pilots was
introduced in February 1915
showing a flying gull in gold
mounted on an enamel oval
of red, white and red,
surmounting a black enamel
shield bearing a gilt crowned
anchor. A new badge was
introduced in January 1918,
a larger oval of green laurel
wreaths surmounted by a
red, white and red shield
bearing the monogram 'K'
of the last Kaiser, Karl. At
the base were the escutcheons
of Austria, Habsburg-
Lothringen and Hungary in
enamel, and across the whole
was mounted a flying gull.
The same badge was
awarded to naval observers
with a white wreath, and the
gull held six lightning
flashes.
*Right:* The ensign of the
*K u K Kriegsmarine* borne on
the tail of Austro-Hungarian
naval aircraft

THE Imperial and Royal Navy of Austria-
Hungary was one of the first to investigate
the military possibilities of aircraft. In 1909
*Linienschiffsleutnant* Viktor Klobucar Rukavina de
Bunic went to France to learn flying and returned to
set up an experimental Naval Air Station near Pola,
the naval base at the tip of the Istrian peninsula
commanding the Adriatic Sea. In 1911 the experimental station was transferred to the island of Santa
Catarina in Pola harbour itself. In the summer of
1912 the Commander of the *K u K Kriegsmarine*,
*Admiral* Rudolf Graf Montecuccoli, made several
flights in a float biplane built by Klobucar and his
engineer Mickl, and he was probably the first
admiral anywhere to fly.

By January 1913 there were ten marine aircraft
at Pola (mostly French-built) and that same month
the first formation flight was made by three aircraft
from Pola to Trieste and back. During the Second
Balkan War, three Donnet-Levêque flying boats
were established at Cattaro successfully to assist the
1st Battleship Division with the blockade of the
Albanian coastline. That same year, 1913, a naval
air training station was established on the island of
Cosada, just outside the Pola naval base, and at the
outbreak of war the Navy had a total of twenty two
aircraft.

Gottfried Banfield who was to be the Austro-
Hungarian Navy's greatest pilot was born in Pola
itself on 6 February 1890, the son of a captain in the
*K u K Kriegsmarine*. He followed his father's example
by entering the military academy at St Pölten in
1910 and thence went to the *Marineakademie* at
Fiume. In 1912 he applied to join Klobucar's tiny
Naval Flying Service and was accepted, learning to
fly at Wiener Neustadt and Fischamend.

During those early experimental days, Banfield
was seriously injured when his aircraft plunged into
the sea shattering his leg, and it was to be a year
before he could fly again; but he was back at Pola
when the fatal shots rang out at Sarajevo 200 miles
to the south-east. The first offensive action of the
naval flying service was on 12 August 1914, a
bombardment of Mount Lovcen in Montenegro,

### Hansa Brandenburg CC

Early unfortunate experiences with floatplanes, and the relatively calm waters of the Adriatic led the *K u K Kriegsmarine*, the Austro-Hungarian Navy, to concentrate on flying boat types even for fighter aircraft. The German Navy by contrast had the rougher waters of the North and Baltic Seas to contend with and preferred floatplanes.

Designed by Ernst Heinkel early in 1916 as a fighter flying-boat for Austria-Hungary's intensifying air war over the Adriatic, the CC was named after the industrialist Camilo Castiglioni. The little wooden-hulled fighter displayed the same 'starstrutting' used on the Brandenburg DI (see pp. 86/7) and a Benz BzIII powered prototype was tested by the German Navy at Warnemünde in February 1917 and some twenty-six were taken into service.

Meanwhile the main customer, the *K u K Kriegsmarine*, had tested the prototype numbered A 13 at Pola and in the hands of Gottfried Banfield it had shot down a Farman in October 1916. Production orders followed and A 14 was the first production aircraft to arrive at Trieste on 16 December 1916, the last being A 49 arriving on 18 June 1917. They were built by Phönix and Ufag and were powered by the native Austro-Daimler or Hiero engines. Armament was a single 8-mm Schwarzlose, although some machines had twin machine-guns fitted.

Banfield flew several fighter flying-boat types including the Lohner M-type numbered L 16, hastily improvised as a fighter in April 1916 with a water-cooled Schwarzlose machine-gun to defend Trieste from Caproni attacks. His next mount, A 11 was a special one-off design by Weichmann named *der Blaue Vogel*, the bluebird, and Banfield scored several victories with it. He also flew A 3, one of seven Fokker EIIIs urgently purchased for port defence in spring 1916. The Hansa-Brandenburg CC, A 24 was his most successful mount however and in this aircraft he had his inconclusive encounter with Baracca's Nieuport 11 over the Isonzo on 10 January 1917.

| | |
|---|---|
| Manufacturer: | Hansa und Brandenburgische Flugzeug-Werke GmbH/Phönix/Ufag |
| Engine: | Austro-Daimler, Hiero, 6-cyl in-line, 185 hp |
| Span: | 9.3 m (30 ft 6⅛ in) |
| Length: | 9.15 m (30 ft 0¼ in) |
| Max. take-off weight: | 1031 kg (2268 lb) |
| Max. speed: | 175 kmh (109 mph) at sea level |
| Ceiling: | 3300 m (10,825 ft) |
| Armament: | 1/2 x Schwarzlose 8-mm |

*Below: Linienschiffsleutnant* Gottfield Banfield (right) and his observer prepare to disembark from Löhner flying boat L 16. It is armed with a water-cooled Schwarzlose machine-gun

A group of Austro-Hungarian naval pilots photographed in 1916. Like their British and German equivalents, they adopted the uniform of their land-based military counterparts and here wear a mixture of dark-blue naval uniform and the 'pike-grey' of the army, with the addition of naval badges and rank insignia

and was followed by attacks on French naval units on 17 October. On 23 October, Antivari in Montenegro was raided by day and on 23 November by night.

The Austrians had it very much their own way in the Adriatic until Italy declared war on 26 April 1915. The Italian naval air station at Venice was only some half hour's flying time from Pola, but the *Sezione Aviazione Marina* had no aircraft capable of standing up to the Austrians until Lohner L 40 was captured intact by the Italians at the end of May 1915 and immediately copied and within 33 days began to be produced in quantity as the Macchi L 1. The strength of Italian naval aviation grew from 39 aircraft in 1915 to 467 in 1917 with ten bases and the seaplane tender *Europa*.

Against this growing strength Banfield energetically organized a defence and kept up the morale of the service and indeed of the whole Austrian Navy with his offensive example. In 1916 he was promoted to *Linienschiffsleutnant* and given command of the naval air station at Lloyd's Arsenal, Trieste. Under his command the air war in the Adriatic was taken right to the enemy—Venice was attacked by the Austrians thirty-six times, while Pola was attacked by the Italians forty-one times. Flying his Lohner L numbered *L 19*, technically a two-seat reconnaissance bomber armed with a single Schwarzlose machine-gun, he led offensive

sweeps into Italian territory making night raids on Venice, Rimini and Ancona, attacking airship sheds, communication targets and military bases in northern Italy and even kite-balloons on the Isonzo Front, where his first four victories were balloons. Intercepting French and Italian attacks on Trieste, he scored three FBA flying-boats shot down and on the night of 1 June 1916 he shot down an Italian Caproni Ca3 three-engined bomber caught in a searchlight beam over Trieste.

In 1916 Ernst Heinkel designed a single seat fighter flying boat for the Austrian Navy, the Brandenburg CC or KDW. Banfield was delighted with the prototype and soon had a chance to put the new aircraft to the test. He met the distinctive Nieuport 11 of the Italian ace Francesco Baracca, with its prancing horse insignia, over the Isonzo battlefield but neither of the experienced pilots could gain the upper hand in the bad weather conditions prevailing. Banfield noted that the Italian's Nieuport with its 80-hp Le Rhône rotary was slower than his 150-hp Austro-Daimler powered flying-boat but much more agile, climbing and out-turning the Austrian aircraft.

On 17 August the naval ace was awarded the *Ritterkreuz des Militär Maria-Theresien-Ordens*, becoming *Freiherr* von Banfield, and ended the war as the hero of the Austrian Navy with eighteen victories.

# Jean Navarre

NAVARRE was one of the first French aces and France was the country which invented the 'ace' system. Like Boelcke he made his name over Verdun, and again like Boelcke he packed into a short career an example to be copied by many who followed him.

When the German offensive broke at Verdun on 21 February 1916 there was only one *escadrille de chasse* located in that sector but within three weeks five more had been rushed in. Among them was *Escadrille N 67* newly equipped with the Nieuport *Bébé*. Among the pilots was Jean Marie Dominique Navarre who was already one of the very few victors of an air duel. Within weeks his name would be known by all of France and his red painted aircraft become an inspiration for the defenders of Verdun.

Jean Navarre was born at Jouy-en-Morin, the son of a wealthy paper manufacturer, and had already used some of his father's money to learn to fly before the war. He was one of the very select band of pre-1914 pilots and held military brevet No 601. His service career began when he joined *Escadrille MS 12* as a *Caporal* flying Morane-Saulnier Type L parasol monoplanes. On the night of 21 March 1915 the *escadrille* took off to intercept a Zeppelin attack on Paris. Navarre took a carbine and a kitchen knife declaring his intention of stabbing the monster to death! Not surprisingly the Zeppelin escaped. These were the very earliest days of air fighting but there was nothing to stop improvization. A Lewis-gun armed Morane flown by Eugène Gilbert claimed a victory on 10 January 1915 and on 1 April Roland Garros first used his deflector device successfully to destroy a German aircraft. On the same date Jean Navarre, flying above the Fismes sector to the east of Reims, managed to bring down an Aviatik with three rifle shots, one having injured the pilot. With Pégoud and Gilbert still about to make their names on the Morane Type N single-seater, Navarre's victory was still a big event and the young *Caporal* and his observer *Lieutenant* Robert were entertained and be-medalled by *Général* Franchét d'Éspérey. At this stage of the war, as with most other air forces, the pilot was the NCO 'chauffeur' for an officer observer.

Nevertheless Navarre was promoted *Sergent* and briefly transferred to flying a Morane N himself before joining *Escadrille N 67* flying the new Nieuport 11 with a Lewis or Hotchkiss firing forward above the propeller arc. He came to Verdun with a reputation already established and immediately justified it. On 25 February he shot down two German aircraft behind the French lines. One came down intact and the crew surrendered and the other in flames on a later patrol. It was the first French double of the war and Navarre became the first French fighter pilot to be cited in the army communiqué of the day. During the next few months his red-painted *Bébé* was both an inspiration to the *poilus* fighting and dying in the rubble below and a taunt to the German *Eindecker* pilots still operating independently over the battlefield. However, by

*Sergent* Jean Navarre with a Morane Type L parasol of *MS12*, late 1915. Navarre wears the officer's blue-grey tunic or *vareuse* of distinctive cut with the aviation service black brassard with the red and white winged propeller badge of a *Sous-Officier Aviateur*

**Sous-lieutenant Jean
Navarre, Verdun, spring
1916**

Nieuport XI patrols low
over the Verdun front

now the French were taking the tactical lead and *Commandant* de Peuty's order for offensive large-scale patrolling made as much impact as the 36 odd Nieuport 11s in the Verdun area had originally made themselves.

Navarre's way of fighting was already out of date and he was to be knocked out of the fighting just as the era of the lone hunter began to slip away. His method of attack was highly individualistic—he would fly up to within a few feet below and behind the enemy somewhat in the manner of Albert Ball, then actually stand up in the cockpit of his rotary-engined and highly unstable Nieuport to sight and fire the wing-mounted Lewis. It was a near suicidal operation attacking an experienced enemy and retribution was not far off. On 19 May 1916 he shot down his twelfth and last German. On 17 June *Sous-lieutenant* Navarre was shot down over the Argonne and severely wounded in the head.

Navarre, France's first ace, had fallen but he recovered sufficiently only to limp on with a severe mental disturbance. His brother was killed in November 1916 and, interred in an asylum in Paris, Navarre could only vent his anger and frustration against his warders. It was two years before he briefly returned to the Front without any result. At the end of the war the mentally crippled ace was brought out of his sheltered retirement once again to fly a new Morane-Saulnier through the Arc de Triomphe as part of the victory celebrations. He never got there. He crashed and died in training for the event on 10 July 1919.

**Nieuport Nie 11**

Gustave Delage's first design for Nieuport, the Type 10 of early 1914, was the company's first biplane and also introduced the sesquiplane layout that was to be a trademark of Nieuport products until 1918. The Type 10, called the '18 Metre' because of its wing area, served successfully with the *Aviation Militaire* and in small numbers with the RFC and RNAS but the company's fame was made by Delage's next design, the tiny Nieuport Type 11. It was based on a pre-war Gordon Bennett racer powered by an 80-hp Gnome rotary and armed with a single Lewis firing over the top wing. Its tiny size earned it the nickname *Bébé* when it entered service in summer 1915 and it was also known, like the Type 10, for its wing area as the '13 Metre Nieuport'.

The *Bébé* successfully challenged the supremacy of the Fokker *Eindecker*s at Verdun and examples supplied to the RFC and RNAS did the same on British Fronts in company with the DH2 and FE2b. Nieuport 11s went to the Dardanelles and were licence built by Macchi in Italy while others went to Belgium and Russia. The Nieuport's qualities so alarmed the German pilots that *Idflieg* urgently studied captured examples and many of its features appeared on the next generation of German fighters. They even commissioned firms to build straight copies (rather as an alarmed German High Command ordered copies of the Russian T-34 tank in 1942) and Albatros, Euler, Alter, Rex and Siemens-Schuckert produced Nieuport copies, the last company's DI actually going into production with a geared-rotary engine and some reached the front line.

The Nieuport 16 appeared in 1916 and was basically a more powerful *Bébé* powered by a 110-hp Le Rhône and mounting a synchronized Vickers.

| | |
|---|---|
| Manufacturer: Société Anonyme des Etablissements Nieuport | |
| Powerplant: Le Rhône 9-cyl rotary, 80-hp | |
| Span: 7.55 m (24 ft 9¼ in) | |
| Length: 5.80 m (19 ft 0½ in) | |
| Max. take-off weight: 480 kg (1058 lb) | |
| Max. speed: 156 kmh (96.8 mph) | |
| Ceiling: 4600 m (15,092 ft) | |
| Armament: 1 x Lewis .303-in | |

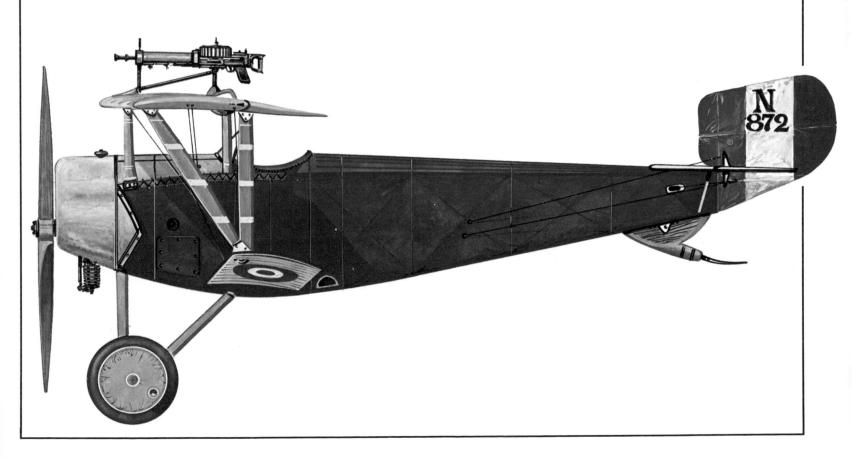

# 1916

THE German High Command's plan for the attack on the French fortress system round Verdun did not envisage a great breakthrough and turning movement but instead it was intended to draw in the whole strength of the French Army and destroy it in a gigantic battle of attrition. In the first weeks of 1916, in conditions of great secrecy, German aircraft were concentrated opposite Verdun to ensure a blockade of German-held airspace. Armed C-type two-seaters were to bear the brunt of this work with available E-types grouped in three *Kampfeinsitzer Kommando*s to assist them in mounting standing patrols.

At first this concentration of strength gained almost complete air superiority over the German lines and well out over the French defences allowing German artillery spotters and bombing aircraft to operate with relative immunity.

After the initial shock the French defence on the ground and in the air stiffened swiftly. *Escadrilles de chasse* were rushed from other sectors under the command of the pugnacious Commandant Tricornot de Rose, *Chef d'Aviation* of Second Army, and concentrated in a group at Behonne, outside Bar-le-Duc. Among them were the *Cigognes*, the Storks, who had already made a reputation under Felix Brocard in the Champagne fighting with Sixth Army. Increasingly French 'blockade-runners' got through directing counter-battery fire and putting out the eyes of the German gunners who had to rely on balloon observation as the German effort in the air became increasingly defensive. Oswald Boelcke flying EIIIs from the left bank of the Meuse saw the deleterious effect standing patrols and long transit flights were having on men and machines and moved three *Eindeckers* forward to Sivry, just 11 km behind the front, with a forward observation post connected by telephone to make the most economical use of aircraft for direct interceptions. Now the French were compelled to use their fighter strength defensively to protect their own reconnaissance machines.

New tactics took the French off guard and the *Cigognes* were badly mauled, Guynemer, Brocard and Deullen being wounded in the month mid-March to mid-April. By mid-April the French had assembled over 220 aircraft including the first Nieuport 11 *Bébés*. The Nieuports were more than a match for the *Eindecker* which was now beginning to show its age. Boelcke noted 'They were sending out as many as 12 fighters to protect two observation machines. It was seldom we could get through this protecting screen to reach the observation aircraft'.

The scale of the air fighting over Verdun was disproportionately multiplied by the fact that the hundreds of aircraft engaged were compressed into a terribly small arena. From the air pilots could see the flash of the long range guns firing and their shells falling like rain on their targets—as week by week the landscape below turned into an obliterated lunar landscape of shell-holes until at last only the bare geometric outlines of the forts themselves were interpretable.

In spite of the prototype specialist fighter organization being made on both sides, the fighter aces of Verdun sought combat and fought singly. Boelcke gained his ten victims by stalking alone and the French aces Jean Navarre and Charles Nungesser hurled themselves at German aircraft with reckless individualism. Nevertheless the lessons of the Verdun air war were clear. Destruction on the ground was wrought by accurately directed artillery fire. This meant denying airspace to the enemy and sweeping defended skies for friendly reconnaissance machines to work. To this end should be developed fast heavily armed machines able to outshoot and outmanoeuvre the opposition, and for maximum effect they should be grouped in mutually self-supporting specialized squadrons.

The fighting at Verdun ended before these doctrines could be applied. The June Brusilov offensive in Russia and the British build-up on the Somme forced the Germans to reduce the pressure and the terrible Verdun battles ended finally in December.

To the north on the British Front, the German advantage had also been checked in the first half of 1916. The 'offensive spirit' still carried RFC and RNAS aircraft into the Fokker infested skies and from January formation flying had reduced the damage to the vulnerable BE2c squadrons at least. But above all new aircraft were coming to redress the balance.

In July 1915 a single-seat pusher fighter armed with a forward-firing Lewis gun designed by the ex-

German soldiers surround a downed Sopwith Pup. The Pup was one of the outstanding Allied designs of 1916 although its impact was only fully felt the following year

Royal Aircraft Factory alumnus Geoffrey de Havilland had arrived in France and been promptly shot down. In spite of this inauspicious start in late 1915 the Airco DH2 had gone into production and on 7 February 1916 Major L G Hawker VC brought No 24 Squadron's DH2s to Bertangles, followed to France by Nos 29 and 32 Squadrons in March and May. Hawker's was the first specialized single-seat fighter squadron at the front and at last in company with the two-seat FE2b the technical edge of the Fokker E-types was blunted.

By the early summer of 1916 the French, German and British commands were digesting the lessons of Verdun. From the drawing offices and factories were coming prototype aircraft to match new tactical doctrines. Four brigades had been formed in the expanding RFC at the beginning of the year and at the end of April Trenchard withdrew fighting scouts from the Corps squadrons with their reconnaissance function, concentrating them in the Army Wings for fighting duties. The operational command of the Royal Flying Corps on the Western Front still had only limited powers. The 1st Brigade RFC was an integral part of 1st Army BEF and so on, and squadrons could not be transferred to another brigade without Army HQ agreement. Day to day orders for army co-operation and fighter patrols came from the relevant Army or Corps. Thus airpower was spread along the British front and a decisive concentration was really impossible to achieve.

The French system was not so rigid and the *Chef de Service Aéronautique au Grand Quartier Général* could more easily move squadrons from Army front to Army front. The French *escadrille de chasse* system had been vindicated while the reputation of the élite fighter *escadrilles* such as those of Groupe de Chaise 12 *Les Cigognes* and *Escadrille N 77 Les Sportifs* enraptured the whole of France.

On 1 July 1916 the Anglo-French offensive opened on the German Second Army front on the Somme. At 7.30 am, after a bombardment which could be heard in London, 100,000 British soldiers climbed out of their trenches and began to walk towards the German wire. On the ground it was a disaster—but in the air the Allies obtained complete local superiority. The RFC brought in three DH2 squadrons and a squadron of Morane Type Ns, their noses liberally daubed with red to avoid confusion with Fokker monoplanes, and the French concentrated four Nieuport *escadrilles*.

The E-types of Second Army's two *KEK*s *Nord* and *Süd* were quickly swept aside and the few newly arrived Fokker and Halberstadt single-seat biplane D-types were rendered ineffective in spite of new co-operative tactics. When the Somme offensive began Max Immelmann had already left the arena, shot down on 18 June, and Oswald Boelcke was away in the East touring the Russian Front and boosting the morale of Germany's Balkan allies. The shock of the Somme and the lessons of Verdun now brought large changes in the German fighter aircraft command structure. Army HQs had previously controlled the *KEK*s but from the beginning of August 1916 they were controlled at Corps level. Then on 10 August the new *Feldflugchef*, *Oberst* Hermann von der Leith-Thomsen, authorized the formation of the first *Jagdstaffel*, grouping the new D-types in a pure fighting formation. *Jasta 1* became operational under *Hptm* Zander with Fokker DIIs on the 24th. On the 11th Thomsen telegraphed a delighted Boelcke in Bulgaria with the news he was to command *Jasta 2*. On the way home at Kovel in Russia he chose *Leutnants* Richthofen and Böhme to fly with him. Boelcke scored his twentieth victory flying a Fokker DIII from Bertincourt for the *Jasta*'s first unit victory on 2 September. Throughout the ensuing weeks he worked up his young pilots to a fighting pitch which matched the efficiency of the new tractor biplanes Boelcke had asked for early in 1916 which were now beginning to arrive from Germany.

In the late summer of 1916 German airpower as a whole underwent a wholesale reorganization. On 8 October a *Kommandieren General der Luftstreitkräfte* was established with *Generalleutnant* Ernst Wilhelm von Hoeppner as first *Kogenluft*, in charge of all German aviation except the Bavarian units which remained under the nominal control of the original *Inspektion des Militär Luft und Kraftfahrwesens (Iluk)* for disciplinary and supply matters, although under the tactical control of the Prussian *Feldflugchef*. The old general-purpose *Feldflieger Abteilungen* disappeared, replaced by *Flieger Abteilungen* under Army HQ control for long range reconnaissance and *Fl Abt(A)*s for artillery co-operation. 'Protection squadrons' were grouped in *Schutzstaffeln (Schusta)* to defend the artillery two-seaters and engage in local ground-attack work, while the long range bombing arm was also reorganized and strengthened. The 1916 plan called for 30 *Jagdstaffeln* each equipped with 16 single-seater D-types to sweep the enemy from the skies of the Western Front.

1916 was the year that the organization of fighter aircraft on the Western Front changed radically, spurred by the technical advance of the synchronized machine-gun and also by the simple question of scale, with hundreds of aircraft being involved in enormous battles lasting many months. These two factors also brought about concomitant changes in tactics. The strategic role of the fighter was still defensive—to keep the enemy out—but this also meant defending the observation and reconnaissance machines which were the eyes of the only offensive bludgeon effective in a war of position—massed artillery. In 1916 ground attack and strategic bombing aircraft were in their infancy but their time was coming.

Even with special fighter squadrons and formation flying, the security of the army co-operation aircraft could not be guaranteed. Trenchard for one proclaimed the doctrine of the offensive, pushing British aircraft into enemy skies to engage enemy fighters there and force their defence line ever back from the front, and the French largely concurred. The RFC attempted to maintain army co-operation operations throughout the hours of daylight and in all but the worst weather with fighter protection being consequently stretched. The Germans worked in one or two periods each day with fighter strength concentrated. The French used both systems as circumstances allowed. German standing orders published in October 1916 stated:

'The present system of aerial warfare has shown the inferiority of the isolated fighting aeroplane; dispersal of forces and a continuance of fights carried out when in a minority must be avoided by flying in large formations up to a whole *Jagdstaffel*.'

The early aces fought alone pouncing on unwary two-seaters and inventing new manoeuvres and personal tactics in the process—but with these developments in tactics and organization the day of the lone hunter were numbered.

On 26 October Boelcke was killed in a mid-air collision. Four weeks later Major L G Hawker was shot down and killed in his outclassed DH2 by von Richthofen flying an Albatros DII. The veterans were leaving the arena (Boelcke and Hawker were both twenty-five) their place taken by the new heroes of the Somme air fighting, the twenty year old Albert Ball and the twenty-one year old Georges Guynemer.

The appearance of the new fast Halberstadt and Albatros D-types with their twin-gun armament again took the RFC and *Aviation Militaire* off guard as the *Eindecker* had done a year earlier. On 30 September 1916 as the Somme fighting sputtered to a close Sir Douglas Haig urgently requested the War Office in London to supply more fighting aeroplanes. Thus the naval squadrons on the Flanders coast with their excellent Sopwith 1½-Strutters and Pups began to be formed into fighter squadrons to join the battle to the south and they would make a great contribution to the coming battles of the spring.

Very youthful RNAS Flight Sub-Lieutenants mourn the crash of a Sopwith 1½-Strutter, one of the most effective Allied aircraft of 1916, serving in both bomber and fighter roles. They wear the khaki RNAS uniform described on page 75

# Max *Ritter* von Mulzer

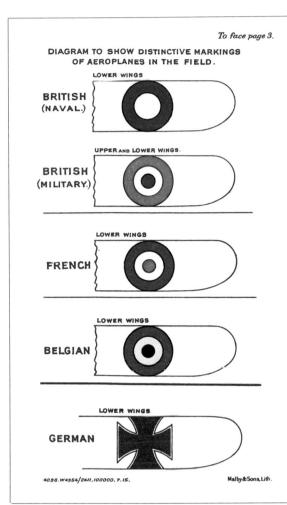

*Far left:* **Leutnant Max Ritter von Mulzer, 1916.** He received the *Pour le Mérite* in July 1916 and the *Militär Max-Joseph Ordern* (inset) of his native Bavaria in September—in effect a knighthood. He wears the very distinctive uniform of the Bavarian *Chevaulegers*— in this case *Regiment Nr 8*— with white facing colour. The single edge of piping to the plastron front has caused more than one celluloid 'ace' to be dressed in this apparently field-grey version of the RFC's maternity jacket. The Bavarian pilot's breast badge was the same as the Prussian except sur- mounted by the Bavarian crown.
*Left:* Weeks after the out- break of war the combatants adopted insignia for their aircraft. This recognition guide was published in Britain in late 1915.
*Below:* The *Militär Max- Joseph Ordern*

LIKE so many other young Germans attracted to the *Fliegertruppe* in the first years of the war, Max Mulzer was a frustrated cavalryman. There had been no glorious charges with lance and sabre, just tours of the trenches or waiting in dreary encampments for breakthroughs which never came. Like von Richthofen he had seen action in the very first months of the war when he won the Iron Cross for a particularly courageous cavalry patrol. He was a Bavarian, born in Kimratshofen near Kemp- ten on 9 July 1893, and on the outbreak of war joined that peculiarly Bavarian light cavalry—the Chevau- legers. On 13 December 1914 he was commissioned *Leutnant* in *Chevaulegers-Regiment Nr 8* and he looked most handsome in the plastron fronted tunic with its single edge of piping. He still sought action however and in mid-1915 successfully applied for transfer to the Air Service.

He reached *Feld-Flieger Abteilung 4* at the end of 1915, passed quickly to *Fl Abt 5*, but his great chance came when he was posted to the famous *Fl Abt 62* at Pontaverger with both Boelcke and Immelmann as his mentors. Immelmann in particular took the young Bavarian under his wing and taught him the new art of single-seat air fighting with the

Fokker *Eindecker* as the instrument. Throughout the spring of 1916 Immelmann and Mulzer flew to- gether, the Saxon and the Bavarian sharing several victories during this period.

On 9 July 1916, at the height of the Somme fighting, Max Mulzer was awarded the *Pour le Mérite*, having shot down seven aircraft to that date. At the end of the month he was appointed to command the new and largely Bavarian *Jagdstaffel 32*. In September King Ludwig awarded him the Military Order of Max Joseph—in effect a Bavarian knighthood—and the doctor's son became Max *Ritter* von Mulzer.

On 26 September 1916 he received orders to collect a new Albatros DI from *Flugpark 6* at Valenciennes. Here was the aircraft that would restore German dominance lost to the Nieuports and DH2s but Mulzer became the very first victim of the new aircraft's design flaw. After only a few minutes in the air a mainplane sheared and the Albatros plunged into the ground. Von Mulzer was dead, and, like several other German aces who followed him, he died testing a machine so that other less experienced pilots should have an ever greater margin of error.

# Oswald Boelcke

OSWALD Boelcke was the greatest example of everything a fighter pilot should be to the generation of German pilots who so closely followed him—indeed he was Germany's first true fighter pilot. He was a brilliant organizer and the guiding intelligence behind much of Imperial Germany's power in the air. He left much more than just a personal example—a set of rules for air fighting and an outline of fighter squadron organization which paralleled in importance the introduction of the synchronized machine-gun itself for the way the first war in the air would be fought.

He was born the third child of six to a schoolteacher who had been rector of the Lutheran School in Buenos Aires serving the large German community in Argentina, before returning home to Gibechenstein near Halle in Saxony where Oswald was born on 9 May 1891.

*Herr Professor* Boelcke was quite content for his older boys to have military careers but it seemed the frail and bookish Oswald would pursue a career in architectural engineering. The glittering military pomp of the Kaiser's Germany was irresistible to the young man and in 1911, two months short of his twentieth birthday, he entered the Prussian Cadet Academy at Coblenz. In August 1912 he was commissioned as a *Leutnant* in the Military Telegraph Service. Here his scientific interest was already equipping him to be the kind of technically-minded soldier that the snobbish military conservatives patronized as they bridled their cavalry chargers. Yet the coming war would be a war of machines and would call on such men over and over again. While at Darmstadt he had his first tantalizing contact with aircraft. He was already a trained telegrapher and had little difficulty transferring to the fledgeling Air Service. After seven weeks at the training school at Halberstadt he qualified in August as an NCO-pilot. It was seventeen days after Sarajevo.

By early September 1914, Oswald was serving with *Fl Abt 13* at La Ferté on the Champagne Front. Flying an Albatros BII with his bearded brother Wilhelm as observer, the workmanlike routine of the Boelcke brothers earned Oswald an Iron Cross 2nd Class in October while a week or so later Wilhelm, the elder brother and NCO observer, was awarded the First Class for having flown more miles of observation patrol than any other German observer on the front. As winter closed down, the pattern of trench lines which now stretched from the Belgian coast to the Swiss frontier had become firmly set. The work of the aviators who had flown off into the unknown in August with such high hopes was now a dreary round of observation patrols and reports.

In November 1914 *Leutnant* Parschau had brought a Fokker AI monoplane to the Boelckes' field and Oswald felt an excitement just like his first glimpse of an aircraft at Darmstadt. A bout of asthmatic trouble took him to a sanatorium early in 1915 and a two-week stay with *Idflieg* ensued but towards the end of April he was posted to the newly

established *Fl Abt Nr 62* under the pugnacious *Hauptmann* Kastner at Döberitz, west of Berlin. At *Abt 62* Boelcke flew an LVG BII, a stable but tame training aircraft equivalent to the RFC's Avro 504, but when the unit went to the front at Douai, he received an Albatros CI—one of the first C-class armed aircraft with a Parabellum machine-gun for the observer. On his first two days of missions with this machine he and his observer engaged four enemy aircraft. Then on 4 July 1915 they engaged a French Morane Type L parasol over Valenciennes. After twenty-five minutes of jousting, Boelcke held his aircraft within range long enough to let his observer *Leutnant* von Wuehlisch bring the French two-seater down with machine-gun fire. Wuelisch got the Iron Cross (Boelcke already had one) and Boelcke the pilot had made his first kill.

This was to be his only victory in a two-seater. In May, in conditions of some secrecy, Anthony Fokker had demonstrated a Fokker EI with synchronized machine-gun, at the front near Verdun. On 19 August, Boelcke shot down a Bristol while testing a demonstration EI and he needed no further convincing. In September he got a Fokker EII with a 100-hp Oberursel rotary engine and within a few days he had won his third victory—another Morane parasol.

Initially the Fokker *Eindecker*s were not seen as offensive weapons but only for defence of the two-

**DICTA BOELCKE**
**The air fighting rules of Oswald Boelcke**

**1:** The best position in aerial combat is that where one can shoot at the enemy from close range without him being able to reply, thus. . . .

**2:** Climb before the attack and dive from the rear. Altitude imparts speed in a dive and widens the patrol area.

**3:** Use natural cover—clouds and the glare of the sun.

**4:** Attack when the enemy is unsuspecting and pre-occupied with other tasks.

**5:** Do not fire until the enemy is within range and squarely in your sights.

**6:** The basic offensive manoeuvre is to turn more tightly than one's opponent thus eventually coming into a position on his tail.

**7:** Never turn your back and run from the enemy, turn and face the enemy with your guns.

**8:** To parry an attack from ahead, turn directly towards the opponent and present as small and as fast a target as possible.

**9:** To parry an attack from behind, enter and maintain as tight a turn as possible to make it as difficult as possible for the enemy to stay on your tail.

**10:** Foolish acts of bravery are fatal. Fight as a single unit and obey the formation leader's commands.

seaters– indeed German tactical doctrine of the time forbade penetration of the enemy's front lines because of the 'secrecy' of the synchronizing gear and the unreliability of the engine. However Boelcke and Immelmann flying machines with such a pronounced ascendancy over the opposition could not fail to give the French and British the ferocious mauling that became known as the 'Fokker Scourge'.

Between 6 July 1915 and 26 October 1916 Boelcke scored forty official victories. Thirty-one were to be two-seaters and the old Farmans, Voisins, and especially the British BEs with their observer in the front seat went down before his forward-firing machine-gun in droves.

In November 1915 Boelcke reported to the Charleville supreme headquarters of the *Feldflugchef Major* Hermann Thomsen and began a series of reports from the front line on tactics, organization and technical summaries of new aircraft types in action. It was an admirably short circuit between commander and the front-line and Boelcke's reports were models of conciseness. When in January 1916 he received the *Pour le Mérite* he became known not just to his own High Command but to the whole of Germany and indeed Europe.

With the *Pour le Mérite* at his neck and the ribbon of the *Ritterkreuz* on his tunic he was not yet twenty-five. He flew the most modern machine available, a Fokker EIV with a 160 hp Oberursel twin-row

rotary and in February 1916 the greatest battle the world had ever seen was about to begin. On 21 February 1916 massed German artillery began to shell the complex of French forts around the ancient fortress of Verdun. Verdun was the crucible for the development of fighter aviation proper. There were still in real terms very few Fokkers available and these few were used singly mainly on escort missions. They were divided into small *Kommandos*, Boelcke first partnering *Leutnant* Notzke at Sivry some seven miles behind the front. Boelcke, now promoted to *Oberleutnant*, used the same aggressive tactics that had already brought him fame and began to prey on the French *escadrilles* brought in to bar the skies above Verdun and where Charles Nungesser and Jean Navarre were beginning their careers. Notzke was killed at the end of April and he was replaced by *Freiherr* von Althaus, although the two Germans did not seek to act as an offensive formation, seeking combat, like their opponents, in individual duels. By 21 May Boelcke's score had risen to eighteen. The next day by the Kaiser's decree he was promoted *Hauptmann*. It was the first time in the Royal Prussian Army that a man of twenty-five had achieved this rank and this was all the more surprising because of his middle class background.

With Boelcke's line to his *Feldflugchef* fully open and his prestige enormously high, his suggestion that the *Kampf und Feldfliegerabteilungen* should be

*Above left:* The flying personnel of Fl Abt 62. Boelcke (left) and Max Immelmann flank the tall *Hauptmann* Kastner (centre), the unit's commander. Furthest left of the back row is Max Mulzer in his distinctive *Chevauleger* uniform.

*Above:* Boelcke, often revered as 'the father of air fighting', thoroughly instructed the pilots of his unit, formulating a set of rules. The basis of the training of the *Luftwaffe's* fighter pilots' of World War II and the tactics developed by Werner Mölders, his rules have substantially survived into the jet fighter age

**Hauptmann Oswald Boelcke, Verdun front, Spring 1916.**
Boelcke was awarded the *Pour le Mérite* on 12 January. On 21 May he was appointed the youngest *Hauptmann* in the Prussian Army

Germany's new élite fighting formation led by Boelcke himself, now Imperial Germany's greatest national hero, and great things were expected of them.

The ascendancy of the Fokker monoplanes however was now long over, their mastery wrested by the DH2 and Nieuport 11. On 27 August Boelcke established his *Jasta 2*'s headquarters at Bertincourt some miles south of Bapaume on the Second Army Front, and on 1 September ferried a new Fokker DIII from the *Armee Flugpark* as his personal machine. Immediately he began intensively to train his pupils and lecture them on every aspect of tactics and their mounts. Every morning he went up alone in the style of 1915, and as Richthofen wrote 'almost daily he had an Englishman for breakfast'. When the complement of new Albatros DIs and Fokker DIIIs was up to strength Boelcke decided the time had come to lead this personally created fighting unit into action and on 17 September *Jasta 2* fell upon the pilots of the RFC like a pack of wolves.

In the first large formation sweep into Allied territory, flying Albatros DIs and Halberstadt DIIs, six FE2d pushers and two BE2cs of No 11 Squadron RFC were engaged and none survived.

Between November and December 1916 *Jagdstaffel 2* completely dominated its sector and together with the other two *Staffeln* the British effort on the Somme was stopped here in the air as surely as the khaki-clad infantry below. *Jasta 2* alone shot down 76 British aircraft for the loss of seven of its own, the new D-class aircraft completely outclassing the DH2 and Nieuport 17. Beginning on 17 September, *Jasta 2* was flown as a flying circus, a complete fighting organization with every available pilot and aircraft being put into the air in one tight formation sweep with Boelcke leading. On the ground however he was still continuing to write the fighter pilot's rule book. He led the squadron but he also remained the teacher. In a frenzy of work he communicated his views to the High Command, visited other squadrons and set up the organizational nuclei of other *Staffeln*.

On 25 October, Boelcke scored his fortieth victory sending a BE down in flames west of Serre. On the late afternoon of the 28th, having already made five sorties that day, Boelcke led a six-aircraft flight in formation up and under a flight of British DH2s. In trying to maintain his defensive position behind his commander's black Albatros DI, Böhme's upper wing tip nudged Boelcke's interplane struts and the top wing began a progressive collapse. With the 160 hp Mercedes engine still churning out power, Boelcke fought for control but at 500 feet he plummeted into the ground and Germany's first great air fighter was killed.

At the funeral, conducted with full Imperial and military pomp at Cambrai Cathedral, von Richthofen carried Boelcke's *Pour le Mérite* in front of the casket. It would prove more than a symbolic gesture.

reorganized into specific fighting units was taken very seriously. The lessons of Verdun were clear and in June 1916 the first *Jagdstaffeln* (hunting flights) were formed. On 18 June Max Immelmann was killed. Boelcke was now worth more as a national morale-builder than a fighting airman and so by order of the Kaiser he was grounded and sent off on a tour of Germany's air forces in Russia, the Balkans and Turkey. At Kovel on the Central Russian Front he selected two men as potential fighter pilot material. One was a thirty-seven year old veteran of German East Africa named Erwin Böhme. The other was a young flier who wore the plastron-fronted tunic of a *Uhlan* regiment. His name was *Leutnant* Manfred *Freiherr* von Richthofen.

On 1 July the great British offensive opened on the River Somme. Four of the new *Jagdstaffeln* were assigned to the German First and Second Armies holding the line. Boelcke was recalled from Bulgaria to lead *Jasta 2*. Böhme and Richthofen joined him as Boelcke's hand-picked hunters, and others came from all over the front. They were the pilots of

## Fokker DIII

With the Fokker monoplane in decline by early 1916, Schwerin's chief designer Martin Kreutzer turned to a biplane layout and an in-line water-cooled engine for the next Fokker fighter, the DI, although few of these mediocre machines were built. The rotary-engined DII followed it closely and although rather better, it inherited some of the DI's faults including its system of wing-warping for lateral control.

The DIII was an attempt to improve performance by strengthening the fuselage to take the 160-hp Oberursel UIII engine. This was a twin-row rotary, a type of engine configuration used in pre-war racing aircraft but notoriously unreliable for military work because of overheating problems, as experience with the Fokker EIV had shown. Later versions of the DIII were fitted with proper ailerons instead of wing warping.

The aircraft's operational career was brief and it was soon replaced on the Western Front by the new Albatros and Halberstadt D-types equipping the first *Jagdstaffeln* from the summer of 1916. Nevertheless Oswald Boelcke flew one successfully, as did other pilots later to be aces, such as Richthofen, Udet and Kissenberth.

Boelcke collected his Fokker DIII number 352/16 from the *Armee Flugpark* on 1 September 1916 and the following day he made the first operational flight of newly established *Jasta 2* in this machine from their field at Bertincourt. That evening Boelcke had his first aerial combat for over two months and in a new aircraft, but he shot down a DH2 escorting a BE2c on a reconnaissance mission. It was his twentieth victory.

Boelcke flew the DIII until *Jasta 2* received its first Albatros DIs and DIIs and from 15 September, with only a month left to live, he flew all missions on the Albatros. Boelcke's DIII 352/16 hung in the Berlin *Zeughaus* for many years as a revered totem of Germany's first war in the air and its first air hero, with a wreath laid beneath it every year on 28 October, until it was destroyed by RAF bombers in 1943.

| | |
|---|---|
| Manufacturer: | Fokker Flugzeug-Werke GmbH |
| Powerplant: | Oberursel UIII 14-cyl twin-row rotary, 160-hp |
| Span: | 9.05 m (29 ft 8⅜ in) |
| Length: | 6.3 m (20 ft 8 in) |
| Max. take-off weight: | 710 kg (1562 lb) |
| Max. speed: | 160 kmh (100 mph) |
| Ceiling: | 4000 m (13,123 ft) |
| Armament: | 1/2 Spandau 7.92-mm |

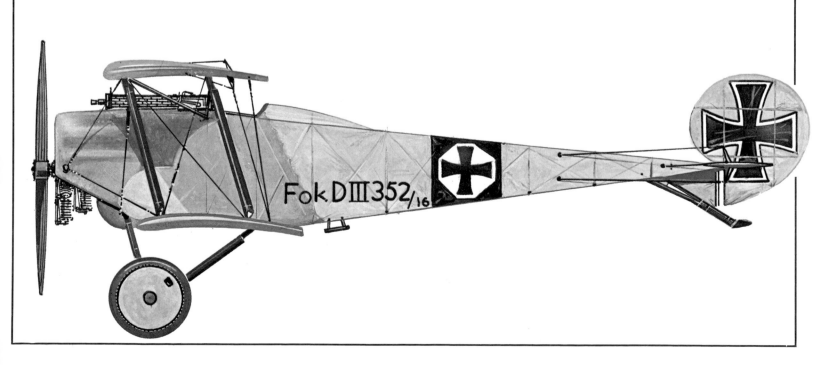

# Max Immelmann

MAX Immelmann and Oswald Boelcke were the two Great German aces of the first part of the war. Immelmann was born in Dresden in Saxony on 21 September 1890. His father was an industrialist who died of tuberculosis when Max was seven. In 1905 the discipline of the Saxon Cadet Academy at Dresden closed round him and in 1911 he was commissioned *Fähnrich* with a railway regiment at Berlin-Schoeneberg. In 1912 he left the Saxon Army to study engineering at the Dresden *Technische Hochschule*, and again like Boelcke his training made him an ideal man for the new age of war waged by machines.

When Germany mobilized for war Immelmann was posted to his old regiment but succeeded in transferring to the *Fliegertruppe*. In November he reported to the flying school at Adlershof and by March 1915 he was passed out as a pilot. The start of his active service was inauspicious when he cracked up two LVG two-seaters in heavy landings but his great chance came when in May he was transferred to *Fl Abt 62* at Döberitz and thence to Douai where he and Boelcke began their unique partnership.

On 4 June, flying an unarmed LVG on a photo reconnaissance mission, Immelmann was engaged by an armed Farman and a lucky French bullet sheared off his ignition. He brought his powerless aircraft safely down in a field near to base and for the feat received the Iron Cross Second Class. He was still in Boelcke's shadow however and when his friend and rival received an armed Albatross C I his

LVG BII equipped with a lashed-up Hotchkiss was passed on to Immelmann. When Boelcke got a new Fokker EIII, Immelmann took over the Albatros. On 30 July 1915, as a newly promoted *Leutnant* he flew a two-seat Fokker M8, an unarmed reconnaissance monoplane but similar to the EIII.

Early on the morning of 1 August, *Abt 62* was roused from its slumbers by the sound of roaring engines and the crump of bombs. Ten RFC BE2cs were beating up the airfield and, by the time Immelmann had sprinted to Boelcke's second Fokker EIII, the British were on their way home. Boelcke got up in pursuit wearing his nightshirt while Immelmann quickly found his way round the unfamiliar machine. Boelcke never fired a shot. He had to turn back with his machine-gun jammed. The Saxon however caught up with the rearmost BE2c near Vitry and fired off some sixty rounds before his machine-gun jammed. Then the British aircraft went into a spin, its pilot wounded in the arm, but landed safely and Lieutenant Reid RFC was taken prisoner. He was Immelmann's first victim.

For this feat Immelmann got the Iron Cross First Class and on 25 August he and Boelcke brought down a Caudron GIV. The next day Immelmann flying alone made his second kill and the day after came another claimed as a Bristol two-seater. More victories followed and in this period of ascendancy Immelmann was able to work out the tactics, including the famous manoeuvre that became known as the Immelmann turn, that a single-seat fighter

The famous manoeuvre known as the Immelmann turn was supposedly devised by Max Immelmann within weeks of first flying Fokker E-types with fixed forward-firing armament. If attacked from behind the turn could be used to put the single-seater above and flying in the opposite direction to the attacker, or to dive down on the victim from behind, by following through round the turn and half rolling again in the process. Against such aircraft as the BE2c with the observer-gunner in the front seat, the advantage of such techniques was absolute

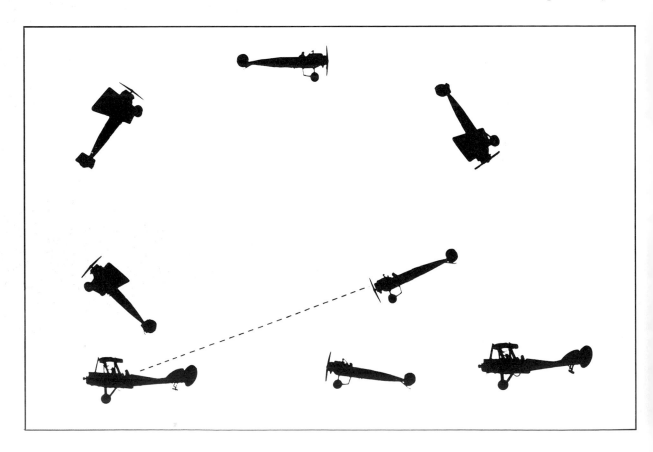

Master and pupil. *Oberleutnant* Max Immelmann (left) and *Leutnant* Max Mulzer (right) at Douai, June 1916

**Leutnant Max Immelmann, 1916.**
Immelmann originally joined a Saxon railway regiment, transferring to the flying troops in May 1915. Within weeks his career as one of the first single-seater aces had begun.

The *Pour le Mérite* was awarded by Prussia in January 1916, and his own state conferred the Saxon *Hansordern* soon afterwards. *Far right :* Immelmann with the wreckage of his seventh victim, a Morane Parasol of No 3 Squadron RFC, brought down on 15 December 1915

armed with a forward-firing machine-gun allowed. It was Immelmann also who set the pace for using the Fokker offensively by aggressive patrolling and stalking Allied machines that crossed the lines. In October Boelcke was detached for bomber escort to Metz and Immelmann became the sole defender of the highly important communications centre of Lille, wherein he gained two more victories to become an 'ace'. When the first *Kampfeinsitzer Kommando*s were formed, Immelmann led his unit at Douai while Boelcke was at Sivry. Both men received the *Pour le Mérite* in January and their fame and exploits were trumpeted throughout the Reich.

Inevitably by the spring of 1916 the Fokker monoplane's advantage was eclipsed by new Allied types but the designer strove to keep the edge. Immelmann tried an EIII with twin machine-guns but twice the interrupter gear failed and he shot his own propeller off. He tried the bigger EIV with a twin-row rotary and mounting three machine-guns but it was so heavy and slow that he soon reverted back to the 100 hp EIII.

By June 1916 the air fighting over Verdun was proving as bloody a mincing machine as the battle on the ground and the British push on the Somme was about to start with great superiority in numbers of aircraft. The *Eindecker*'s advantage had been more than checked. Great things however were hoped of the new *Jagdstaffeln* and the skill of Immelmann and Boelcke still held the morale of the air service and indeed the German people high. Then on the morning of 18 June Immelmann took off with three other pilots to patrol a sector near Lens. He never came back. His aircraft broke up in mid-air after a fight with seven British FE2bs of No 25 Squadron. There are three versions of how it happened. The British records indicate that Corporal J H Waller firing a Lewis from the FE's front cockpit simply shot him down. The second is that anti-aircraft fire was responsible and the third that once again the Fokker's primitive synchronizing gear had failed and the Saxon ace had 'shot himself down'. Whatever the cause it was a severe blow to German morale and signalled the end of the Fokker ascendancy that Max Immelmann had done so much to ensure. The 'Eagle of Lille' had taken fifteen Allied aircraft with him.

**Fokker EIII**

Before the war Anthony Fokker built several rotary-engined monoplanes which were based on then currently successful French practice. His M5K and M5L (K and L indicating short and long wing span) monoplanes served modestly as reconnaissance aircraft in the first year of the war and were not particularly successful. When Garros's Morane Type L with its crude forward-firing device was captured in April 1915, an M5K airframe was used for ground testing of Fokker's interrupter gear. Thus it was that a fragile and underpowered monoplane of 1913-vintage became transformed into one of the very first predatory fighters intended specifically as a destroyer of other aircraft.

From 1 June 1915 deliveries of the EI began and Fokker himself eagerly demonstrated its potential to excited front-line pilots. Construction was simple—the fuselage was of welded steel tube, and the wings were of wood, flexible enough to allow later control by wing-warping. Control cables ran from the wings anchored to the rear spar and over pulleys at the apices of upper and lower pylons to join at the control stick. The undercarriage was of steel tube, and the airframe was skinned in varnished fabric.

The original 80-hp Oberursel rotary of the EI was replaced by a 100-hp Oberursel UI on the EII entering service in September 1915 but the main production model was the EIII which featured further detail refinements. With an increased wing span, the EIII was flown normally with a single 7.62-mm synchronized Spandau, although some were flown with two guns incurring a weight and performance penalty.

For all its improvization, the Fokker EIII was an entirely new kind of fighting aircraft. It was issued, usually in pairs, to two-seater units to fly close escort. In the summer of 1915 both Boelcke and Immelmann were with *Fl Abt 62* one of the first units to get the new Fokker. Their first example EIII 37/15, arrived at Douai in July and was nominally Boelcke's but Immelmann scored his first victory flying this machine on 1 August when the airfield was attacked by British aircraft. With the RFC flying practically defenceless BE2s, the EIII's technical edge was absolute. Immelmann pioneered offensive

patrols rather than close escort, reigning almost unopposed in the skies above his sector between October to January 1916— while he was developing single-seat fighter tactics which remained effective for years to come.

Fokker meanwhile built an enlarged EIII powered by the 160-hp twin-row rotary Oberursel UIII but it was far too heavy and unreliable, and the EIV was an operational failure. Immelmann tried one powered by a captured 160-hp Le Rhône, mounting three machine-guns but this experiment was equally unsuccessful.

| | |
|---|---|
| Manufacturer: | Fokker Flugzeug-Werke GmbH |
| Powerplant: | Oberursel U I 9-cyl rotary, 100-hp |
| Span: | 9.52 m (31 ft 2¾ in) |
| Length: | 7.2 m (23 ft 7½ in) |
| Max. take-off weight: | 610 kg (1342 lb) |
| Max. speed: | 140 kmh (87.5 mph) |
| Ceiling: | 3505 m (11,500 ft) |
| Armament: | 1 x Spandau 7.92-mm |

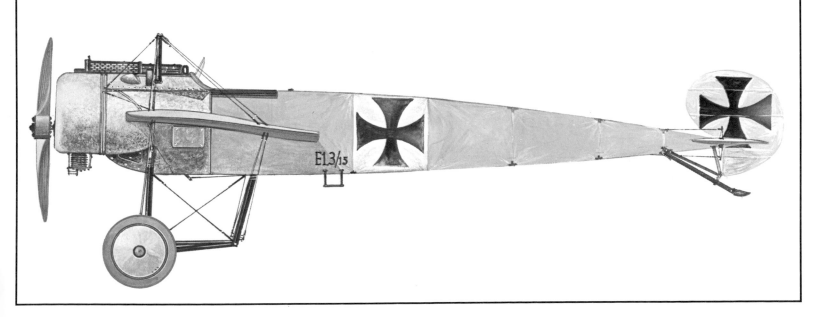

# Lanoe George Hawker

First of the British aces,
Major Lanoe G Hawker
VC DSO, victor of nine
aerial combats

WITH the name of a hunter, and with the manners of a shy young subaltern, Lanoe George Hawker was the Royal Flying Corps' first fighter ace. He was born on 30 December 1890, some four months before Oswald Boelcke, Germany's first fighter pilot hero. Hawker became a cadet at the Royal Naval College, Dartmouth, and later transferred to the Army's Royal Military Academy. In 1911 he was commissioned in the Royal Engineers, the same year as its Air Battalion was formally founded. On the foundation of the Royal Flying Corps the following year he was selected for pilot training and took his Aero Certificate-winning final test flight on a Deperdussin in March 1913.

When the Royal Flying Corps went to France, Hawker flew an RE5 of No 6 Squadron across the Channel with it. In October 1914 he saw the German advance on Antwerp from the air. In April 1915 he set out in a BE2c with three crude Melinite bombs and some hand grenades to bomb the Zeppelin shed at Gontrode near Ghent. Running the gauntlet of heavy ground fire he planted his last bomb on the huge target from a height of 200 feet. For this exploit Hawker was awarded the DSO.

The operational RFC squadrons in France in early 1915 had one or two single seat scouts attached for fast unarmed reconnaissance, but, when early in the year German aircraft increasingly began to intrude over the British lines, rifle and carbine armed scouts were sent up to try to intercept them. The problem of both flying and fighting from the cockpit of a single seater seemed insurmountable. In his earliest experiment Hawker mounted a single-shot hunting rifle lashed to the fuselage to fire at an angle clearing the airscrew—but the degree of skill needed to make a crabwise attack and fire a deflection shot at an enemy aircraft was more than considerable. A happier solution of Hawker's was a Lewis gun mounted over the top wing of No 6 Squadron's Bristol Scout No 1611 to fire along the line of flight. After the Gontrode raid Hawker was in constant action over the Ypres salient, taking a bullet in the foot from ground fire on 22 April, but he was soon back in action. On the morning of 25 July flying No 1611 he attacked an Aviatik C-type two-seater sending it down into the German lines. On a second patrol in the afternoon he attacked another Aviatik over Houthulst Forest driving it down with a damaged engine. Returning on the same patrol over Hooge he attacked an Albatros two-seater from out of the sun. The German observer countered with fire from his Parabellum until the German aircraft turned over throwing the observer into space at 10,000 feet. The blazing aircraft fell in British lines where it continued to burn for fifteen minutes. Three in one day.

Hawker received the Victoria Cross for the day's exploits. It was considered he had shown bravery of the highest order 'as the enemy's aircraft were all armed with machine-guns, and each carried a passenger as well as a pilot'. It was the third RFC/

## Scale of Working Clothing for an Aeroplane Squadron, RFC Army Order 155

| | Per Squadron |
|---|---|
| Boots, knee RFC | 25 pairs |
| Caps, fur lined | 25 |
| Gauntlets, observers' | 12 |
| pilots' | 12 |
| Gloves, chamois leather* | 12 |
| Goggles with Triplex glass | 25 |
| Glass for goggles (night or dark-tinted pairs) | 25 |
| Helmets, aviation | 8 |
| Jackets, leather | 27 |
| Masks | 25 |
| Overshoes, gaitered | 25 |
| Trousers, leather | 27 |
| Jean clothing, or brown drill combination suits | 2 per man biennially |

*For use in cold weather by men doping wings in the open.

RNAS Victoria Cross and the first to be awarded for an aerial combat.

When No 24 Squadron formed at the end of 1915 with DH2s, it was the first British single-seat fighter squadron. Its commander was Hawker, the hero of the RFC and now promoted Major at the age of twenty-five. On 7 February 1916 they arrived at Bertangles in France and immediately began intensive patrol flying north of the Somme as a way of working up and training. After a few weeks Hawker's pilots felt more confident. From 25 April the encounters with Fokker E-types increased and the DH2 showed it could more than hold its own. In October Boelcke had his fatal mid-air collision during an engagement with DH2s of No 24 squadron. No 24 claimed seventeen enemy aircraft in June and twenty-three in July. By November the score was seventy and Hawker's own official score stood at nine confirmed victories.

The RFC's pusher fighting aircraft, the DH2 and the two-seat FE2b, bettered the Fokker E-types and wrested mastery of the air over the Somme. With

December 14, 1916.

**FLIGHT**

# GAMAGES

### The Leading Naval, Military, :: :: and Aviation Tailors. :: ::

**LEATHER COAT FOR AVIATORS.**
The newest pattern, as approved by Officers in the Navy and Army.
In Black Chrome, dressed Leather, lined warm tweed  price **84/-**
Do., made with Camel Fleece lining  ...  ...  ...  ,, **95/-**

**AVIATORS' BREECHES.**
Black Leather Breeches, wool lined  ...  price **37 6** and **42/-**
Tan Leather Breeches, wool lined...  ...  ,, **42/-** ,, **63/-**

**AVIATORS' CAPS.**
The "**Brooklands**" (as illustrated). In black or brown leather,
with protective rolls for the ears, and strap and buckle for chin.
Finest quality.  Lined Sanitary Wool, **8/6**; Fleecy wool, **12/6**

**LEATHER AVIATION HELMETS.**
For R.N.A.S., **39/6**  R.F.C., in brown, **39/6**
Full length, Government Pattern, **55/-**

**AVIATORS' BOOTS.**
The "**A.W.G.**" High Legs, Quality "A"  ...  price **50/-**
Also made in Quality "B"  ...  ...  ...  ,, **55/-**
This "B" boot is also made with black uppers for Naval Airmen.

**ROYAL FLYING CORPS SERVICE JACKETS.**
In Serge and Cashmere  ...  ...  ...  **50/-** and **55/-**
**BREECHES**  ...  ...  ...  **25/- 30/- 35/-**
**SERVICE JACKETS** in Whipcord and Barathea,
**63/- 70/- 84/-**
**BREECHES**  ...  ...  ...  **30/- 35/- 42/-**
The above prices include badges and buttons.

**BRITISH WARM COATS,** fleece lined,
**50/- 55/- 63/- 84/-**

**THE "FLANDERS" WAISTCOAT.**

**CHAMOIS LEATHER WAISTCOAT.**

SPECIAL OFFER.
Can be worn open or buttoned up.
In fawn fleece...  ...  ...  **14 9**
Also in soft tan leather, warmly
lined  ...  ...  ...  **27/6**
Fleece lined  ...  ...  ...  **30/-**

With long sleeves and back of same
leather.  Very warm and comfortable.
Does not take up much room under
Jacket.  Natural colour in Brown
Chamois  ...  ...  ...  **30/-**
Extra long in Dark Brown  ...  **35/-**
Superior quality, extra long, Brown
or Grey  ...  ...  ...  **50/-**

R.N.A.S. Officer's Uniform.

**ROYAL NAVAL AIR SERVICE UNIFORMS**
FOR OFFICERS in 48 Hours.
**Blue Beaver Great Coats,** complete with Shoulder
Straps  ...  ...  ...  ...  **£5 5 0**
**Fleece British Warms,** complete with Shoulder
Straps  ...  ...  ...  ...  **£4 10 0**
**Super Reefer Jacket, Waistcoat and
Trousers**  ...  ... £4 15 0 and **£5 5 0**
**Cap and Badge**  ...  ...  ...  **£0 17 6**

R.N.A.S. British Warm.

## HOLBORN, LONDON, E.C.

*When communicating with advertisers, mention of "Flight" will ensure special attention.*

35

*Far left:* Table of protective clothing officially allotted to an RFC squadron in 1915. *Left:* Gamages advertises its wares for 1916. Note they could tailor an officer's uniform within 24 hours. The knee-length coat in 'chrome leather', brown for the RFC and black for the RNAS, with its chest slant pocket, was the British flyer's trademark

**Lieutenant L G Hawker, No 6 Squadron RFC, Bailleul, France early 1915.**
Issue RFC protective clothing at this stage of the war included leather trousers and gauntlets but there was still room for personal improvisation as evidenced here. *Flight* magazine's editorial for 19 September 1915 lambasted airmen for their habit of 'wrapping themselves in large sheets of a daily paper when a visit to a fashionable London store would suffice. The fur cuirass worn by our troops at the front is obtainable here made in rabbit or goatskin. Mr Kent of the aviation department at Gamages would be happy to assist'

the appearance of the new Albatros and Halberstadt D-types from September the sturdy and manoeuvrable DH2 was outclassed.

On 23 November No 24 Squadron's 'A' Flight commander Capt J O Andrews led four DH2s out over the Somme battlefield with Hawker flying as an ordinary member of the patrol in No 5964. Andrews spotted a formation of five Albatros biplanes heading east. They were new DIIs of *Jasta 2* trailing their coats and leading the British aircraft deeper over the German lines. As the Germans began a slow climb one of the tired old DH2s developed engine trouble and turned for home, closely followed by a second. Hawker and Andrews flew on. Just as the 'A' Flight commander fell on the tail of an Albatros, another shark-nosed German aircraft locked onto Andrews' tail, and a stream of bullets smashed into the spinning rotary engine, its mass protecting the pilot. As his engine revolutions fell away, Andrews turned and headed for his own lines, losing height and wagging his tail as he went throwing off pursuers. He landed safely at Gillemont leaving his commanding officer alone.

Hawker had gone for a second DII. At the first burst of Lewis fire, the Albatros banked round sharply. The pilot was Manfred von Richthofen, victor of fourteen air combats.

Thus far his victories had been over two-seaters with two BE12s and a Martinsyde G.100 single-seater, both types being stable 'sitters' in an aerial combat. Ten of Richthofen's victories had been the result of long careful stalking pursuits. Hawker was something different, even in the outmoded DH2. Richthofen employed his well-tried tactics of simple pursuit, using the Albatros's advantage of speed and climb, against Hawker's tighter turning circle. After repeated circling to the right and then to the left, the Englishman throttling back at the apogee of his turn, sideslipping at maximum bank to break up the deadly symmetry of the chase—the pair had lost 5000 feet and were now down to 3000 feet. There was less and less height left for Hawker to turn into speed.

Hawker was running out of fuel as well as altitude. He tried a series of loops and for a matter of seconds the German filled his sights—the Lewis however could not deliver a fatal burst of fire in a few snapshots and at last Hawker broke off completely and turned desperately for his own lines. With his outrigger tail weaving from left to right threshing the air like a landed fish, Hawker was using every trick he knew to throw off his pursuer and still losing height to try and gain speed. At 100 feet he was almost grazing the broken tops of the stripped trees punctuating the battlefield but they could offer no shelter. Richthofen had already fired nearly 900 rounds from his twin belt fed machine-guns. From sixty yards he fired a final burst as Hawker tried to turn and offer a last defence. Unprotected by the engine, he was hit in the head and the hero of Royal Flying Corps plunged into the ground.

### De Havilland DH2

When Geoffrey De Havilland joined the Aircraft Manufacturing Company at Hendon in June 1914, he brought with him experience of the pusher 'Fighting Experimental' types he had worked on previously at the Royal Aircraft Factory. The DH1 two-seater pusher armed with a single Lewis machine-gun bore more than a passing similarity to the FE2 but this first Airco machine was destined for the relative obscurity of Home Defence and the Palestine Front. Next from De Havilland was the DH2, a slightly scaled down version of the DH1—but a single-seater, designed in the spring of 1915 as a fighting scout.

The wings were of wood and fabric and the tail structure borne at the end of four cross-braced metal tube beams anchored to the rear wing spar. Churning away within the bird cage structure was a 100-hp Gnome Monosoupape rotary engine, which on later production machines demonstrated a fatal tendency to hurl one of its nine cylinders through part of the structure.

The whole point of the pusher layout was to relieve the pilot of the frustrations of trying to fire a machine gun from a tractor single-seater. There were still considerable problems however. The prototype No 4732 featured a mounting for the Lewis on the port side of the cockpit. This machine was sent to France in July 1915, but on 9 August it was forced down behind enemy lines and its pilot died of his wounds. Despite the poor start the DH2 was ordered into quantity production, now featuring a modified gun mounting. The front of the nacelle was revised with the Lewis mounted centrally on a free mounting that allowed it to be traversed from left to right and elevated upwards and downwards. The idea seemed excellent—combining a manoeuvrable gun platform with all the tactical advantages of a free weapon—but in practice it simply did not work. Pilots could barely fly their tricky mounts and lay the gun at the same time, let alone change Lewis drums after every 47 rounds in a thunderous slipstream.

Hawker's squadron No 24 was the first to form with the new fighting scout followed to France by RFC Squadrons Nos 29 and 32 on 25 March and 28 May 1916. Hawker who had been experimenting with airborne armament from the earliest days did not like the flexible Lewis, nor the frequent changing of drums. He reportedly devised a double drum with Air Mechanic W L French and employed it successfully. As for the 'wobbly' mountings as the pilots described them, the gun when elevated actually fouled the control column. Hawker at first tried clamping the muzzle of the gun so that it fired straight forward, but the scheme was officially forbidden. A spring clip allowing the gun to be both free and fixed (invariably flown fixed) was described as the 'best compromise with red tape'.

Flown in this way the DH2 was remarkably effective in action, considering its outmoded concept, being highly manoeuvrable and with its lightness and large diameter four bladed propeller it had an excellent rate of climb. For all its apparent fragility it was basically tough and the rear mounted engine afforded the pilot some protection from stern attacks. It was however slow. The high drag of the pusher layout's 'built in tailwind' prevented the aircraft from picking up speed even in a long dive. This factor, plus the Albatros DII's great margin of power, gave Richthofen a crucial advantage in Hawker's last fight.

The death of Hawker symbolized the regained supremacy of the German fighters over the Western Front at the close of the Somme fighting. Nevertheless the DH2 squadrons had to fight on out-gunned and outflown as they were. On 20 December 1916 No 29 Squadron lost five DH2s out of six in one fight, under the guns of five Albatros DIIIs. Nevertheless withdrawal of the DH2 only began in March 1917. Nos 24 and 32 Squadrons still flew DH2s during the Battle of Arras and still had some on charge during the Battle of Messines in June, until at last completing re-equipment with DH5s.

Some lingered on in Palestine and Macedonia—two were unsuccessfully tried out in 1917 as anti-Zeppelin fighters—but most ended up as trainers in the United Kingdom finally retiring in the autumn of 1918.

| | |
|---|---|
| Manufacturer: Aircraft Manufacturing Co Ltd | |
| Powerplant: Gnome Monosoupape 9-cyl rotary, 100-hp | |
| Span: 28 ft 3 in (8.6 mm) | |
| Length: 25 ft 2½ in (7.6 m) | |
| Max. take-off weight: 1441 lb (653 kg) | |
| Max. speed: 93 mph at ground level | |
| Ceiling: 14,000 ft (4267 m) | |
| Armament: 1 x Lewis .303-in | |

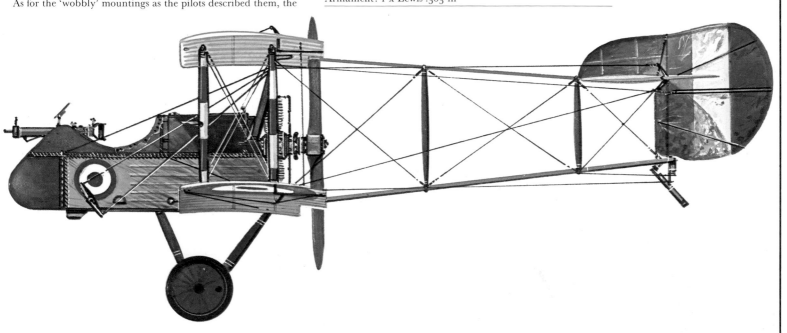

Albert Ball

Captain Albert Ball in an
SE5 at the still snowbound
airfield at London Colney
during No 56 Squadron's
working up period, March
1917. Ball did not at first like
the new fighter from
Farnborough and made
several modifications
including removing the
original windscreen and
fuselage Vickers machine-
gun

**2nd Lieutenant Albert Ball RFC, summer 1916.**
Ball wears army service dress with the collar and cap badge of the Sherwood Foresters, the regiment he joined at the age of eighteen on the outbreak of war

HE was not a 'Hun-hater', and the shy young man was embarrassed by the adulation that the British press whipped up, yet Albert Ball was the first British pilot to become a national hero until his life was cut violently short at the age of twenty.

He was born in Nottingham on 14 August 1896, and like so many other children born on the brink of the new century, he spent much of his childhood delightedly tinkering with engines and electrical circuits. On the outbreak of war he volunteered for the Sherwood Foresters and was gazetted as a Second Lieutenant in October 1914. Throughout the early summer of 1915 he took flying lessons at his own expense on an old Caudron, cycling from the transit camp pitched on Ealing Common to the Ruffy-Baumann School at Hendon, and got his Royal Aero Club certificate in October. He was then attached to the RFC and by January 1916 he had his wings. At last in February he was posted to France to join No 13 Squadron RFC flying BE2cs at Savy airfield. His baptism of fire was not long in coming. On 20 March he crash-landed a BE2c damaged by anti-aircraft fire, but during the next six weeks he was constantly in action, choosing to fly the squadron's sole single-seater, a Bristol Scout, whenever he could and all the time aching to be free of the cumbersome BEs and fly fighters proper. His chance came early in May when he was transferred to No 11 Squadron and to his delight got his hands on the sensitive control of a Nieuport.

He was soon in action and on 22 May drove down an Albatros DI and an LVG and over Douai airfield on 1 June he did the same to a Fokker and an Albatros. On 26 June he destroyed a German observation balloon using incendiary bombs, and on 2 July he sent a Roland CII crashing smack into the Mercatel-Arras road to gain his first confirmed victory. At the end of the month his MC was gazetted but meanwhile Ball, after a brief period of leave, had been posted back to a two-seater squadron, No 8 at Bellevue still flying BEs. Ball saw it as a punishment for his 'swell-headedness' but nevertheless used his unforgiving BE2d to undertake offensive missions even forcing a balloon observer to take to his parachute.

On the day after this mission, 10 August 1916, Ball was posted back to No 11 Squadron with the rank of Lieutenant, and began a run of victories throughout the month establishing him as the most successful British scout pilot to date. At the same time he was evolving his own tactics requiring tremendous degrees of skill and timing. He would dive head on at an enemy formation, scatter any semblance of a cohesive defence, then fasten tightly under the tail of a chosen victim, to rake its belly with upward fire from the upper-wing mounted Lewis-gun. His Nieuport was rigged to be tail-heavy allowing a greater stability at altitude and freeing both Ball's hands to manipulate the Lewis and its drum ammunition supply. Ball attacked, shot and escaped very quickly. He was a

### Bristol Scout

Like the Nieuport *Bébé* the Bristol Scout was derived directly from a pre-war racing aircraft and Frank Barnwell's design was exceptionally clean and fast for its day. The Bristol Scout appeared however when neither armament nor tactical organization were adequate to make it an outstanding military aircraft. If it could have been fitted with a synchronized machine-gun when it first went into action in September 1914, it would have been the most efficient military aircraft at the front. As it was, the Germans got there first with the otherwise very inadequate *Eindecker* and later with the tactical grouping of the *Jagdstaffeln*.

The original design was completed in February 1914 at Filton and recorded a speed of 95 mph (152.8 kmh). Two went to France with the BEF (Type B's) and orders for more were placed by the RFC and RNAS and these 'Scout Cs' began to be delivered from February 1915, and along with the BE2c, the Bristol was one of the first aircraft of the war to be ordered into quantity production.

These single-seat aircraft were at first unarmed, seen very much as fast scouts, although every combination of small arm was taken aloft. Like the *Eindecker*s the Bristol Scouts were allocated piece-meal to two-seater squadrons as escorts. The Scout D appeared in November 1915 with detail airframe alterations but more important had some provision for armament. A Vickers machine-gun was fitted firing through the airscrew via Challenger synchronizing gear, although many pilots preferred an overwing-mounted Lewis.

Albert Ball had his first flight on Bristol Scout No 5316 attached to 13 Squadron then flying BE2cs, on 29 April 1916. This Scout was normally reserved for 'experienced' pilots but after pestering his squadron commander for weeks Ball at last was allowed to fly it round the aerodrome, delighting in its speed and manoeuvrability after the lumbering BEs. On 5 May he flew another Scout No 5313 on a lone patrol over German lines but nearly shot off his own propeller while testing his guns with their primitive synchronizing gear.

No 11 was one of the first RFC squadrons to be allocated solely to 'fighting duties'. Ball flew one of the Bristol Scouts,

No 5326 and on 15 and 16 May he succeeded in driving down two Albatros C-types and another Albatros and an LVG on the 22nd while flying the same aircraft. Ball was soon afterwards delighted to receive a new Nieuport 16 and after his unfortunate experience with the Bristol in which he nearly repeated Immelmann's feat of shooting himself down, he eagerly experimented with the new Foster mount and an over-wing Lewis.

From mid-1916 Bristol Scouts were progressively withdrawn and allocated to training duties. Albert Ball again flew a Scout during his brief stay as a fighting instructor with No 34 (reserve) Squadron at Orfordness where he managed to overturn a Bristol Type C No 5554 escaping unhurt.

| | |
|---|---|
| Manufacturer: | The British and Colonial Aeroplane Co (Bristol) |
| Powerplant: | Gnome 7-cyl rotary, 80-hp |
| Span: | 24 ft 5 in (7.4 m) |
| Length: | 20 ft 7 in (6.30 m) |
| Max. take-off weight: | 1195 lb (542 kg) |
| Max. speed: | 95 mph (145 kmh) |
| Ceiling: | 15,500 ft (4724 m) |
| Armament: | 1 x Vickers .303-in/1 x Lewis .303-in |

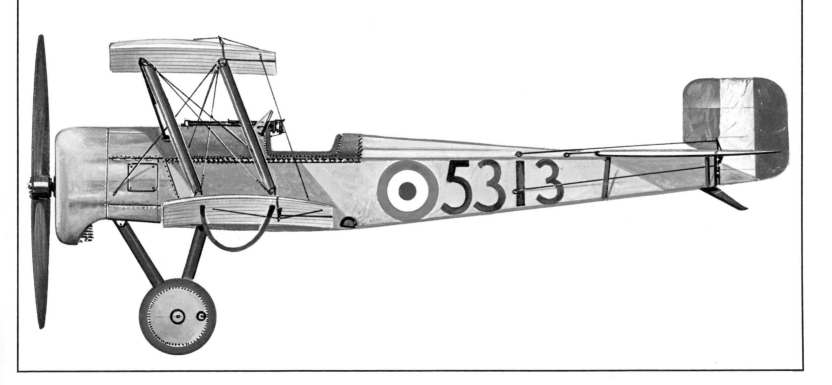

lone hunter who could attack a formation and win, taking advantage of their surprise and defensive pre-occupation with station-keeping.

In late August he was allocated to No 60 Squadron at Filescamp which had just been pulled out of the line and re-equipped with Nieuports having suffered near-disastrous losses.

No 60's Commander, Major Smith-Barry, recognized the shy and temperamental young man's ability to wage a successful individual war and gave him a roving commission. This period coincided with the arrival of the first *Jagdstaffeln* on the British Front but Ball's solitary habits and skill saved him from the onslaught, and the Englishman's score rose relentlessly, his Nieuport 17 with its bright red spinner slicing through formations of enemy two-seaters, mainly LVG and Roland CIIs, with deadly effect. On 1 September Ball's squadron was transferred back to his old base at Savy. On the same date General F A Higgins wrote of Albert Ball '. . . He has forced twenty German machines to land, of which eight have been destroyed . . . during this period he has forced down two hostile balloons and destroyed one.' When Ball was sent back to England on 4 October he had in fact decisively shot down nine German aircraft. His importance to Britain's war effort however lay not in how many German two-seaters he had knocked down, but in the effect his exploits had on the sagging morale of the Royal Flying Corps at a time when, like the infantry below whose blood soaked the chalk of the Somme valley, they had been checked by a numerically inferior enemy but one possessing better equipment and better tactics.

Ball hated his sojourn as an instructor and repeatedly applied to be returned to France. There were some breaks however from the routine at No 34 (Reserve) Squadron at Orfordness on the bleak East Anglian Coast. During his stay in England he was fêted by the press and civic dignitaries. He had the MC and now the DSO and Bar and the Russian Order of St George. He made tours of aircraft factories and Austin Motors of Birmingham, designed and built a fighter, the Austin-Ball AFB1, based on his ideas, typically with an upward firing Lewis.

The frustrations of seniority did not end for the twenty year old however when he was posted to the newly forming No 56 squadron at London Colney in Kent as commander of 'A' Flight, and the young man found his time taken up with administrative duties for several weeks. The new squadron however was a long way from his training unit. In March 1917 the whole of the RFC had been combed for its most experienced and pugnacious fighter pilots to form a new squadron equipped with the Royal Aircraft Factory's latest product, the SE5 fighter. Ball was not at all enthusiastic preferring the agility of his rotary Le Rhône-engined Nieuport to the Hispano-Suiza V8-engined SE5. He removed the windscreen, the upper wing tank and the fuselage Vickers and lowered the pilot's seat on his SE5,

A4850, and he kept a Nieuport, B1522, just to make sure. At last, after six weeks of acclimatization, on 7 April, No 56 Squadron flew to France and its base at Vert Galand.

Ball's career began all over again and he fought in much the same way as he had before. On 22 April Ball led the squadron's first sortie in the SE5 but it was indecisive. Turning to his Nieuport on the next day he scored the squadron's first confirmed victory by sending an Albatros CIII down in flames. Later that day flying the SE5 he shot down the Albatros DIII of the commander of *Jagdstaffel 12*. That was no easy two-seater and Ball began to warm to the qualities of the SE5, especially its stability as a gun platform.

In the first days of May he sent down nine more black-crossed aircraft, single and two-seaters, until on 6 May, flying his Nieuport B1522, he sent down the red-marked Albatros DIII of *Vizefeldwebel* Jäger of *Jagdstaffel* 20 over Sancourt. It was his forty-fourth victim—it was also to be his last.

No 56 Squadron with its cream of experienced pilots and equipment was unusual within the RFC. The British did not generally band together their best pilots into special units such as the French *groupes* and German circuses, but No 56 was an exception. They must have met Richthofen's *Jasta 11* on several occasions reporting clashes with 'all red scouts' in the squadron war diary, but they never found Richthofen himself. Ironically the 'anti-Richthofen' squadron, with Albert Ball as its inspiration, was to meet disaster at *Jasta 11*'s hands on Monday 7 May 1917.

Early that Monday morning Ball flew an uneventful patrol escorting Sopwith 1½-Strutters of No 70 Squadron. At 1800 hours Ball again took off in SE5 A4850 leading an eleven strong patrol of SE5s over the area of Cambrai-Douai, east of Lens. In a three-pronged stack, two fours and a three, the formation flew into towering cumulus cloud and began to lose cohesion over Bois-sous-Bourlon near Cambrai well inside the German lines. The lowest flight found the enemy 3000 feet below them, six Albatros DIIIs, and went into the attack. But the Germans too had been flying in a stack and two more *Jastas* of *Jagdgeschwader 1* followed No 56 Squadron down to ambush the ambushers. The battle broke up into flailing individual contests. Five of the SE5s went down in the desperate and confused fighting and Albert Ball himself was seen to fly into a dense cloudbank. He was never seen again by his airborne comrades. Germans on the ground saw an aircraft come out of the cloud with its propeller stopped and crash into the ground near the village of Annouellin.

Albert Ball was found dead at the controls, his body badly mutilated by the crash, but no bullet had hit him or his aircraft. Ball the inspiration of the RFC was dead, some eleven weeks before his twenty-first birthday, and had taken forty-four German aircraft with him. King George V presented a posthumous VC to his parents on 21 July 1917.

# Robert Alexander Little

MANY pilots from Britain's dominions wore the uniform of the Royal Naval Air Service. R A Little was one such, an Australian, born in Melbourne, Victoria, on 19 July 1895. He was just twenty when he qualified as a pilot at Hendon in October 1915 and three months later was commissioned as a probationary Flight Sub-Lieutenant at Eastchurch. By June he was at the Naval Air Station at Dunkirk fulfilling the function of the naval pilots in France at this time by undertaking reconnaissance along the coast and making strategic attacks on German installations in occupied Belgium. By Autumn 1916 however the RNAS was being drawn into the land battle further south and had the task of forming the personnel at Dunkirk into fighter squadrons to fight under RFC command. Thus was born the famous 'Naval Eight'—No 8 (Naval) Squadron—on 25 October with Fl Sub-Lt R A Little among its first pilots.

Under Squadron Commander G R Bromet they began with three flights of Nieuport 17s, Sopwith 1½-Strutters and Sopwith Pups but by December it was the first all-Pup squadron in action. Little and his fellow naval pilots were delighted with the new aircraft. On 11 November, Little made his first kill, an Aviatik C1, while flying a Pup N5182 and by December had claimed two Halberstadts.

On 1 February 1917 Naval Eight handed over its Pups to No 3 (Naval) Squadron who took their place in the line with the RFC while Naval Eight's personnel went back to Dunkirk to reform with a more formidable fighting machine—the Sopwith Triplane. At the end of March the squadron flew south to Auchel, on the Third Army Front near Arras. Opposite them at Douai, once the home of Boelcke and Immelmann, was the HQ of Manfred von Richthofen's Albatros DIII-equipped *Jasta 11*.

While the RFC squadrons with their obsolete equipment were being bloodily mauled, the naval Triplanes at least cowed the *Jasta* pilots and Little

An F N Birkett graduation photograph of R A Little (*left*) at Hendon in October 1915. The aircraft is a Caudron GIII widely used by the British and French for training—as was the bigger twin-engined Caudron GIV of 1916, seen in RNAS service (*above*)

**Flight Lieutenant R A Little RNAS, October 1916.**

Dress regulations for the RNAS were promulgated by Admiralty Order on 26 June, 1914. It read: 'Officers of the Royal Navy graded as flying officers wear the uniform of the Military Branch of the Royal Navy but of the relative rank which they hold in the Royal Naval Air Service, with the addition of an eagle on the left sleeve above the distinction lace and on the left shoulder strap.'

The anchor on cap badge, buttons, full dress epaulettes and sword belt was replaced by the eagle.

Royal Marine and Army officers attached to the RNAS wore their original uniform with the eagle on the left breast, as did RNAS officers wearing the khaki uniform.

In October 1917 new regulations ordered the wearing of the eagle on both cuffs and shoulder straps and, further: 'Observer officers wear the uniform of their rank in the Royal Navy with the addition on each sleeve above distinction lace and on each shoulder strap of a gilt badge consisting of an "O" with wings.'

Changes in the cuff rank system were introduced at the same time, illustrated *opposite*.

In January 1918 non-graded or non-flying officers of the RNAS were granted a gilt badge of a winged 'A' to be worn instead of the eagle

was by now a master of this highly manoeuvrable machine. Flying with another great Australian naval triplane exponent, Fl Cdr C D Booker, he got a *Jasta 11* Albatros over Lens on 7 April. On 24 April he attacked a DFW CV, put a bullet through its oil tank, and then followed its glide down to a field behind the Allied lines. The German made a perfect landing but Little's triplane turned over on landing and the German pilot (who had been a Rhodes scholar at Oxford before the war) had to help his notional captor out of the upturned Sopwith, remarking 'it rather looks as if I shot you down, not me'.

In spite of this humiliation, Little's victory log lengthened throughout May. By the 26th it totalled twenty-eight and by the end of July he had destroyed thirty-seven enemy aircraft. The DSO and Bar to his DSC were gazetted on 11 August 1917 and the Bar to his DSO on 14 September 1917.

In the summer of 1917 Little was recalled to RNAS Dover for instructional and administrative duties where he tried a new Sopwith Dolphin and a Spad. He could not stay out of the fighting for long, however, and was posted back to Naval Three, soon to become 203 Squadron RAF commanded by Raymond Collishaw. His appetite for air fighting was insatiable. When not sharpening his eye on the airfield's rabbits with a .22 rifle, he would lead offensive patrols with scant regard for danger. On one occasion he attacked a particularly effective German *Flak* battery near La Bassée by flying in at 7000 feet, spiralling earthwards in a controlled 'falling leaf' spin and finally flattening out at very near ground level to scatter the amazed gunners with machine-gun fire and then hedge-hop home.

On the day Richthofen was killed, 21 April 1918, Little flying a Sopwith Camel picked off the rearmost aircraft in a formation of twelve from *Jasta Boelcke*. Six avengers turned angrily on Little's Camel and shot his controls away. The aircraft went down to within 100 feet of the ground before flattening out with a jerk. Little, having unstrapped his seat belt against standing orders, was thrown clear as the Camel ploughed into the ground north of the Forest of Nieppe. Two enemy aircraft followed him down to rake the wreck with fire, but Little was out and still fighting, blazing away with his Webley until some British infantry joined in with Lewis guns. On 28 May Major Booker, Little's comrade from Naval Eight and now Commanding Officer 201 Squadron RAF, was summoned to the scene of a crash where a Camel had come down in the French lines. He got a terrible shock—the pilot still at the controls with a bullet through his heart was Little. The previous evening Little had taken off in Camel B6318 in an attempt to intercept German Gotha bombers making a night raid. It seems that he was killed by one of the Gothas' defensive gunners, while blinded by a searchlight beam, and crashed. He was buried in Wavans cemetery and Australia had lost its foremost fighter pilot. Booker died of wounds three months later.

## Sopwith Pup

The Sopwith Pup has been called a 'masterpiece' and 'the perfect flying machine'. Yet when it appeared in 1916, by the standards of the time, it was underpowered and beginning to look underarmed. Nevertheless its balanced airframe extracted the maximum from its 80-hp Le Rhône engine and its light wing loading made it a delight to fly. Equally important, it could hold its height better than the opposition and with its sensitive controls was fully aerobatic up to 15,000 feet.

The prototype Pup first flew in February 1916, a redesign by Herbert Smith of a 1915 personal aircraft of Harry Hawker. The name was unofficial. The Admiralty's bald 'Type 9901 80-hp Scout' designation was soon forgotten as were their official attempts to suppress the nickname 'Pup'.

In May 1916 the prototype was assessed by 'A' Squadron RNAS at Furnes and the naval pilots were delighted. The Admiralty placed large orders for the Pup with Sopwith and Beardmore and the RFC did likewise with Whiteheads and the Standard Motor Co.

On 15 October 1916, No 1 Wing RNAS detached No 8 (Naval) Squadron to serve under the RFC. With them went the six Pups of 'B' Flight. By November it was the first all-Pup squadron in action, and in spite of engine troubles and gun-jamming, the Pups soon proved their effectiveness.

Flt Lt R A Little started making his name with Naval Eight on Pups. Flying N5182 he shot down an Aviatic CI on 11 November, a Halberstadt on 4 December, and a two-seater on the 20th. By the end of 1916 Naval Eight's eighteen Pups had accounted for 20 enemy aircraft. On 1 February, the Squadron handed over its Pups to No 3 (Naval) Squadron and went back to Dunkirk to reform with Triplanes, an aircraft of which Little was to become a brilliant exponent.

The first RFC squadron to form with the Pup was No 54 which arrived in France on Christmas Eve, 1916. Other users were Naval Nos 3, 4 and 9 and RFC Nos 46 and 66 and through the dreadful spring of 1917, and at Ypres, Messines and Cambrai, the Pup was one of the few British scouts able to hold its own against the latest Albatros D-types.

### Royal Naval Air Service:

*Top:* Squadron Commander
*Centre:* Flight Sub-Lieutenant
*Bottom:* Flying Officer

*Top:* Wing Commander
*Centre:* Observer Lieutenant
*Bottom:* Warrant Officer 2nd Grade.

*Top:* Wing Captain
*Bottom:* Flight Commander

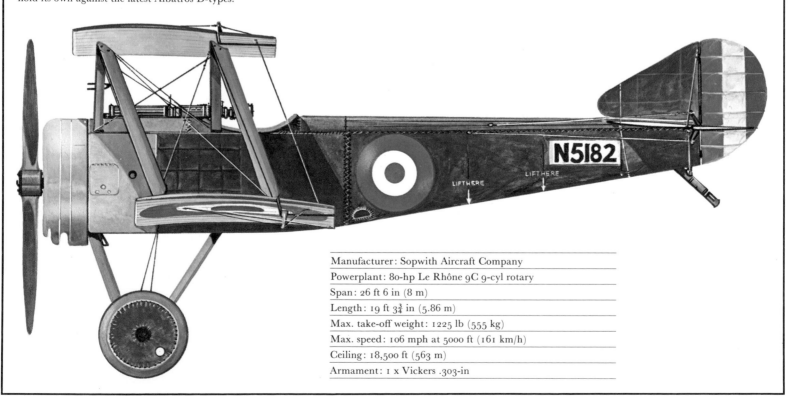

| Manufacturer: Sopwith Aircraft Company |
| --- |
| Powerplant: 80-hp Le Rhône 9C 9-cyl rotary |
| Span: 26 ft 6 in (8 m) |
| Length: 19 ft 3¾ in (5.86 m) |
| Max. take-off weight: 1225 lb (555 kg) |
| Max. speed: 106 mph at 5000 ft (161 km/h) |
| Ceiling: 18,500 ft (563 m) |
| Armament: 1 x Vickers .303-in |

# Georges Guynemer

GEORGES Guynemer held an almost spiritual grip on the imagination of his fellow Frenchmen. During his brief career he shot down fifty-four enemy aircraft, twenty-one fewer than René Fonck, yet he was and remains a symbol of France's suffering and resolution during their *Grande Guerre*. A plaque in the Panthèon in Paris enscribed with the name Guynemer calls its charge 'a legendary hero, fallen in glory from the sky after three years of fierce struggle'. There is no body interred to join France's sleeping heroes. Guynemer disappeared on his last flight and it is assumed that the crashed aircraft and its pilot were pulverized by a British artillery bombardment. Every French schoolchild knew however in that last winter of the war that France's greatest and youngest hero 'flew so high he could not come down again'.

Georges Marie Ludovic Jules Guynemer was born in Paris on 24 December 1894, the son of a prematurely retired professional army officer. After an undistinguished career at the Compiègne *Lycée* he was smitten with the aviation mania that consumed pre-war France. In August 1914 however successive recruiting officers turned down the frail and sickly-looking young man. When a military aircraft force-landed on the beach near the family's holiday villa in Biarritz, the nineteen year old conceived a bold plan. He talked his way into the confidence of *Captaine* Bernard Thierry, commander of the military airfield at Pau. By 21 November he was in the Service—as a student mechanic. A bit of discreet string-pulling by Guynemer *père* amongst his St Cyr class-mates, secured the young Guynemer a transfer to a flying school. He made his first solo on

*Below, from top to bottom:*
The Cross of a chevalier of the *Légion d'Honneur*, awarded to Guynemer on 24 December 1915.
The *Médaille Militaire*, awarded to Guynemer on 4 August 1915.
The *Croix de Guerre*, instituted in April 1915 and awarded to Guynemer on the 21st

10 March 1915 and three months later, now promoted *Caporal*, he was posted to *Escadrille MS 3* stationed at Vauciennes near Villers Cotterets. A bare month after his arrival at the front Guynemer scored. Piloting a Morane Parasol he pursued an Aviatik until his observer managed to shoot it down. On 4 August came the *Médaille Militaire*, such an unusual event was the destruction of an enemy aircraft at that time. When the squadron re-equipped with some of the first Nieuport 11s to reach the front, Guynemer found in the single-seater scout with its forward firing machine-gun the fighting machine he had been waiting for. On 5 December 1915 he made an uncorroborated kill, and three days later a confirmed victory, an LVG two-seater. 'The passenger fell out at Bus', he noted grimly in his log, 'the pilot at Tilloloy.' Six days later

*Left: Capitaine* Guynemer by the upturned wreckage of a Spad SVII.
*Above:* An earlier mishap— Guynemer with broken-propellered Nieuport.
*Top:* Guynemer and Nieuport '*Bébé*': he named his aircraft '*Le Vieux Charles*' (*Le Miroir* 9 April 1916)

**Capitaine Georges Guynemer, 1917.**
Guynemer was awarded many of the honours of France and her Allies. Apart from decorations and *palmes* he received twenty-six other citations.

Some French aviator officers continued to wear the pre-war dark-blue uniform long after the horizon blue uniform was introduced in 1915. Officers transferred to the *Aviation Militaire* continued to wear the uniform of their original unit with the addition of aviation badges and squadron photographs of the period present a widely varied selection of dress

he downed another two-seater and damaged a second. At this stage of the war, this record was already exceptional and on Christmas Eve 1915, Georges Guynemer's 21st birthday, he was awarded the Cross of the *Légion d'Honneur*.

Two months later the storm broke at Verdun with the German High Command resolved to draw the French armies into a gigantic battle of attrition. Guynemer, already highly decorated, was commissioned as a *Sous-Lieutenant*, but he was shot down on his second flight with a bullet in the left arm and superficial face wounds. He was in hospital for a month while his squadron *Escadrille N 3* fought bitterly over Verdun and the reputations of other French airmen climbed even higher. A formidable gathering of fighter pilots, men like Hertaux, Duellin, Dorme, De La Tour and others under the command of the pugnacious Felix Brocard, were founding the reputation of the élite fighter formation known for the symbol emblazoned on their aircraft—*Les Cicognes*, the Storks.

Guynemer rejoined his squadron in time for the Battle of the Somme, and in the bitter fighting he further perfected his own air fighting techniques, favouring a frontal attack where all the most vulnerable parts of an enemy aircraft were concentrated. By the end of July, Guynemer's score had risen to eleven but in September his career was to enter a new phase.

In July 1916 the prototype of a new aircraft, the Spad SVII, had flown at Villacoublay and structurally it was the antithesis of the agile Nieuport. What it lacked in manoeuvrability however it amply made up for in an improved rate of climb, a higher top speed and ceiling. By the autumn of 1916 the first production models were reaching the frontline and they went to the foremost squadrons first. *Escadrille N 3* became *SPA 3* and similarly Guynemer transferred the name *Vieux Charles* from his Nieuport to his brand new Spad.

With the new aircraft, the rate of the Frenchman's scoring rose dramatically. On one day, 23 September 1916, he shot down three Fokkers within five minutes only to be shot down himself by a French 75 field-gun. Guynemer fell for some 4000 feet escaping from a violent crash landing and actually hitting the ground some moments before his last bullet-riddled victim of that morning still spiralling earthwards.

Guynemer went on scoring multiple victories at regular intervals. By January 1917 he had claimed his thirtieth victim, making him the Allied ace second only to Albert Ball. On 18 February at the age of twenty two, he was promoted to *Capitaine* and his exploits were trumpeted throughout France. Guynemer seemed only capable of exceeding the accolades and on 25 May four enemy aircraft fell to his guns in one day. France was running out of honours to pin on Guynemer's tunic. On 5 July 1917 General Franchet d'Espérey presented him with the rosette of an *Officier de la Légion d'Honneur*. The citation read—'Heedless of danger he has become for the

**Spad SVII**

The availability of Marc Birkigt's Hispano-Suiza V 8 and the talents of Spad's chief designer Louis Bêchereau combined in late 1915 to produce a fighter which broke the ascendancy of rotary-powered types and which was to start a strain of aircraft on which many aces made their names. Although it was the antithesis of its great contemporary the Nieuport, the Spad made up in speed and strength what it lacked in manoeuvrability. Its lack of dihedral made it more sensitive however than many of its rotary-powered contemporaries.

The prototype SVII first flew at Villacoublay in April 1916 powered by a 140-hp Hispano-Suiza and armed with a single Vickers synchronized by a Birkigt designed gear. Bêchereau's preceding Spad models included the extraordinary A2 to A5 'pulpit-fighters' but here was an obvious winner, and the French Government placed large orders. By the autumn of 1916 the first production models were reaching the front line. One hundred SVIIs were built in Britain by the British Blériot & Spad Co and twenty more by Mann Egerton. These had originally been ordered by the RNAS but they traded their Spad orders for Sopwith Triplanes and the British Spads went to Nos 19 and 23 Squadrons RFC, and some served with No 72 in Mesopotamia.

It served with numerous *escadrilles de chasse* including *Les Cicognes* and more went to Belgium and Russia. In Italy they eventually equipped five *squadriglie* including Baracca's *91ª*. In December 1917 the USAAS brought 189 Spad VIIs, allocating them to Pursuit Squadrons, and sent the rest home as trainers.

| | |
|---|---|
| Manufacturer: | Société Pour Aviation et ses Dèrives |
| Powerplant: | Hispano-Suiza 8Aa V-8, 150-hp |
| Span: | 7.82 m (25 ft 7¾ in) |
| Length: | 6.15 m (20 ft 2 in) |
| Max. take-off weight: | 740 kg (1632 lb) |
| Max. speed: | 191.5 kmh (119 mph) |
| Ceiling: | 17,500 ft |
| Armament: | 1 x Vickers .303-in |

*Above:* Général Franchet d'Espérey presents 22 year old Guynemer with the rosette of the *Légion d'Honneur* at Bonnemaison airfield, Champagne on 5 July 1917. In the background are the Spad SVIIs and pilots of Guynemer's unit, *Escadrille SPA3, Groupe de Chasse 12—Les Cigognes.*
*Right:* G. Boillot was awarded the *Légion d'Honneur* in March 1916 following a combat in which he shot down an Aviatik and himself crashed with his tail virtually severed by enemy fire. This photograph of Boillot with his Nieuport Type 11 *Bébé* appeared on the front page of the monthly magazine *Le Miroir* of 4 June 1916 shortly after he had been killed in combat during the intense fighting on the Alsace front. The caption says 'the celebrated aviator is pictured with his aircraft several minutes before his last take-off. Surrounded by five 'fokkers', Boillot attacked them and brought down one of his adversaries before he was brought down in his turn'

enemy the most redoubtable adversary of all.' With his score at 45 and his propaganda utility immense, he came under strong pressure to take a rest from operations. Guynemer refused and was to ignore even greater pressures later.

That spring and summer of 1917 the air war over the Western Front reached a deadly new pitch of intensity. Guynemer was a veteran at twenty-two, his statistical chances of survival long since used up. Guynemer himself knew his end must be near. For France his image had become almost an icon, a talisman of victory, but in those photographs of 1917 the large dark eyes seemed to sink ever deeper into the thin pale unsmiling face and the medals on his chest weigh down his sparse frame. His father, the old soldier, knew the signs and tried to persuade his son to rest. Guynemer was a prisoner of his own reputation. He went back to the front telling his father—'if one has not given everything one has given nothing'. It was the kind of attitude that sustained France through the Battle of Verdun and drew the French armies back from the edge of disaster in 1917.

The *Escadrille* moved from the Nancy sector to the British Front on the Flanders coast. *Groupe de Chasse 12* as a whole moved to St Pol near Dunkirk to bolster the RFC while Haig's Flanders offensive bogged in the mud below. On the day before his arrival, Guynemer's old friend Alfred Hertaux was seriously wounded. The aircraft themselves were showing the strain of prolonged combat with worn out engines and dud machine-guns. On one day alone Guynemer had to make three forced landings due to defective aircraft.

Not only the aircraft were worn out. Their pilot had spent all his former passion. He flew and fought now almost by autonomic reflex, his eyes fixed trance-like on some unseen avenger, and the old skills were becoming daily more blunted.

On the morning of 11 September, Guynemer took off from St Pol at 8.35 am in a combat-weary Spad SXIII accompanied by *Sous-Lieutenant* Bozon-Verduraz. Over Poelcapelle the two Spad pilots staged a conventional quarter and rear attack on an enemy two-seater. Unseen to the veteran Guynemer, a flight of Albatros DVs was flying top cover and fell on the two Spads from 3000 feet higher. Bozon turned in time and escaped. Georges Guynemer was never seen again by his comrades.

For a week *Les Cicognes* kept a mournful vigil for their greatest stork, but the skies stayed silent.

A report received via Spain told that German infantry had reached the wreck and identified the pilot as Guynemer from his papers. He had died from a bullet through the head. Later a German newspaper claimed one Kurt Wissemann, a two-seater pilot, as Guynemer's victor but he was to fall some weeks later to René Fonck's guns. All the human evidence was to be destroyed. On that same morning of 11 September, a British bombardment obliterated both pilot and aircraft and sealed under tons of clay the mystery of Guynemer's death.

# Raoul Lufbery

Gervais Raoul Lufbery, one of the original American volunteers of the *Escadrille Lafayette*

WHILE the government of the United States stood away from the great European conflict of 1914-17, a number of young Americans were physically caught up in the fighting. Some came deliberately to defend European civilization from the ravening Hun. Others were adventurers and soldiers of fortune or they were drawn by the ties of birth to the defence of their old country. One such young American was Norman Prince, born in Massachusetts in 1887, who died for France 15 October 1916. He was a shy lawyer who had become fascinated by flying, so obsessed in fact that he enlisted in the French air service in 1915. Along the way he proposed forming a unit of volunteer American flyers to fight at the front and eventually the French authorities listened.

So was born the *Escadrille Americaine* on 16 April 1916 with seven American NCO pilots and two French officers to command them. In addition to Prince there gathered the ex-Foreign legionnaire William Thaw who had been in the French air force since Christmas 1914, Kiffin Rockwell a medical student from N Carolina, and Victor Chapman who had been a student in Paris in 1914, got caught up in the war, and who had also joined the Foreign Legion. Two volunteers from the American Ambulance Field Service, James McConnell and Eliot Cowdin also joined, as well as the Texan stunt flyer Bert Hall.

Of this original nucleus of seven only three were to survive the war and of the thirty-eight Americans who eventually served in the unit, nine were killed in action and one died of injuries after an accident.

They formed first at Luxeil in the Vosges to begin operations as *N124* but as a propaganda exercise *l'Escadrille Americaine* misfired. The Germans brought pressure on neutral America who in turn put pressure on France and the first result was that *Americaine* was dropped for *Lafayette*, the French

hero of the American revolution whose name Pershing was to invoke on his landing in France a year later. The pilots themselves were fêted by the press but for a time they were kept in *grand luxe* limbo by the authorities, anxious not to lose an American pilot in action. At last they were drawn into the desperate air battle over Verdun and one by one the *Escadrille* members went down. Thaw was severely wounded and Chapman was shot down, the first American airman to be killed in the war, on 23 June 1916. In September Kiffin Rockwell went down causing a great stir in the American press and two weeks later Norman Prince crashed after returning exhausted from the raid on the Mauser Werke at Oberndorf and later died of his injuries.

Raoul Lufbery missed this first calvary of the American aviators at Verdun although he had been a front line pilot of the *Aviation Militaire* since October 1915. After the losses of June-July the French forces were again combed out for American nationals to take their place in the *Lafayette*. Lufbery came to the *Escadrille* along with some seasoned veterans like James Hall and Charles Nordhoff, but there were many others less experienced. They all would continue to build the near legendary tradition of the *Volontaires Americains*.

Lufbery was born in France of French parents on 14 March 1885 and emigrated to America with his parents at the age of six. At seventeen he ran away from home and began a remarkable peregrination through Europe and the Middle East, back across America and at last in 1908 to the Philippines as a rifleman with the US Army. In 1910 he began a journey through South-East Asia which brought him in 1912 to Saigon and an encounter with an aviator named Marc Pourpe. Pourpe had come to French Indo-China with a Blériot monoplane to show the inhabitants of France's far-flung empire

**Sous-Lieutenant Raoul Lufbery, spring 1917.** Lufbery wears the *Croix de Guerre*, the *Médaille Militaire* and the cross of the *Légion d'Honneur*. He was the first American to win the British Military Cross, bestowed on 12 June 1917.

Lufbery was commissioned a Major in the USAAS in November 1917 but remained in French uniform until January 1918

The Sioux warrior insignia of the *Escadrille Lafayette* used from April 1917 and borne on the fuselage of Lufbery's Spad

the wonders of aviation. Lufbery was suitably impressed and persuaded Pourpe to take him on as his mechanic. On the outbreak of war they were in France. Pourpe immediately enlisted in the air service but Lufbery as an American was directed towards the recruiting office of the *Legion Etrangère*. Within weeks however Lufbery managed to join Pourpe at *Escadrille N 23* as his mechanic and when his patron was killed soon afterwards, Lufbery himself was given permission to fly. On 29 July he received his brevet after training on Maurice Farmans and in October 1915 he was posted to *Escadrille de Bombardment VB 106*. Six months of bombing missions followed until, like another bomber pilot, René Fonck, he was sent for training as a fighter pilot. He soon got over any initial clumsiness at the controls of a Nieuport and at last on 24 May 1916 he was sent to the *Escadrille Lafayette*.

Success came quickly and by mid-August he had four victories. On 12 October promoted to *Adjutant* he scored his fifth victory on the same bomber escort mission which claimed Norman Prince. He was the first American to win the British Military Cross adding this award to the *Croix de Guerre* and *Médaille Militaire* of France.

When the United States came into the war they had virtually to build an air force from scratch, but the expertise tied up in the *Escadrille Lafayette* at first went largely untouched. Lufbery was commissioned as a Major in the USAAS on 7 November 1917 but he remained with the *Escadrille* until 5 January 1918 when he was sent to the huge new base at Issoudun with an administrative job. While Lufbery's desperately needed experience was being wasted, on 18 February the *Escadrille* was formally absorbed into the USAAS with William Thaw as commander of the rechristened '103rd Aero Squadron USAAS'.

Now many of the Lafayette veterans were spread around the new American squadrons and Lufbery himself was assigned to the 95th Aero Squadron and soon afterwards to command the 94th Aero Squadron. On 19 March he led the first air patrol by an American unit over enemy lines with Rickenbacker and Campbell, leading these brand new arrivals to war in the air with all the experience of three years of fighting.

On the morning of Sunday 19 May 1918 Lufbery took off in a Nieuport 28 to intercept a single German two-seater. He made one attack, then swerved, it seemed, to clear a jammed machine-gun. While the men of his new command watched from the ground, to their horror they saw Lufbery's aircraft burst into flames. As flames poured from the engine, Lufbery sideslipped trying to extinguish the blaze. Desperately he climbed out of the burning cockpit and tried to retain control from astride the fuselage. It was all in vain. He plunged to his death from some three thousand feet into a flower garden in the village of Maron, just north of Nancy. Gervais Raoul Lufbery was buried in a French hillside with American military honours.

# 1917

IN August 1916 the military leadership of Germany changed and with it German strategy. After the failure at Verdun, Falkenhayn was packed off to Rumania and replaced by the heroes of the Russian Front, Ludendorff and Hindenburg. The new Commanders quickly recognized that the depredations of the Verdun fighting and the terrible defensive battles on the Somme had exhausted any offensive capacity left to the German Army on the Western Front—at least in the new year of 1917.

As early as November 1916 a British long range reconnaissance aircraft reported the beginnings of a formidable defensive zone under construction far back behind the Somme area. It was part of Ludendorff's great plan to withdraw to a highly organized defensive zone codenamed the *Siegfried Stellung* or Hindenburg Line, behind which the German Armies could regroup and, further, release reserves of men and material to seek decisions in Russia and Italy by bolstering their ailing Austrian allies.

The recently organized *Jagdstaffeln*, now equipped with Albatros DIIIs represented a fine offensive instrument but in 1917 their role on the Western Front would also be defensive. With the afternoon sun at their backs, westerly prevailing winds to bear them homewards if they sustained battle damage and with most of the fighting going on over their own lines covered by a highly organized reporting system to guide interceptions and record kills, the German fighter pilots enjoyed more than a technical advantage in the first months of 1917.

New tactics were paying off. The *Sperrefliegen* or barrage patrols of Verdun had been abandoned and instead *Jastas* were brought to readiness and ordered up by the *Gruppenführer der Flieger* at Corps HQ amply informed by special air protection officers (*Luftschutz Offiziere*) stationed well forward, enabling them to intercept an enemy incursion in strength. Sections of four to six aircraft were sent up from airfields close to the front line, led by an experienced pilot, his aircraft suitably distinguished by a personal marking or a long fabric streamer. Training and pilot selection had also greatly improved. A special fighter school was formed at Valenciennes at the end of November 1916 and here, along with the new drafts from the single-seater schools at Grossenhain and Paderborn, many of the surviving individualists of the *KEK* and early *Jasta* days were re-educated in the arts of formation flying and aerial fighting with new twin-gun high-performance aircraft.

Against this defence the Royal Flying Corps would come in April with tragically outmoded equipment, inadequate training and inflexible tactics—and the result was the terrible mauling for the Royal Flying Corps known as 'Bloody April'.

During the German retreat to the Hindenburg Line, the period of maximum danger for the disengaging armies, bad weather and the efficiency of Second Army's *Jastas* kept the great secret from prying airborne eyes. In February/March, sixty Allied intruders were brought down for the loss of only seven German aircraft. Then on 24 February a flight of RFC Sopwith Pups reported dumps burning and villages abandoned. On 17 March a two-week British advance began through the desolated abandoned Noyon salient, and the RFC had to rapidly improvise mobile warfare tactics such as infantry contact patrols and even cavalry co-operation.

With the fluid British front sealed by the Hindenburg Line, German air strength was switched to the Aisne to await the expected French offensive which *Général* Robert Nivelle had openly promised would rupture the German line within 24 hours. A British operation against Arras was to be a preliminary to this great Allied offensive to be carried out, Nivelle proclaimed, with 'violence, brutality and rapidity'.

In spite of repeated plans for the expansion of the RFC made in 1916 and the subsequent re-organization of the supply of pilots, engines and airframes in Great Britain, the supply position of the RFC in France on the eve of the Arras offensive was miserable. Through the winter of 1916–17 there had been continual postponement of deliveries both to replace obsolete aircraft and for the establishment of new squadrons. Training requirements had been progressively stiffened and made more technocratic throughout 1916 and there was no shortage of officer volunteers but there was still a serious shortfall of skilled mechanics and riggers. The early mistakes of sending all RFC personnel and aircraft to France had seriously handicapped early attempts at expansion and large-scale pilot training, as had the absorption of pre-war skilled mechanics into the infantry—many of whom were now just casualty statistics on the Somme.

The total strength of the RFC and RNAS grouped on the First and Third Army Fronts for the Arras offensive was twenty-five squadrons, with some 365 serviceable aircraft of which a third were single-seat fighters—Spad SXIIs, Nieuport 17s, Martinsyde Scouts, Sopwith Pups and the Triplanes of the Naval Squadrons, plus a squadron of the new two-seat Bristol Fighters of which great things were expected. Corps aircraft were still largely BE2s in various sub types with some of the first of the new Royal Aircraft Factory RE8s designed to supersede them. The pusher FE2b and Sopwith 1½-Strutter squadrons were detailed for offensive patrols or reconnaissance and night bombing. One squadron, No 56, with some of the best pilots of the RFC was forming in England with the SE5 single-seater but these were not used over the lines until 23 April. Facing this British line up was the German Sixth Army its airspace defended initially by five *Jastas*, eight by the end of the month. Along the whole British front between Lille and Peronne the RFC/RNAS could count 754 aircraft including 385 fighters. The two German armies opposite them could muster 264 aircraft, 114 of them being fighters. The main German strength in fact faced the French where *Commandant* de Peuty, in command of the large scale *groupement de combat* on the Aisne was telling his pilots that their task was to seek out and destroy the Germans wherever they were.

On 4 April, a full five days before an artillery and gas bombardment opened the battle on the ground, the British opened the Arras offensive in the air. The intention was to force German fighters back from the front line to leave a swept zone for the Corps aircraft to operate unmolested. It had worked on the Somme but it did not work against the new *Jagd-staffeln* with their Albatros DIIIs. In those five days 75 British aircraft were shot down, and 105 pilots lost. Replacement pilots, gunners and observers, sucked into the battle with only the scantiest training, youth and a tragic enthusiasm to sustain them, did not have time to learn the practical lessons of survival and the statistical life of aircrew at the front began a progressive drop to three weeks as morale and tactics deteriorated.

The début of No 48 Squadron's Bristol Fighters was disastrous. Out of a patrol of six F2As on 5 April only one returned undamaged and four had fallen victim to von Richthofen and four of his comrades from *Jasta 11*. The Nieuport 17s of No 60 squadron were given a similar mauling by Richthofen on the 7th. Attacks against kite balloons at heights often below 200 feet brought one to one losses to ground fire. The new RE8s very quickly acquired a reputation for a fatal tendency to spin and in action they were only a little less vulnerable than the BE2s. On the 13th an entire patrol of six RE8s was wiped out by Richthofen's unit, all the pilots and observers except two being killed.

Amongst these disasters there were some Allied successes. Douai airfield, the home of Richthofen's *Jasta 11*, was bombed on the night of April 5/6 by FE2ds of 100 squadron. The Sopwith Triplanes of the Naval Squadrons 1, 3 and 8 more than held their own, and this was the type on which Little, Dallas and Booker made their names. Collishaw's Black Flight of Naval Ten Triplanes joined them in mid-May. Captains Albert Ball and W A Bishop in Nieuport Scouts had considerable success flying and fighting alone, and Ball was an inspiration to the RFC in its darkest hour until he was killed in an SE5 on 7 May.

If the German fighter units needed an inspiration they had it in von Richthofen. *Jasta 11* scored 89 victories in April, twenty-one of which were credited to the *Rittmeister*. The eight *Jagdstaffeln* engaged had an average daily strength of only seven aircraft, and could be airborne up to four times a day at the height of the fighting. Strict formation grouping and the efficiency of the ground reporting service localized defensive firepower and British intelligence estimated the operational strength the RFC was facing to be far higher than it actually was. Above all the German pilots were supremely confident in their machines, their tactics and in the example of the *Staffel* leadership. Single German pilots would impudently attack the large formations the British were forced to send out as escorts for the vulnerable Corps aircraft; in the fast Albatros DIII

they could dive, score and break away before the inexperienced escort pilots could react.

It was the same on the French front. Nivelle's much vaunted offensive stalled bloodily on the Chemin des Dames on Day One, 16 April. The staff work of the four aviation *groupes* assembled for the battle was badly muddled and the French units were not ready when the offensive started. They were facing the main German air strength, some 480 aircraft, which showed their teeth on the first day attacking the French observation machines, and the old Farmans and Voisin pushers were as vulnerable as the BE2s of the RFC. The French creeping artillery barrage lost cohesion and the advancing infantry walked straight into intact wire and machine-gun positions. After two weeks of grotesque losses the French Armies were near to cracking.

Haig launched a relief offensive on the 23rd on a nine mile front and the patterns in the air of the first two weeks of April, with a lull from the 16th to the 20th due to bad weather, repeated themselves on an even larger scale. On the evening of the 23rd there was one of the first really large-scale dog-fights of the war lasting over an hour with scores of machines involved filling the sky with weaving aircraft.

As at Verdun, sheer scale was changing the pattern of air fighting. The German *Staffelführers* would lead their six to ten aircraft towards the battle area in rigid formation but once an action

developed it broke up into many individual contests. The SE5 pilot Cecil Lewis recalled a dog-fight of May with thirty machines engaged—'a pilot would go down on the tail of a Hun, hoping to get him in the first burst; but he would not be wise to stay there, for another Hun would almost certainly be on his tail, hoping to get him in the same way. Such fights were really a series of rushes, with momentary pauses to select the next opportunity—to catch the enemy at a disadvantage, or separated from his friends.'

The 25 British squadrons engaged in the Battle of Arras lost 316 aircrew killed and missing in April against 114 Germans, but these losses should be put in perspective. On the ground British casualties were 84,000, German 75,000. On the Aisne the French lost 120,000 men in five days. But the battles of 1917 could not be fought, let alone won, without air power and this terrible drain on trained aircrew could not be sustained indefinitely by the RFC and the *Aviation Militaire*. New aircraft were coming from the factories to redress the balance it was true but now eyes turned covetously towards the United States, at war with Germany since 6 April, with its vast reserves of manpower and its supposedly mighty industrial base.

The German High Command understandably reacted with alarm. The aerial expansion programme of October 1916 was incomplete, industrial capacity was under tremendous strain, and raw material shortages were causing ever increasing production problems. In early June *Kogenluft* and *Idflieg* met to endorse a huge expansion plan called appropriately the *Amerikaprogramm*, calling for the establishment of 40 new *Jagdstaffeln* and 17 Artillery *Flieger Abteilungen* within a matter of months. The bases of production were to be restructured, aircraft production was to be doubled, training expanded with 24,000 new recruits including a complete new fighter school and such essentials as the production of aircraft machine-guns, lubricating oil and aviation fuel was to be greatly increased. The single-seater high performance fighter was recognized as the primary unit from which the rest of air power sprang, and the utmost effort was to be directed towards gaining technical superiority. The America plan also recognized the effectiveness of *ad hoc* groupings of *Jagdstaffeln* in larger formations and had envisaged and achieved the permanent formation of a new large unitary command, the *Jagdgeschwader* or fighter wing. The first was formed on 23 June 1917 when *Jasta 3 4, 6, 10* and *11* were formed into *Jagdgeschwader 1* under the command of von Richthofen.

Similar decisions and plans were being made in Britain and France. The intrusion of German bombers over southern England stirred up a clamour for an effective response. Lt-Gen Smuts' report to the

An Albatros D III captured by the RNAS. The impact of this aircraft on the RFC was devastating in the spring of 1917. The naval fliers, however, had aircraft such as the Sopwith Triplane which could match it

War Cabinet dated 17 August 1917 recommended a unified independent air service directed by an Air Ministry and an Air Staff. This report was to be the birth certificate of the Royal Air Force formally constituted eight months later. The French were feeling the great strain of supplying aircraft and engines not only to their own forces but to virtually all the combatant Allies, as well. At the same time the command went through an unhappy period. In February 1917 Barés was dismissed and replaced by *Commandant* de Peuty as *Chef du Service Aéronautique au GQG* and the *Service des Fabrications de l'Aviation* underwent some rapid changes of directorship in the first half of 1917 while a highly critical French press talked of a deep crisis in aviation.

By mid-May 1917 however the French Armies themselves were in near complete disarray. On 15 May Nivelle was replaced by Pétain, the hero of Verdun, and the mutinies which followed the disaster on the Aisne were quelled. There would be no more fruitless offensives—Pétain would wait for 'the tanks and the Americans'.

To take the pressure off the French and with the objective of clearing the Flanders coast of U-Boat bases, Haig planned a new British offensive in the Ypres salient dominated by the high ground of Messines-Wytschaete. Approximately 500 aircraft were concentrated for an attack on a 10,000 yard front giving an initial superiority of four to one. The attack was heralded by the usual massive bombardment, then on 7 June a million pounds of high explosive blew the top off the Messines ridge. Temporary air superiority was gained at first but the Germans were able to bring in units from the largely dormant French Front to swing the balance.

In the Arras fighting and the subsequent battles in Flanders, ground attack techniques became ever more elaborate and more extensively used on both sides. The German *Infantrieflieger* or contact patrol flights had proven their worth since the Somme, now at the end of 1917 specialized and highly effective armoured two-seaters such as the all metal Junkers J 1 began to equip them. From September the *Schutzstaffeln* or protection flights began using the new CL-types from Halberstadt and Hannoveraner, and at Cambrai their use as offensive ground attack weapons was crucial in the counter-attack of 30 November against the British armoured incursion, itself pressed home in co-operation with low-flying aircraft, particularly DH5s.

In preparation for a renewed offensive in the new year, the *Schusta* were re-organized as *Schlachtstaffeln* or battle flights. An *OHL* document of February 1918 stated their purpose—'The object of the battle flights is to shatter the enemy's nerve by repeated attacks in close formation and thus to obtain a decisive influence on the course of the fighting.' The large-scale expansion of the *Schlasta* became a priority in readiness for a renewed offensive in the spring, by which time thirty of these units were to be in existence.

The German strategic defensive on the Western Front, against which the British and French had repeatedly dashed themselves in 1917, was matched by an offensive effort by the Central Powers elsewhere. The German priority was to keep Austria-Hungary in the war. The Austro-Hungarians had been fighting on two fronts since Italy's declaration of war in 1915. The Russian 'Kerensky' offensive of July 1917 badly shook the Austrian Armies in Galicia but rapid German stiffening and the October Bolshevik revolution rescued the Dual Monarchy and bolstered its fragile military power for a little while longer at least. In early 1917 the *Luftfahrtruppen* had been re-organized and re-equipped largely along German lines, at first with the Brandenburg DI single-seaters and later with more effective licence-built Albatros DIIs and IIIs. The fighting unit was the *Fliegerkompagnie*, abbreviated to *Flik*, a fighting *Jagd* role being designated by *J* suffix, such as the famous unit *Flik 41J* commanded by the Austrian ace of aces, Godwin Brumowski. Attempts to form larger units with a nominal strength of 16 to 20 aircraft on German *Geschwader* lines were hindered by shortages of aircraft—there were only seven *Flik (J)*s in mid-1917—as well as the outmoded doctrine of restricting single-seaters to escort of army co-operation aircraft. Help however was on the way in the shape of powerful German reinforcements released from the Western Front.

The Italians also had their problems. In early 1917 the *Aeronautica del Regia Esercito* was reorganized with each Army having its own attached air formation containing a varying number of *Squadriglie*. By the time of the Eleventh Battle of the Isonzo, the Italian assault launched on 18 August 1917, the *squadriglie da caccia* had been virtually completely equipped with French types, Spad SVIIs, Nieuport-Macchi XVIIs and the first Hanriot HD1s. By October there were fifteen fighter squadrons defending the front, but the equipment of the reconnaissance squadrons, mainly Caudron GIVs and Savoia-Pomilio SP2s was very outmoded.

From September onwards, under careful German supervision, a new Fourteenth Austrian Army (seven of its divisions and most of its artillery were German) was assembled behind the Tolmino-Caporetto area. The Albatros-equipped *Jastas*, newly arrived from the Western Front, swept the Italians from the skies and the reconnaissance machines were able to complete their work unmolested. On 24 October the Austro-German storm troops crashed against the Italian Second Army's Front and streamed through it at Caporetto, not stopping until they reached the Piave. German flying units were able to use Italian airfields, often captured with all their facilities intact, and throughout the three-week advance they engaged in strenuous ground attack work in the manner of the Flanders fighting. The British and French rushed 11 divisions to Italy to restore their shaken ally and the British despatched 90 aircraft including 54 Sopwith Camels to form the new VII Brigade of the Royal Flying Corps.

# Raymond Collishaw

T HIRD on the list of British aces, second to W A Bishop as Canada's greatest fighter pilot and the top naval ace of World War I, Raymond Collishaw in addition was leader of one of the most famous Allied fighter units of the war—the 'Black Flight' of Sopwith Triplanes.

He was born in Nanaimo, British Columbia, on 22 November 1893. While still in his teens he served as second mate on a tramp steamer and in 1911 he sailed with Scott to the Antarctic. By 1914 his taste for adventure had not been quelled and from Canada's Fishery Protection Service he transferred to Britain's Royal Naval Air Service at his own expense and by the beginning of 1916 was a qualified pilot assigned to coastal patrol duty. On 2 August 1916 he joined No 3 Wing RNAS, the so-called 'Sopwith Sailors', who were constituted at Luxeil-les-Bains with a motley collection of equipment to make strategic bombing raids on the German industries of the Saarland. On 12 October 1916 the wing set out to attack the *Mauser Waffenfabrik* at Oberndorf. Collishaw flying a single-seat Sopwith 1½-Strutter escorted an Anglo-French bombing force of 24 aircraft on the 223 mile round trip and saw off a Fokker DII that attacked the formation. On 25 October he downed two more of the same type over Luneville while ferrying a new aircraft from the wing's field at Luxeil.

On 1 February 1917 he was transferred to No 3 (Naval) Squadron at Marieux flying Sopwith Pups commanded by another Canadian, Sqn Cdr R H Mulock. On 4 March Collishaw claimed an Albatros DIII, and one week before the Battle of Arras opened, Collishaw went to No 10 (Naval) Squadron at Furnes on the Flanders coast to take command of 'B' Flight. He was newly promoted Flight-Commander and hand-picked four other redoubtable Canadians to follow him. They were to become one of the most successful units of the war.

At the core of 'Naval Ten' were the five Canadians, Collishaw himself, Flt Sub-Lts Ellis Reid of Toronto, J E Sharman from Winnipeg, J E Nash of Hamilton and M Alexander of Montreal—all of them in their early twenties. They flew the Sopwith Triplanes of the ominously named 'Black Flight'—the engine cowling, wheel disc covers and metal forward fuselage decking all being painted black with the names in white lettering: *Black Maria*, *Black Death*, *Black Sheep*, *Black Roger* and *Black Prince* of Collishaw, Sharman, Nash, Reid and Alexander.

While the RFC's aerial offensive above Arras was breaking bloodily against the Albatros *Jastas*, in the area around Dunkirk where Naval Ten operated with its Triplanes, it was a different story. While these formidable fighting machines were being used to protect the Channel approaches, the RFC squadrons to the south were being decimated. On 28 April Collishaw caught a Roland over Ostend and scored three more times during the first twelve days of May while patrolling the coast. Meanwhile reports of this strange three-winged fighter that could perform outstanding aerobatic feats were

**Squadron Commander R Collishaw RNAS, February 1918.**
Men of the Royal Navy fighting on land adopted khaki uniforms early in 1915 and the practical example of the Royal Naval Division was quickly followed by the Royal Naval Air Service in France. The wearing of khaki by naval officers was finally regularized by an order issued in October 1916. The uniform was only to be worn outside the United Kingdom but this was often ignored.

The regulations specified a standard Army pattern four-pocket tunic with lapels. There were no distinction marks on the shoulder straps but rank marks were as on the blue uniform except that the gold lace was replaced by plain khaki braid. The RNAS-pattern buttons were of bronze instead of gilt and the cap was the blue naval cap with a khaki cover. The gilt eagle was worn on the left breast. Trousers were drab serge or khaki drill, breeches Bedford Cord, to be worn with a drab shirt and tie, and Sam Browne belt

*Above:* A portrait of Collishaw taken in 1916. The rag in the special chest pocket would be used to wipe oil from the goggles, a necessary item for any pilot of rotary-engined aircraft

filtering down to the embattled squadrons, both British and German to the south.

Finally on 1 June 1917 Naval Ten was drawn into the battle and put under No 11 Wing RFC stationed at Droglandt. Immediately the black-nosed triplanes made their presence felt. Four enemy aircraft went down before Collishaw's guns in five days. On 5 June he brought his score to thirteen with the destruction of an Albatros two-seater. On 6 June he shot down three Albatros DIIIs in the course of one action and for this feat he was awarded the DSC; he was gazetted on 20 July 1917. On 15 June Collishaw shot down three Halberstadt D-types and an LVG two-seater bringing his victory total to twenty-three.

By now the *Jasta*s who had had it their own way for so long were alarmed. Ground observers were urgently alerted to look out for the three-winged aircraft and *Jasta 11* was given priority orders for their destruction. On 25 June the rival formations

*Far left:* Flt Sub-Lt Collishaw at Manston, Kent, June 1916 serving with No 3 Wing RNAS.
*Left:* Collishaw (seated, centre) as Squadron Commander of No 3 Squadron RNAS, February 1918. Naval, including RNAS, officers were ordered to remove their caps' wire stiffeners in 1917 as they interfered with ships' compasses.
*Below:* Major Collishaw, despite RAF rank, wearing a naval monkey jacket, with men and Sopwith Camels of No 203 Squadron RAF (ex-No 3 Squadron RNAS) at Izel-les-Hameau, July 1918. Note mixture of RFC, khaki RNAS and lone RAF uniforms

*Right:* Clayton and Shuttleworth built Triplane N5366 of 'Naval 10', at Droglandt, summer 1917.
*Below:* Triplane of an unidentified RNAS squadron cracked up on landing. The official history of the spring 1917 air fighting recorded: 'The sight of a Sopwith Triplane formation in particular induced the enemy pilots to dive out of range.' Collishaw destroyed seven enemy aircraft and drove down seventeen out of control between May and June 1917

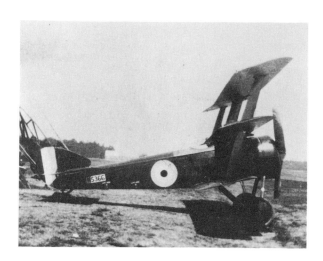

*Right:* An unidentified RAF officer, still wearing RNAS uniform, inspects a captured Nieuport 17 of the Red Army. Collishaw commanded No 47 Squadron RAF engaged in fighting in South Russia from June 1919 until April 1920

met over Quesnoy and the German veterans found the Sopwiths as slippery in the air as they had been led to expect. Only *Leutnant* Karl Allemenröder, von Richthofen's deputy, scored a victory shooting down Nash in *Black Sheep*. The Germans however were shaken. Allmenröder split the *Jasta* in two attempting to build a tactical trap to ensnare the Black Flight but his plan went wrong and the lower formation was caught by Collishaw before the German top cover could pounce. *Black Maria* cut Allmenröder's green and white Albatros DIII away from his formation and with a burst of fire sent *Jasta 11*'s deputy commander diving into Lille's outskirts.

For the first three weeks of July the indomitable Canadians continued to maul the Germans. On 6 July Richthofen himself was shot down and wounded by the gunner of an FE2d fighting in a defensive circle until Collishaw himself arrived with four Triplanes and drove away the attackers without loss to themselves.

By 28 July his score was thirty-seven and he was sent back to Canada for two months' leave. On his return to France on 26 November after a brief spell as an instructor he joined the RNAS Seaplane Defence Station at St Pol as 'A' Flight Commander. On 29 December 1917 he was given command of the unit now retitled No 13 (Naval) Squadron equipped with a formidable new aircraft again from the Sopwith stable. The experienced Collishaw quickly learned the unforgiving habits of the Sopwith Camel and despatched two seaplanes and an LVG. At the end of January Collishaw, took over No 3 (Naval) Squadron, another Camel unit based at Bray-Dunes near Dunkirk. When Ludendorff's great offensive opened in March the unit was at Mont St Eloi, near Arras but Collishaw himself was tied up with administrative duties. On 1 April however when the RAF was formally constituted, he was commissioned as a Major and placed in command of the Camel-equipped No 203 Squadron. In June he was back in action and through the next four months while up against the formidable last generation of German fighter aircraft he scored twenty more victories including ten Fokker DVIIIs. On 1 October 1918 he was promoted Lieutenant-Colonel and was only twenty-five years old. He was withdrawn from the front line and joined the other famous Canadian airmen like Bishop and McKeever who at the time were laying the administrative foundations for a Royal Canadian Air Force.

The November Armistice was not the end of the air combat however for Raymond Collishaw. In July 1919 the No 47 Squadron RAF under his command was sent to southern Russia to aid the White General Denikin against the Red Army. Here he scored more victories including an Albatros DV.

Raymond Collishaw's sixty-two victories included forty-two destroyed (and one shared) and nineteen seen to go down out of control. This great Canadian ace also had over 100 indecisive fights in which a further fifteen aircraft were driven down but not claimed.

## Sopwith Triplane

The success of the Sopwith Pup led its designer Herbert Smith in the spring of 1916 to try a bold aerodynamic experiment. The triplane formula with its decreased wing-span and increased wing area should enhance manoeuvrability and rate of climb at the same time. The result was the Sopwith Triplane first test flown by Harry Hawker on 30 May 1916. The Admiralty eagerly snapped up the unconventional aircraft and sent the prototype N500 to France for combat tests with the RNAS in June 1916. For the naval pilots who tested it, its aerobatic qualities and its phenomenal climb came as a revelation. Less than a quarter of an hour after its arrival in France it was sent up to attack a German aircraft and the squadron's diary reported that it could reach 12,000 feet in only 13 minutes.

Both the RNAS and the RFC now placed production orders but, after an urgent request from Field-Marshal Haig following the ravages of the Somme fighting urging 'a very early increase in the numbers and efficiency of our fighting aeroplanes', the Admiralty began to form squadrons to work with the depleted RFC (Naval 8 was the first) and make large transfers of aircraft, airframes and engines. In February 1917 all the Spad SVIIs on order for the RNAS were transferred to the RFC in return for their Triplane order. From the original order for 400, only 144 were delivered (N5420-N5494, N6290-N6309 from Sopwith, N533-N538, N350-N5389 from Clayton and Shuttleworth; Oakley's, N5910-N5834, only delivered three).

The prototype's 110-hp Clerget rotary was replaced on production machines by a 130-hp Clerget 9B. Armament was a single Vickers with Scarff-Dibovski synchronizing gear, although N533-N538 had twin Vickers and one Triplane was unsuccessfully tested with a Lewis gun.

Deliveries of the Triplane began in November 1916 and by mid-February of the new year, with the Battle of Arras a few weeks away, Naval Squadrons Nos 1, 8, 9, 10, and 12 were re-equipped with the type. In the crisis of April, Naval Squadrons, 1, 8 and 10 were ordered south to the rescue of the RFC and the impact of the Triplane squadrons was immediate.

In the hands of such pilots as Flt Lt R A Little, Flt Sub Lt R S Dallas, and Flt Cdrs R J Compston and C D Booker, the Triplane gave the Germans a shock which reverberated right into their aircraft design departments who began an urgent search for an answer to this 'secret weapon'.

The Triplane served almost exclusively on the Western Front but one went to Russia and one more was flown by Fl Lt J W Alcock in the Aegean. As early as July 1917 however the Triplane began to be replaced by the Camel and in mid-October the last operational squadron, Naval One reluctantly gave up their tractable Triplanes for the unforgiving Camel.

| | |
|---|---|
| Manufacturers: | Sopwith Aircraft Company |
| Powerplant: | Clerget 9Z 9-cyl rotary, 110-hp/Le Rhône 9-cyl, 110-hp |
| Span: | 26 ft 6 in (8 m) |
| Length: | 19 ft 6 in (5.9 m) |
| Max. take off weight: | 1415 lb (641 kg) |
| Max. speed: | 116 mph (176 km/h) at 6000 ft (1828 m) |
| Ceiling: | 29,000 ft (8839 m) |
| Armament: | 1 x Vickers .303-in |

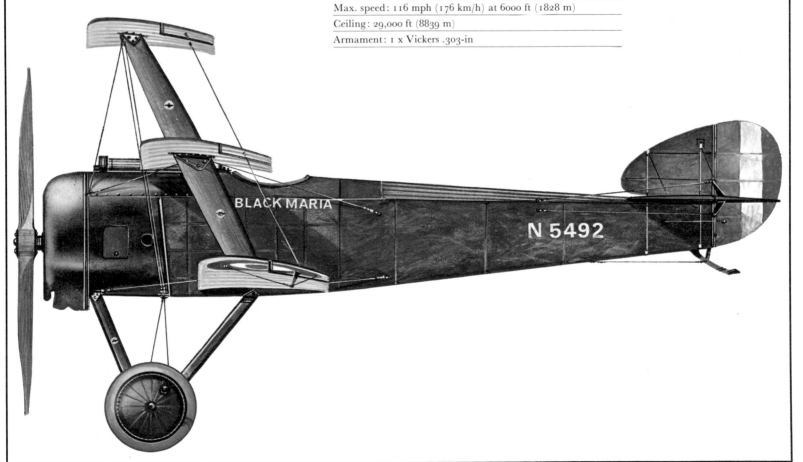

BLACK MARIA     N 5492

Captain W A Bishop
portrayed in the cockpit of
Nieuport Scout B1566, May
1917. He was awarded the
DSO on 2 May, and the
Victoria Cross on 11
August 1917

Bishop shot it down at 1000 feet. The Canadian ran the gauntlet of five more DIIIs now angrily seeking vengeance on the bullet-ridden Nieuport which had wrought so much havoc—but flying low and fighting back nausea, Bishop got back to his airfield. He personally congratulated the station armourer whose care of the Nieuport's single Vickers kept it blazing away through this lone action. For this extraordinary mission Bishop was awarded the Victoria Cross, gazetted on 11 August 1917.

Bishop's technique was to attack to the point of recklessness, but tempered with skilful flying and marksmanship. Now he realised he should exercise restraint having 'got so far in the game and past its most dangerous stages'. Shooting he concluded was the all important skill and of this he had plenty, going back to his days of hunting in the woods of Ontario. Nevertheless he still continued to fly and fight to the limit. His score reached forty-five and Bishop was promoted Major. He was awarded a Bar to his DSO and this coincided with the award of his VC by King George V in London. A few days later loaded with honours he sailed from Liverpool for Canada and a well-earned home leave. He stayed somewhat longer than he had anticipated, not only did he get married but he also embarked on a recruiting tour on behalf of the Dominion government.

Early in 1918 Bishop was back in England as chief instructor at the Aerial Gunnery School, but on 13 March 1918, with the German offensive at its height, he was posted to command his own squadron —No 85. Although under official pressure not to

risk his valuable life he opened his score in spectacular fashion all over again. With two weeks to go before being posted to a staff job in London, he shot down no fewer than twenty-five enemy aircraft, twelve of them in the last three days and all in a total flying time of thirty-six-and-a-half hours.

Like Boelcke in 1916, Bishop was of immeasurably greater value as a symbol than as a destroyer of enemy aircraft. In just over one year he had shot down seventy-two enemy aircraft confirmed, but, unlike Boelcke, he was destined to survive the war. His 'unidentified two-seater' driven down on 19 June 1918 was his last victory. On 5 August his secondment to the RAF was formally terminated and he was attached to the Canadian HQ as a Temporary Lieut-Colonel of the Canadian Cavalry. His work was now purely administrative and in October he went back to Canada once again pursuing plans for the creation of the Canadian Air Force. By the time he returned to France, the war was two months over.

After a distinguished career in Canadian business and public life, Bishop wrote and lectured extensively on his wartime experiences, but the commitment to the service whose traditions he had so uniquely helped to found still called. As an Air Vice Marshal RCAF he was chairman of the Air Advisory Committee to the Minister of National Defence 1938-9 and throughout World War II he was Director of the Royal Canadian Air Force. Air Marshal W A Bishop died on 11 September 1956.

**Nieuport Nie 17**

Many of the leading aces of France and Britain began their careers on the Nieuport 17. It became one of the most successful fighting aircraft of the war with a career which lasted longer than most.

The nimble French fighter first reached the front on 2 May 1916. *Escadrille N 57* got them first, but the shortage of British-built scouts in 1916 led to large orders from the RFC and RNAS. The Nieuport 17 was the favourite mount of Capt Albert Ball who exchanged it only very reluctantly for an SE5 and Bishop scored thirty-six of his confirmed victories in the type, flying it until 28 July 1917. *Les Cicognes* flew the Nieuport until replaced by Spads and Guynemer and Nungesser made their reputation with it.

The first RFC examples had a Lewis gun mounted on the overwing rail devised by Sergeant Foster RFC in October 1916, but later machines in addition featured a synchronized Vickers. Le Prieur electrically fired rockets could be mounted on the characteristic V-struts for 'balloon busting'. By the spring of 1917 however the Nieuport 17 was beginning to appear seriously underarmed.

Late-production aircraft were fitted with 130-hp Clerget engines (17*bis*) and the Nieuport 23 widely used by the RFC had detail changes to improve aerodynamics. The Nieuport 17 was supplied liberally to France's Allies including Italy and Russia where it was licence built. Britain and Belgium used them and a large number were made available to the AEF squadrons in 1917-18 as much-needed pursuit trainers.

*Right:* W A Bishop photographed with his Nieuport Type 17 Scout B1566 of No 60 Squadron RFC in 1917

| | |
|---|---|
| Manufacturer: SA des Etablissements Nieuport | |
| Powerplant: Le Rhône 9J 9-cyl rotary, 110-hp | |
| Span: 8.22 m (26 ft 11 in) | |
| Length: 5.74 m (18 ft 10 in) | |
| Max. take-off weight: 565 kg (1246 lb) | |
| Max. speed: 177 kmh (110 mph) at 2000 m (6562 ft) | |
| Ceiling: 5300 m (17,388 ft) | |
| Armament: 1 x Lewis/1 x Vickers .303-in | |

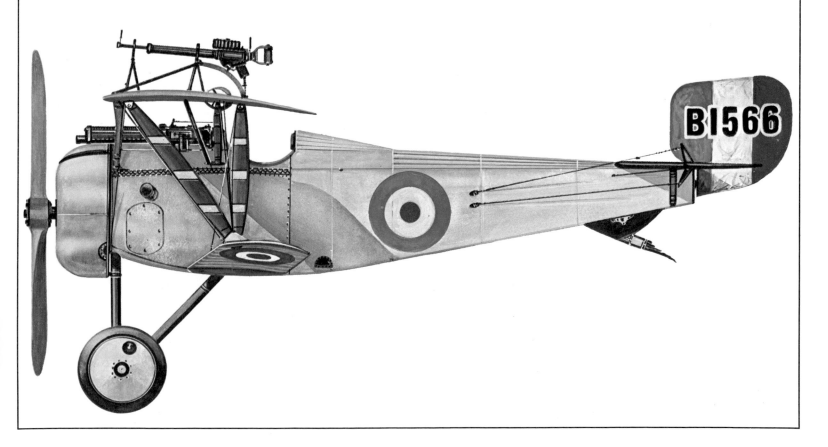

# Godwin Brumowski

THE institution which held the multi-national empire of the Hapsburgs together, perhaps even more than the monarchy itself, was the Imperial and Royal Army of Austria-Hungary. Godwin Brumowski was a typical product of the system, a professional artillery officer born in Wadowice, Galicia on 26 July 1889, of Polish parents; he went on to become the Dual Monarchy's highest scoring pilot gaining all his victories on the Italian Front. When Italy declared war on 15 May 1915 the thin resources of the *Luftfahrtruppen*, already embattled in Poland, Galicia and the Balkans, were stretched even further. Godwin Brumowski as an officer of *Feld-Artillerie Regt Nr 6* was at the time fighting in Russia and had been since the outbreak of war, but, late in 1915, he transferred to the *Luftfahrtruppen* as an observer, quickly gaining a reputation for bravery tempered by reliability. He received no formal pilot's training but rather showed an aptitude encouraged by his various NCO 'Chauffeurs'. As a pilot he quickly showed a natural ability and soon was in command of a *Fliegerkompanie* (*Flik*) equipped with a mixture of observation and single-seat scout aircraft.

By early 1915 the Italian effort in the air was increasing with better aircraft and new tactics. Meanwhile Brumowski had a chance to see for himself the new German organizational methods being evolved on the Western Front. When he returned to the Italian Front in late 1916 he could try some of them out at a time when new and effective single-seat types were beginning to reach the Austrian squadrons. Brumowski's *Flik 41(J)* (J)—*Jagd* or fighting)—was equipped with the Brandenburg DI, the unmistakable 'star-strutter' which was comparable with its Western Front contemporaries in everything except armament. Its single Schwarzlose machine-gun was mounted above the wing in a faired casing, but to reduce stoppages caused by condensation Brumowski had the ammunition belt on his aircraft (numbered 65.53) disengaged from its drum and spread in layers inside the casing. Meanwhile he devised a macabre badge for his formation, again like Western

*Left:* Godwin Brumowski, Austria-Hungary's highest-scoring fighter pilot.
*Above:* The macabre badge adopted by Brumowski in 1917, a white skull on a black background.
*Right:* a portrait of *Offizierstellvertreter* Julius Arigi, the most decorated *Unteroffizier* of the Austro-Hungarian army, and victor of 32 aerial combats.
He was born in Teschen in October 1895 and joined *Festungsartillerieregiment Nr 1* (facing colour red) in March 1914, transferred to an airship detachment, and qualified as pilot in November 1914. He fought in Russia, the Balkans and on the Italian front where his career as a single-seat fighter pilot took off in 1917. In spite of all his successes he was never promoted beyond NCO

**Hauptmann Godwin Brumowski, Italian Front, 1917.**

There was no distinct uniform for the *Luftfahr-truppen* other than the balloon badge worn on the collar patch, officially introduced for the airship detachment on 19 September 1910. The collar patch retained the colour of the wearer's original unit.

A distinct uniform for aviation troops was designed in 1915 and approved by the Kaiser but it was not introduced, and no particular protective clothing was officially approved.

A pilot's breast badge was introduced on 11 September 1912 consisting of an oval oakleaf wreath with green enamel inlay. At the top was a crown with red enamel inlay and at bottom a white shield with the Emperor Franz Josef's monogram 'FJI' in red enamel. In the centre was a hovering eagle in black, later in gold.

On the accession of Karl, the monogram changed to a 'K', then in October 1917 a new badge was introduced with the same eagle, wreath and monogram but surmounted by the imperial crown of Austria and the St Stephen's crown of Hungary.

Miniature versions of these badges were popular and often worn on the various items of headgear including the cylindrical *kappe*

Front practice, and a distinctive white skull on a black background appeared on *Flik 41's* machines.

Godwin Brumowski was constantly frustrated in his attempts to take the lessons of the German experience and organize the *Jagdkompagnien* into large patrolling groups. He was thwarted by shortage of aircraft and the official policy of using fighters as bomber and reconnaissance escorts, integrated into the army co-operation squadrons. Two-seater aircraft still had production priority but slowly however Brumowski managed to encourage the formation of other *Jagdkompagnien* as proper fighting scout units equipped with up to twenty aircraft.

In mid 1917 the new generation of single-seat scouts began to reach the squadrons including the excellent Oefag-built Albatros DIII. Reluctantly Brumowski exchanged his Brandenburg for the new machine but he was soon converted. Again he made personal modifications and in emulation of the great von Richthofen, his flight of six DIIIs was painted red emblazoned with the white skull on the fuselage.

By now Brumowski had scored six victories. On 17 July he shot down a Voisin and on 11 August shot down a Nieuport and a Caudron. By the end of the month he had sent a total of nineteen Italian aircraft to their doom. Then in October 1917 Austro-German forces broke through the Italian Front at Caporetto and caused a near complete collapse. German air units were transferred from the Western Front and for a time the black-crossed aircraft of the Central Powers achieved air superiority. Brumowski and his pilots in formations of up to eighteen aircraft operated with great success and he and Frank Linke-Crawford, his most successful squadron member, competed eagerly at the expense of the *Aeronautica del Regio Esercito*.

On 4 October Brumowski flying with Linke-Crawford despatched an Italian balloon. Two days later the same pair destroyed two seaplanes and two Nieuports on the 23rd. By December his score had risen to twenty-seven. The shattered Italian air crews grimly dubbed their vulnerable SP2 pushers the *Sepoltura Per 2*, the 'Sepulchre for two'.

This time of easy victory was short-lived however. The Royal Flying Corps rushed three squadrons of its latest Camel fighters to repair the sundered front and the Italian flying units themselves were reorganized and re-equipped. In March 1918 the German *Jasta*s were withdrawn for the last great offensive effort in France and the *Luftfahrtruppen* were left to carry on the battle with thirteen depleted *Jagdkompagnien* and deepening logistic problems. Nevertheless *Hauptmann* Brumowski led his squadron gallantly to the end against increasing odds and added to his victory tally all the time. He ended the war with thirty-five victories, the highest-scoring pilot of the Imperial and Royal forces.

After the war Brumowski continued to serve in the tiny air force of the Austrian Republic but was killed when an aircraft he was flying in as a passenger crashed at Schiphol airport on 3 June 1936.

**Brandenburg DI**

The Austro-Hungarian Empire was lucky that the Trieste millionaire of Italian extraction Castillo Castiglione was a loyal supporter of the dual monarchy. Not only did he have financial interests in the aircraft factories of Phönix at Vienna and Ufag (Ungarische Flugzeugwerke AG) at Budapest within the boundaries of the Empire but before the war he had bought the Hansa und Brandenburgische Flugzeugwerke GmbH, established on the Havel 30 miles east of Berlin. The technical director of Hansa-Brandenburg was a young man with large spectacles and a genius for designing aircraft named Ernst Heinkel. The man who was later to build one of the world's first jet aircraft began therefore by designing products for the defence of the Hapsburgs.

In early 1916 Heinkel designed the DI for the *Luftfahrtruppen* and with little else available, the fighter went into production at Phönix and Ufag in the late summer.

The fuselage was deep and ungainly but the DI's most unconventional feature was its four V-strut wing bracing which earned it the name 'Starstrutter' or the 'Spider'. As a fighting aircraft it had its drawbacks. The pilot's forward vision was obstructed and the non-synchronized 8-mm Schwarzlose machine-gun was inaccessible during flight being contained in a fairing above the top wing.

The Brandenburg DI was built in two series. Forty-eight of the Series 28 were built by Phönix powered by a 160-hp Austro-Daimler and another forty-eight similarly powered DIs were built by Ufag. The later Phönix built machines had a low-aspect ratio fin and rudder and this feature was continued on the more conventional and more successful later Phönix fighters, the DI to DIII.

Godwin Brumowski thought well of the Brandenburg DIs which equipped his *Flik 41J* from the end of 1916 to mid 1917 when they were replaced by Albatros DIIIs (Oef), but he modified his Ufag-built aircraft 65.53 by disengaging the Schwarzloses's ammunition belt from its drum and laying it out in layers within the casing to reduce stoppages due to condensation.

| | |
|---|---|
| Manufacturer: | Hansa-Brandenburg and sub-contractors |
| Powerplant: | Austro-Daimler 6-cyl in-line, 160-hp |
| Span: | 8.5 m (27 ft 10⅔ in) |
| Length: | 6.35 m (20 ft 10 in) |
| Max. take-off weight: | 920 kg (2028 lb) |
| Max. speed: | 190 kmh (118 mph) |
| Ceiling: | 5000 m (16,404 ft) |
| Armament: | 1 x Schwarzlose 8-mm |

A Brandenburg D I of the
*K u K Luftfahrtruppen* in flight
over the northern Adriatic

# Ivan Smirnoff

**Sergeant Ivan Smirnoff, 1916.**
He wears a winged propeller and the Roman numerals 'XIX', of the 19th Squadron, on his shoulder straps

*Above:* Smirnoff was awarded the Cross of St George while serving in the infantry in 1915.

The Russian Order of St George was instituted by the Empress Catherine II in 1769. The silver cross for the 5th class of the order for NCOs was awarded to Smirnoff.

*Far right:* 2nd Lt Smirnoff (second left, front) and men of the 19th Squadron photographed in early 1917

WHEN Russia went to war in August 1914 Ivan Wassiliwitsj Smirnoff was nineteen, born in Vladimir on 30 January 1895. He enlisted in the 96th (Omsk) Infantry Regiment and after Russia's ponderous mobilization, Smirnoff plodded wearily west with his unit. As the Eastern front congealed into winter stalemate Smirnoff was wounded, awarded the Cross of St George and hospitalized. From his bed he could see aircraft landing and taking off from a nearby flying field and like many infantrymen saw a better way of fighting.

Early in 1915 he transferred to the XIX Corps Air Squadron at Lutzk commanded by Alexander Alexandrovich Kazakov. Each army Corps had an *Otryad* of six aircraft, later ten aircraft attached to it, but each squadron could have anything up to six different types of aircraft. The problems of keeping them serviceable were enormous and Russian air power was scattered thinly over a vast front. At the end of 1916 there were only 724 aircraft available and in some sectors they could offer no effective opposition to the Germans and Austro-Hungarians. By 1916 however some local grouping of fighter strength had been made in fighter wings (*Istebitelnyi Divisyon*) and by 1917 in four-*otryad* strong groups.

Smirnoff fought and flew with XIX Corps for two years flying Morane Type Ls, Morane Type Ns and Nieuport 17s, French types only, and rose to 1st Lieutenant from Sergeant. On 10 November 1917 he shot down a German aircraft near Gusyatin. It was his twelfth victory and made him the fourth ranking Russian ace after his commander Kazakov with seventeen and P B D'Argueff who scored most of his fifteen victories in France. The naval fighter ace Alexander de Seversky, like the Austrian Gottfried Banfield, made his name on fighter flying boats and scored thirteen victories. By the time Smirnoff scored his last victory, the military power of Kerensky's Provisional Government had crumbled and the Bolsheviks were in power in Petrograd. He was warned by his mechanic that all officers were going to be shot and so he disappeared managing to reach a White or counter-revolutionary controlled area and find passage for England. He became a Major in the RAF and served as an instructor at the Central Flying School Upavon. Smirnoff went back to Russia as a technical expert with General Denikin's White Army in the South but once again had to flee when the Whites were driven to the Black Sea in December 1919.

## Morane-Saulnier Type N

The Morane-Saulnier Type N made its debut flown by Roland Garros at the flying meeting held at Aspern outside Vienna from June 21-28 1914 where it took several prizes. On the last day of the contest, Franz Ferdinand was shot dead at Sarajevo—and pilots and aircraft dispersed as Europe began its month-long stumble towards war.

Garros conducted his machine-gun armament experiments with a Morane Type L parasol but soon after his capture in April 1915, his friend Eugène Gilbert applied the armoured airscrew technique to a Type N, named appropriately *Le Vengeur*. Four French *escadrilles* used the type later in the year and Jean Navarre of *MS 12* and Adolphe Pégoud of *MS 49* flew the armed aircraft successfully.

The Morane was fast, with its circular section fuselage and huge domed spinner it was aerodynamically advanced and highly manoeuvrable for a monoplane. But their aircraft remained what it basically was—an armed improvization based on a pre-war racing aircraft. Landing speed was high and it was notoriously difficult to fly. According to one RFC Morane pilot 'Our main preoccupation once having got into the air was to get down again'.

The Royal Flying Corps had ordered the aircraft in May 1916 and 80-hp Le Rhône powered 'Morane Bullets', shaken by the depredations of Fokker E-types, armed with Lewis guns saw some action during the Battle of the Somme. High hopes were placed in 110-hp Le Rhône powered developments called the Type I and an extended range version the Type V, but by October these too had been withdrawn from the front.

The main user of the 110-hp Morane was the Imperial Russian Air Service. A number of Morane Ns were supplied to Russia in 1916 and reportedly an example was constructed at the Moscow Dux factory the same year.

The supply and maintenance problems of operating foreign built aircraft in Russia were immense. Nieuport 11s for example arrived at the front without guns. Captain Kazakov, Smirnoff's commander, tried and failed to beg a precious British Lewis from a crashed Sikorsky *Ilya Mouromets* bomber,

until his mechanic rigged up his *Bébé* with a water-cooled Maxim mounted to fire obliquely.

The awful Spad A2 'pulpit-fighter' had to stay in front-line Russian service much longer than it should, indeed it should never have been there at all, and only at the very end did the Russians receive fighter aircraft of Western Front standards in the shape of some Spad SVIIs—but by then it was too few and far too late.

Eighteen 110-hp Moranes were in Russian operational service on 1 April 1917 and down to eleven by July—all serving on the Rumanian or Southwestern Fronts, including Smirnoff's XIX detached at Lutsk, two hundred miles west of Kiev.

Again the Russian Moranes were flying and fighting long after their contemporaries had been retired from the Western Front and some of them survived the 1917 revolution.

| | |
|---|---|
| Manufacturer: Société des Aéroplanes Morane-Saulnier | |
| Powerplant: Le Rhöne 9C 9-cyl rotary, 110-hp | |
| Span: 8.24 m (27 ft) | |
| Length: 5.81 m (19 ft 2 in) | |
| Max. take-off weight: 510 kg (1122 lb) | |
| Max. speed: 176 kmh (110 mph) at ground level | |
| Ceiling: 4000 m (13,000 ft) | |
| Armament: 1 x Vickers .303-in | |

Nieuport 17 of the 19th Squadron captured by Austrians in 1917

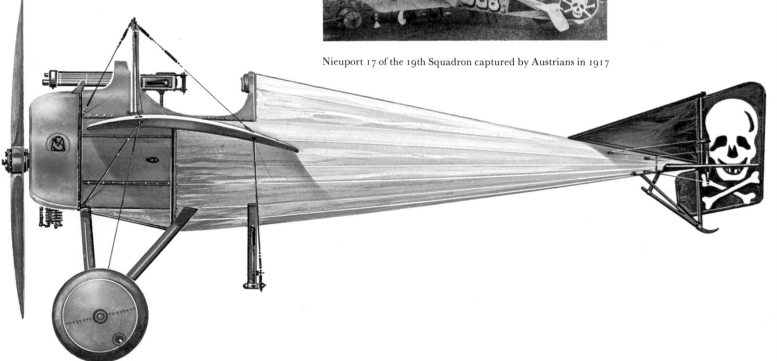

Charles Nungesser

Nungesser carried his macabre symbol from aircraft to aircraft refining it as he went. His first Voisin of 1915 bore a crude skull and cross-bones. His Spad SVII dubbed *Le Verdier* (Greenfinch) carried the definitive marking complete with coffin and candles

LIKE so many of the first military pilots, Charles Nungesser was a frustrated cavalryman. In the first month of the war, looking dashing in the operatic uniform of the 2ème Hussars, he had already earned a citation for bravery during the French Army's retreat to the Marne. But Nungesser was never really destined to make war carrying a sabre and wearing red trousers—he was very much a child of the new machine age.

He was born in Paris on 15 March 1892 and as a boy he was a passionate sportsman. While attending the *Ecole des Arts et Métiers* at Valenciennes he had already formed an ambition to be a racing driver or an aviator. He ran away to South America and flew one of the first aircraft in Argentina soloing on his very first flight. When unable to fly he indulged his appetite for adventure by racing motor cycles and enormously powerful motor cars.

By the outbreak of war he was back in France and the dashing hussar managed to escape from the

**Sous-Lieutenant Charles Nungesser.**
By late 1916 Nungesser was already the bearer of the cross of the *Légion d'Honneur*, the *Médaille Militaire* and the *Croix de Guerre*. He wears the 1914 uniform of blue *képi* with regimental number, red trousers with blue piping and black officer's tunic of his original regiment, the *2éme Hussards* with the insignia of a qualified aviator and the red and white sleeve badge of a *Sous-Officier Aviateur*

German armies advancing on Paris by capturing a German staff car by shooting the occupants and driving at high speed to safety. He had already exchanged his horse for the internal combustion engine successfully and Nungesser asked the General directly who awarded him the *Médaille Militaire* for the exploit for a transfer to the Flying Service. His wish was granted.

On 22 January the already experienced pilot began training as a military aviator and on 8 April 1915 he reported to his first operational unit, *Escadrille VB 106* based at St Pol flying Voisins. After six months as a particularly aggressive reconnaissance pilot, Nungesser was sent with *VB 106* to Nancy where while flying a new Voisin he shot down an Albatros. The *Croix de Guerre* soon followed and Nungesser went on leave to await his conversion course to the new *avions de chasse*.

In November 1915 the new fighter pilot reported to *Escadrille N 65* forming with Nieuport 11s at his old base at Nancy. Nungesser revelled in his own brand of morbid humour and the *Bébé* was adorned with all the black symbolism of violent death. A crude death's-head first appeared on his Voisin in early 1915 and the skull and cross-bones, a coffin and candlesticks all contained in a black heart, adorned all his subsequent aircraft. The town of Nancy was treated to the sight of this grim reaper in the sky when he beat up the town at thirty feet to earn himself eight days suspended arrest.

On 29 January 1916 three weeks before the Battle of Verdun opened, Guynemer suffered a serious accident. Testing a new Ponnier biplane, the aircraft spun into the ground just after take-off. Nungesser was pulled from the cockpit with a dislocated jaw, a perforated palate and two broken legs. Within two months he was flying again, hobbling to his aircraft on crutches. By the end of March he was back with *N 65* and in the first week of April he made up for lost time over Verdun shooting down several enemy aircraft and balloons. The pilot like his aircraft however was soaking up yet more punishment. His lip was clipped by an explosive bullet. His jaw was broken again in a forced landing and his knee was dislocated in a crash between the lines. Nungesser had to spend as much time recovering as he did at the front and meanwhile *N 65* relocated at Bar-le-Duc was suffering terribly itself. In the first weeks of May, three-quarters of its pilots were put out of action killed or wounded. When the Battle of Verdun finally came to an end the incredible Nungesser was as patched and repaired as his aircraft. By December he had scored twenty-one victories. He returned to hospital to have his badly knitted fractures broken and re-set. He was at last officially ordered to rest and agreed on condition that he would be allowed a roving commission on his return to combat.

Nungesser returned to battle in May 1917. He had a new Nieuport with a 130 hp Clerget in place of the more usual 110 hp Le Rhône. Based at first on the Channel coast he shot down six aircraft in two

**Nieuport Nie 23**

The Nieuport 17 represented one highpoint of the small highly manoeuvrable rotary-engined fighter armed with a single machine-gun. By late 1916 the supremacy of this formula was being challenged by the faster, heavier, water-cooled engined types such as the Albatros DIII and Spad SVII. However, rotary engined fighters such as the Camel stayed in the fore-front with engines of ever greater power until the end of the war.

The Nie 23 was a development of the Nieuport 17, in every way identical except it was slightly heavier and powered by a 120-hp Le Rhône rotary. Designer Gustave Delage's sesquiplane formula was continued in the subsequent Nie 24 and Nie 27. The unsuccessful Nie 28 of mid-1917 had wings of equal span but employed a high-powered rotary engine. The last wartime design, the superlative Nieuport-Delage NiD 29 of late 1918, employed a large in-line engine, the 300-hp Hispano-Suiza 8Fb, and, modified, remained in service until 1928, as the NiD 29C.1.

| | |
|---|---|
| Manufacturer: SA des Establissements Nieuport |
| Powerplant: Le Rhône, 9-cyl rotary, 120-hp |
| Span: 8.10 m (26 ft 10¼ in) |
| Length: 6 m (19 ft 8¼ in) |
| Max. take-off weight: 585 kg (1,287 lb) |
| Max. speed: 185 kmh (115 mph) |
| Ceiling: 5050 m (16,560 ft) |
| Armament: 1 x Vickers .303-in. |

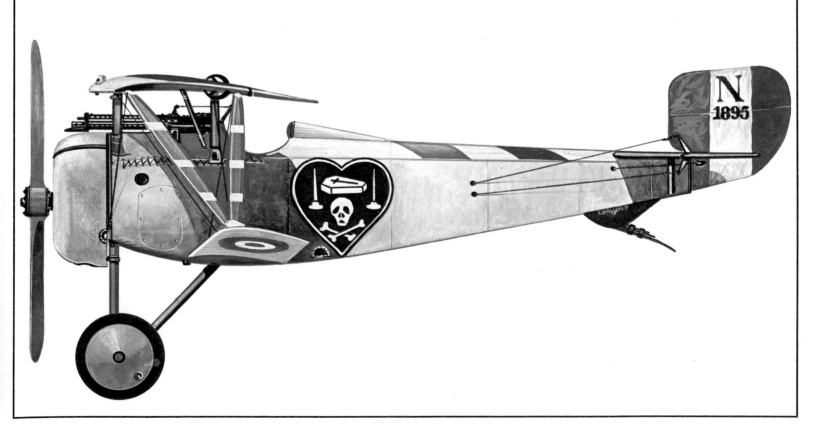

Nungesser was loaded with the military honours of France and her Allies. In this portrait he wears the Cross of the *Légion d'Honneur*, the *Médaille Militaire*, the *Croix de Guerre* with twenty-seven *Palmes*, Britain's Military Cross, Belgium's Order of Leopold II and *Croix de Guerre*, Romania's Order of King Ferdinand, the United States' Distinguished Service Cross, Serbia's Karageorgevic Cross, Portugal's *Croix de Guerre*, and medals of Russia and Montenegro

to and from his aircraft. On 12 September he set off from Dunkirk to fly to Paris when he was set on by a solitary Halberstadt DII, itself well behind the Allied lines. After a fight lasting half an hour Nungesser landed at Le Touquet in despair with his fuel exhausted. The German also landed and with a wave he opened the throttle and took off again. Nungesser took it as a personal humiliation.

The Allied air forces had suffered more than humiliation throughout the spring of 1917 and Nungesser bore the scars of his many close encounters with death. That September the terrible news of Guynemer's disappearance further shook the morale of the *Aviation Militaire*. Nungesser was given only a slight respite when for a period in the autumn of 1917 he undertook the combat training of new pilots. He was a master of the art of air fighting. One of his pupils reached a score of five in as many days.

Then in December returning to Paris at night in one of the powerful touring cars in which he revelled, he struck a patch of ice at speed and the car overturned. Nungesser was thrown clear but again seriously injured. His faithful mechanic Pochon lay dead in the wreckage. Nungesser was once again in hospital and for the rest of the war his returns to the front were interrupted by frequent spells of hospitalization. He scored his 40th victory flying a Nieuport 23 on 16 July 1918 but his great rival René Fonck had already inherited Guynemer's mantle with a score of forty-five. On 14 August Nungesser scored again with two balloons but once again he was slightly wounded. The next day he brought his score to forty-five and earned his fifteenth citation. At that score, and laden with honours from the French and Allied governments, he finished the war.

Nungesser was immensely popular in France. Like a champion boxer, his scars only heightened his attraction for women and with his flamboyant cars, his taste for Paris night-life and his medal encrusted tunic he was the archetype for many celluloid aces who followed him on a flickering screen. The legend however overtook the man. When the lionizing of the Paris *salons* began to pall, he founded a flying school at Orly with a war-surplus Morane-Saulnier A1. The venture failed and so he went to America with a Hanriot HD-1 again bearing his grim wartime insignia. Even these years of wild barnstorming could not appease his taste for adventure and he resolved to join the race to cross the Atlantic east-west from Paris. He commissioned an aircraft from Levasseur, a flotation-equipped modification of their PL8 three seater built for the new French carrier, the *Béarn*.

On 8 May 1927 at first light the white aircraft set off from Paris and crossed the Channel coast at Le Havre 1½ hours later. *L'Oiseau Blanc* was never seen again. The aircraft flew on into the dawn haze until the drone of its Lorraine engine could be heard no more. Nungesser flew into legend ten years after Guynemer.

weeks. The Germans soon knew the ace was back and on 12 May a single Albatros dropped a message challenging Nungesser to a single combat over Douai. When the Frenchman got there six enemy fighters were waiting. The grimly marked Nieuport shot down two of them in flames and the rest of the pack scattered.

German perfidy was not the only additional danger in this most dangerous of environments. The same day as the German challenge, Nungesser was attacked by a haplessly blundering RFC pilot whom he had no alternative but to shoot down. After this broad stripes of red, white and blue were added to the cockades on the top wing.

On 16 August Nungesser sent his thirtieth victim, a Gotha, crashing into Houthulst forest. But physically he was at the end of his strength and his faithful mechanic, *Soldat* Pochon, had to carry him

# René Fonck

RENÉ Fonck was the Allied Ace of Aces, and he was France's highest scoring pilot. He never gained the kind of wild adulation that surrounded Guynemer. He fought in a way that some found too mechanical, despatching his opponents with a clinical precision in contrast to Guynemer who flew headlong at his opponents and took their bullets in the process. Fonck was the calculating ace who attained his score only five fewer than Richthofen by means of careful tactics and superlative marksmanship. The attention and care he lavished on his guns he gave equally to an understanding of his opponents' strengths and weaknesses. That is why Fonck survived and his opponents did not.

He was born in the Vosges on 27 March 1894 and, although born a country boy, like Guynemer he was gripped with all the excitement of flying at a time when France really did lead the world in aviation. In 1914 upon mobilization he was posted to Dijon and spent five dismal months training as an engineer. In February 1915 he was transferred to flying training at Le Crotoy and by late spring he had qualified. He was soon in action as a reconnaissance pilot on elderly Caudron GIIIs and GIVs covering the region round Corcieux in his native Vosges. While flying a Caudron GIV over Münster he drove away an unarmed German two-seater with some rifle shots fired from the shoulder, a typical encounter in these very early days of air fighting. The greatest danger at this time was ground fire and during this period with *Escadrille C 47* as an observation pilot Fonck had several narrow escapes.

The old Caudrons were already outclassed but in July 1916 in time for the Somme battles, they were fitted with fixed forward-firing machine-guns. They were certainly no fighters. Nevertheless Fonck spoke well of the machine and even managed to force a Rumpler down behind French lines where the terrified crew surrendered. *Escadrille C 47* was still flying Caudron GIVs when it transferred to a new airfield at Fismes in Champagne in March 1917. A few days later Fonck and another Caudron were attacked by five Albatros DIIIs but in spite of the odds Fonck turned and fought. While his wingman *Sergent* Raux crashed in flames Fonck shot down an Albatros and managed to extricate his unwieldy *bimoteur* from what should have been certain death.

Fonck had long since filed a formal request for transfer to an *escadrille de chasse*. This second confirmed victory made the bureaucracy wake up and the man destined to be France's greatest fighter pilot was sent on a conversion course at Plessis-Belleville. Then on 15 April 1917, to his utter delight, he was posted to *Groupe de Chasse No 12*—the Storks themselves and he joined *SPA 103* commanded by *Capitaine* d'Harcourt. The newly fledged *Cicogne* proved himself quickly. On 3 May he caught two enemy two-seaters and shot one of them down using only some twenty rounds. Two days later he shot down a Fokker in a flailing dogfight and less than a week after that a Rumpler went spinning

down in flames from 18,000 feet under his guns. His score was now four.

On 25 May Fonck was away on leave. On that day his namesake René Dorme, a veteran ace of the *Cicognes* with a score of twenty, was shot down by *Oberleutnant* Hans Berr. On 12 June having returned to his *escadrille*, Fonck attacked two Albatroses diving in his Spad VII from out of the early morning sun. The first was immediately despatched. The second turned but Fonck outfought him and he too was shot down. It was Hans Berr, himself victor of nine combats. René Dorme was avenged.

In July 1917 the *Cicognes* left the Vosges front to come to the aid of the RFC in Flanders. Flying from Dunkirk they began large-scale ground-attack operations and began also to fly in large formations themselves to counter the new German tactics. Fonck took six or seven pilots with him on offensive patrols, starting his less-experienced pilots off with attacks on observation balloons. His *ingénues* could have had few better teachers of air fighting.

11 September 1917 was the Storks' black day when Guynemer failed to return from his last combat. Twelve mournful days later *Commandant* Brocard had abandoned hope and he told Fonck so. Within minutes the normally impassionate and ice-cool Fonck was flying alone towards the German lines intent on revenge. He found a two-seater and, diving from out of the sun, he put a short burst into

René Fonck photographed in 1916 as a twenty-two year old *Sergent*, already the bearer of the *Médaille Militaire* and the *Croix de Guerre* with three *Palmes*

**Sous-Lieutenant René Fonck, 1917.**
Fonck wears the horizon blue uniform with the addition of the flying insignia introduced in 1914. *Below:* Officer's collar insignia for qualified aviators; Breast badge for qualified aviator; Sleeve badge for *Sapeur-Aviateurs* (NCOs). *Sous-Officer Aviateurs* had the extremities of the wings in white and for officers the whole badge was in gold

the pilot from very close range. The aircraft looped wildly and the gunner was catapulted into space, nearly hitting Fonck's machine before plummeting earthwards. It was a particularly terrible revenge, and on 30 September Fonck actually shot down *Leutnant* Wissemann, the two-seater pilot the Germans were claiming had shot down Guynemer.

By mid January of the new year, the Flanders offensive had long since bogged down in the mud with appalling losses and the French squadrons were withdrawn to cover Verdun once again. It was no quiet sector and Fonck's score continued to rise steadily in the first weeks of 1918. By March the *Cicognes* were back at Fismes on the river Vesle in Champagne and, with Guynemer dead, Fonck, Deullin and Madon were all on the same score with only Nungesser ahead of them. Nungesser however was still recovering from his December car crash and Fonck was to overtake him on 29 March.

On 9 May 1918 René Fonck shot down six German aircraft in a single day. On his first sortie he despatched a two-seater and two escorting fighters in under 45 seconds with almost arrogant precision. They all crashed within 400 yards of each other. Having landed to refuel, he then despatched a two-seater attacking out of cloud cover. Five minutes later he was stalking a large formation of fighters, picked off the last of them and a few seconds later he sent the formation leader earthwards before Fonck himself turned and sped back to safety leaving his patrol area littered with the blazing wrecks of German aircraft. By the early evening his incredible sextuple victory had been confirmed. The *Croix de la Légion d'Honneur* was not long in coming, presented to him by *Général* Débéney, commander of First Army.

By mid-July Fonck was regularly scoring multiple victories and the sky was as regularly full of enemy aircraft. At the end of May the Germans launched a major offensive on the Chemin des Dames and surged ten miles across the Aisne and once again the élite *Cicognes* fought desperately where the Allied front was most threatened. On 15 July with their airfield overrun, the *Cicognes* were ordered to a new airfield at Noblette north of Châlon. On the same day six German divisions managed to cross the Marne at Dormans but it was the last gasp of a stalling offensive. On 18 July a major French counter-offensive launched with American support began to pinch out the threat. In the air the Americans provided the First Pursuit Group with 70 Nieuports and Spads to join what was already a formidable concentration of aircraft on both sides and an equally formidable gathering of fighter pilots.

Fonck continued to score doubles and trebles and on 1 August his score at fifty-seven topped that of Guynemer himself. On 14 August he attacked a formation of three head on sending them all down to crash in a 100 yard circle with a typically economical number of bullets in each one. With the German offensive halted, the tempo of air fighting

*Left:* René Fonck practises his marksmanship with a sporting carbine. Such skill made him an outstanding air fighter and he could despatch an opponent using a minimum of ammunition. *Below left:* The famous flying stork badge of *Escadrille SPA3*. Miniatures of *Gruppe de Chasse 12*'s stork badges were often worn on the tunic

did not decrease. With the Allied armies swinging on to the offensive and the morale of the German Army beginning to crumble, the German air forces continued to put up a stubborn resistance with excellent new equipment. In August Fonck shot down eleven aircraft in ten days. On 26 September he scored another sextuple victory and but for a machine-gun stoppage he might have scored two more. On 1 November he shot down a two-seater that incredibly at this last stage of the war was dropping propaganda leaflets on French trenches. It was his seventy-fifth and last victim. His own unofficial score stood at 127. Fonck was twenty-four years of age.

René Fonck knew exactly why he was so good. He wrote . . . 'To obtain good results, you must also know how to control your nerves, how to have absolute self-mastery, and how to think coolly in difficult situations.' He could wait until his enemy made a mistake—'giving way to nervous irritation' as he put it—and then, by firing his almost arrogantly short bursts straight into the enemy's vitals, despatch them sometimes with only three bullets. He was a supreme marksman who was as at home behind a sporting target rifle as behind the twin Vickers of a Spad SXIII firing deflection shots at diving speeds of 200 mph.

He was showered with medals including the *Croix de Guerre* with twenty-eight *palmes*, the British MC and MM, the Belgian *Croix de Guerre* and the Serbian Karageorgevic Cross.

It was not just combat that inspired René Fonck. He loved flying and after the war became an outstanding racing and demonstration pilot. He nearly beat Lindbergh across the Atlantic but his big Sikorsky readied for the attempt in September 1925 never left Long Island in the United States. From 1937-39 he was *Inspecteur de l'Aviation de Chasse* for the *Armée de l'Air*, a post somewhat akin to Udet's in the *Luftwaffe*. In 1940 however the spirit of self sacrifice enshrined in the Guynemer legend had temporarily left France. Fonck with all his first war prestige was a valuable emissary for Vichy France and, whereas other ex-members of the *Cicognes* like Alfred Hertaux, Taracson and Desérin returned from Buchenwald and elsewhere as heroes of the Resistance, Fonck's wartime career was tinged with a charge of collaboration. He died in relative obscurity in Paris in June 1953.

# Manfred *Freiherr* von Richthofen

TO the men he led he was simply *der Rittmeister* —the Captain. To the world he was and is the 'Red Baron'—the very epitome of a fighter ace and the stuff of legends. The propaganda machines of the Kaiser's and Hitler's Germany put the Richthofen legend twice through the distorting prism of political expediency and yet it remains uniquely fascinating. He shot down more enemies of the Fatherland than any other of Germany's pilots of World War I. He shot down more aircraft than any other pilot of World War I. He was a supreme professional in a new and deadly profession and led and organized fighting men under extreme conditions by his own example and unwavering self-discipline.

Manfred von Richthofen was born on 2 May 1892 into the kind of aristocratic family of middle rank who were the backbone of the Prussian military tradition. The career of the eldest son was obvious from the start—the army. At the age of eleven he went to military school at Wahlstatt and thence to the famous Royal Prussian Military Academy in Lichterfelde near Potsdam. The harsh discipline was relieved by visits on leave to the Richthofen estate at Schweidnitz in Silesia with its stables of fine horses and plentiful game to sharpen the *Jungherr's* already excellent marksmanship.

At Easter 1911 he joined a crack regiment of lancers—*Ulan-Rgt Nr 1 'Kaiser Alexander III'* named after its former Colonel-in-Chief, the Emperor of Russia—and in the autumn of 1912 he was commissioned *Leutnant*. Two years later the crisis of August 1914 abruptly ended the glittering round of peacetime regimental life. On 2 August Manfred led his troop of *Ulanen*, their flat-topped *czapkas* covered in drab cloth, across the border into Russian Poland. Two weeks later his unit was switched west

and crossed Germany by train. Soon they were nosing into Luxembourg and into France itself. Within weeks however his unit was halted on the Meuse and first hasty defensive scratches in the soil were hardening into trench lines. The day of the cavalryman was over.

Manfred to his great chagrin became a supply-officer but at the end of 1915, after months of frustration, he secured a transfer to the Air Service as an observer. He did well in the four week training course at Cologne and soon was in action again on the Eastern Front but this time seeing the battlefield not from a horse but from the observer's cockpit of an Albatros BII.

In August 1915 he was transferred west once more to join the clandestine unit known as the *Breiftauben Abteilung Ostende*—'The Ostend Carrier Pigeon Unit', established under *Major* Siegert to pioneer long-range bombing techniques. Richthofen was not at home with these large, slow and comparatively ineffective aircraft and eagerly returned to C-type aircraft. With his pilot *Leutnant* Osteroth, he shot down a Farman with his flexible Parabellum but the kill was not confirmed. Meanwhile he had asked his old pilot and friend from the days in the east, *Leutnant* Zeumer to teach him the mysteries of actually piloting and without much more formal training he made several successful solos. He officially qualified as a pilot on Christmas Day, 1915.

Meanwhile von Richthofen had met Oswald Boelcke quite accidentally on a long train journey to Metz and the experienced and already idolized fighter pilot told the eager young observer of the qualities of the Fokker *Eindecker*. Again however Richthofen's ambition to become a fighter pilot was to be frustrated. In March 1916 he was back on the Verdun front piloting an Albatros C-type. He had fixed a machine-gun to fire forward above the propeller arc and using this device he shot down a Nieuport but again it was unconfirmed. A few flights on a Fokker monoplane only further tantalized the fighting spirit in Richthofen until once again he was switched to the other end of Germany's two front war.

Stationed at the vital rail junction of Kovel, in Galicia, *Kampfgeschwader Nr 2* was heavily embattled throughout June-August 1916, bombing and strafing the waves of Russian infantry which broke on the Austro-German front in General Brusilov's offensive. Richthofen never shot down any of the new Russian machines he may have encountered but it was in Russia ironically that his chance for greatness came. Oswald Boelcke who was making a tour of air units on the Eastern Front selected the young *Leutnant* as a suitable candidate to join him in *Jagdstaffel 2*, the new fighting formation that it was hoped would re-establish German air ascendancy on the Western front. His career as an ace had effectively begun.

On 17 September 1916 Boelcke selected four pilots including von Richthofen to accompany him on the *Jagdstaffel's* first offensive patrol. Flying

Uhlans with their distinctive *czapka* helmets, exercise with their section machine-gun just before the outbreak of war. It was men like this that the twenty-two year old von Richthofen led into Poland in August 1914. Officers who transferred to the Flying Service kept the uniform of their original regiment and Richthofen kept his distinctive lancer uniform throughout his career

Richthofen leads his men in salute under inspection by the Kaiser at Courtrai in early 1917

Albatros DIIs they met a formation of eight BE2cs and some FE2bs over Cambrai and after a long stalk, Boelcke led his novices into the attack aiming to break up any defensive formation on the first pass. Richthofen opened fire much too early, turned then fired again mortally wounding the two man crew of an FE. Richthofen had effectively brought down two aircraft already but neither had been confirmed. This time he had to make sure—he landed and half ran over the shell-torn ground to the wreck of the FE to arrive just as the dying crew were being extracted from the smashed aircraft. That night he ordered a silver cup from a Berlin silversmith as a commemorative trophy. It would be the first of a great deal more.

Manfred von Richthofen scored quickly averaging one a week. He sought air fighting whenever possible and collected relics from his downed victims as once he collected boars' heads in the dark Silesian forests. When Richthofen made his sixth claim by 17 October, his mentor Boelcke had scored thirty-five. A week later the master had scored forty but it was to be his last. The death of Boelcke on the 28th although a great blow did not dampen Richthofen's enthusiasm for combat and he even made a kill on the morning of Boelcke's funeral ceremony on 3 November.

On 23 November 1916, von Richthofen shot down the leading RFC ace of the time, Major Lanoe Hawker, called 'The English Boelcke', in an epic battle in which the technical advantage of the German's Albatros DII over Hawker's DH2 played as much a part as anything else. Richthofen was already undeniably an ace however and the award

of the *Ordre Pour le Mérite* normally given to survivors of fifteen victorious air combats was only a few months away. He got it on 16 January 1917 and with it his first command, *Jasta 11*.

Richthofen was sad to leave *Jasta Boelcke*, as his old squadron was renamed, but now as commander of his unit he could seek as much combat as his appetite demanded and his appetite seemed insatiable. The wintry spring of 1917 at first restricted flying and broke up the rhythm of Richthofen's scoring. The disaster for the RFC of 'Bloody April' changed all that however and his scarlet-painted Albatros was everywhere shooting the near defenceless British BEs and antiquated pushers out of the sky.

*Jasta 11* included in its ranks some of the finest fighter pilots of the whole war, men such as Richthofen's brother Lothar, Kurt Wolff, Karl Allmenröder, Bruno Lörzer, Karl Schaefer and later Werner Voss. In contrast to the British practice of spreading talent and experience thin along the front, here was a unit containing the cream of a generation equipped with excellent fighting machines—and Richthofen wanted his enemies to know it. Hence the all scarlet machine of the *Staffelführer* and the scarlet and second colour of the *Jasta* members he led. The gaudy appearance of this 'flying circus' as the RFC pilots dubbed it however belied the deadly efficiency of their fighting.

To further increase organizational efficiency it was decided to localize the striking power of the *Jagdstaffeln* by banding four of them into a *Jagdgruppe*. *Jasta 11*, along with *3*, *4* and *33* went into action as an independent fighter wing on 30 April

**Rittmeister Manfred Freiherr von Richthofen, 1917.**

Postcard portraits of von Richthofen in his elegant lancer uhlanka tunic, *Pour le Mérite* glittering at the neck, sold in many thousands during the war as his fame grew and this image remains one of the most powerful symbols of the fighter 'ace'.

A short leather coat often favoured by von Richthofen was equally stylish but the rigours of open cockpit flying in winter demanded something more practical. Up to late 1917 and the development of specialised clothing on both sides, keeping warm was largely a matter of personal improvisation.

Here the *Rittmeister* wears a close fitting pigskin helmet, a cut down army greatcoat with fur collar, and goatskin boots

1917 the day that von Richthofen went on leave. Reorganized on his return and now comprising *Jagdstaffeln 11* (Wolff), *6* (Dostler), *10* (von Althaus) and *4* (von Doering), this unit became the true 'Richthofen circus' known after 26 June as *Jagdgeschwader 1*. *JG 1* was centred on Courtrai with Richthofen and *Jasta 11*'s headquarters at Marcke. *Jasta 4* was at Ceune, *Jasta 6* at Bisseghem and *Jasta 10* at Heule. The average age of the *Jasta* leaders grouped in the *JG 1* was twenty-five and that of the pilots themselves a mere twenty-one. The men they were facing were certainly no older.

The high period of an already meteoric career was about to begin. On 22 March 1917 von Richthofen was promoted *Oberleutnant* and a few weeks later *Rittmeister*, the rank equivalent to Captain for members of cavalry regiments, of which von Richthofen nominally still was. In spite of the burden of administrative work, von Richthofen flew whenever he could until, with the new *Jagdgeschwader* itself hardly organized—its leader was ignominiously shot down. While attacking a formation of six FE2ds of No 20 Squadron RFC, a bullet from the Lewis gun of 2nd Lt A E Woodbridge fired at extreme range clipped the left side of Richthofen's skull and sent his red Albatros DVa spinning out of control until he regained consciousness at some 500 feet, recovered, and was able to make a crash landing before crawling out and collapsing beside his aircraft.

The great circus ringmaster had fallen, and the pilots of his command were stunned. With a shaven head swathed in bandages he slowly recovered in hospital at Courtrai tended by a pretty nurse and amply photographed for the newspapers. The visits by his *Geschwader* members and the reports from the front however merely hastened his impatience to get back into action. At last on 25 July 1917 he returned to Marcke and he had some significant new information. The *Geschwader* was to be re-equipped with Fokker triplanes, the tiny pugnacious DrI designed as a pure fighting machine able to outshoot and outmanoeuvre any opposition. Richthofen was delighted. Here was the finely balanced dog-fighting machine he had waited for since praising the Sopwith Triplane's qualities in April. He told his eager pilots the new aircraft were 'as manoeuvrable as the devil' and that they could 'climb like monkeys', but there were to be some disappointments.

Meanwhile on 28 August the new machines arrived amidst great excitement. On 2 September Richthofen scored his sixtieth victory and his first with a DrI when he sent an RE8 down over Zonnebeke. The next day he led a formation of Albatros DIIIs from the cockpit of his triplane, and they met action with a patrol of Sopwith Pups. Richthofen reported the triplane to be 'undoubtedly better and more reliable than the English machine'.

It was not all going the *Geschwader*'s way. The new British scout opposition, Camels, SE5as and Bristol Fighters was getting stiffer by the week and No 56 Squadron RFC consistently denied Ger-

## Albatros DIII

By the winter of 1916 the Albatros DI and DII with their twin Spandau machine-guns and high-powered in-line engines had successfully won back German aerial predominance lost to the DH 2 and Nieuport 11. With their success in the newly organized *Jagdstaffeln* established, the Albatros-Werke team led by *Dipl Ing* Robert Thelen designed a new model, the 'L 20' repeating many features of the earlier aircraft but with a new wing cellule layout and V-type interplane struts, and a high compression Mercedes DIII engine giving better performance at altitude.

Construction followed that of the DII, the fuselage being of semi-monocoque plywood and composite spruce and plywood wings. The radiator was at first positioned centrally in the upper wing, but after combat damage coolant leaks scalded several pilots, it was relocated to the starboard of the upper wing centre section. Pilot visibility was much enhanced, the sesquiplane layout copying Nieuport practice and affording a much better downward view.

From January 1917 the first DIIIs began to reach the *Jagdstaffeln*. By November nearly 450 were in service and formed the main equipment of most of the *Jastas* now operating in large formations, and the DIII was the chief instrument of the RFC's agony during 'Bloody April'. By the autumn of 1917 however they were outclassed by the new Allied fighters, Camels, Spad VIIs and SE5as, and were being progressively replaced by new types including the Albatros DV and DVa.

Richthofen scored his first victory in an Albatros DII No 491/16 while with *Jasta 2* on 17 September 1916 and in this aircraft some months later he shot down Major Lanoe Hawker's DH2. Richthofen's new command, *Jagdstaffel 11*, was equipped with DIIIs in late January and on his second patrol in the type on 24 January Richthofen engaged a formation of FE2bs driving one down with an injured pilot and a bullet-ridden motor. However Richthofen had to force land himself in this action when his top wing cracked as he came out of a dive. He transferred briefly to a Halberstadt DII but came back to his all-red DIII before the onslaught of April where his aircraft D 789/17 rapidly earned the name *le petit rouge* from the Allied pilots. On 23 June 1917 he transferred to a new Albatros DVa having accounted for thirty-five of his victories in the Albatros DIII including the brief interlude on the Halberstadt DII.

Manufacturers: Albatros Werke GmbH and subcontractors

Powerplant: Mercedes DIIIa 6-cyl in-line, 160-hp

Span: 9.05 m (29 ft 8¾ in)

Length: 7.33 m (24 ft 0 in)

Max. take-off weight: 886 kg (1949 lb)

Max. speed: 165 kmh (108 mph)

Armament: 2 x Spandau 7.92-mm

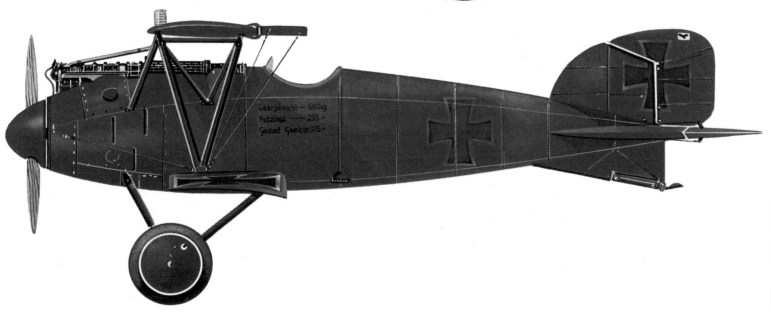

Cappy airfield, 21 April 1918. Pilots of *JG 1* await orders for take-off. Manfred von Richthofen is fourth from the right in one-piece flying suit without parachute harness

Flattening out from his dive, Brown lost Richthofen and May as they seemed to continue on their deadly chase for at least another 1600 yards.

With May convinced his end had come and about to plunge into the Somme in despair, the young Canadian looked round and saw his pursuer do a 'spin and a half and hit the ground'. The triplane bounced and skidded to a halt the right way up. It was some two miles behind the front line in a sector held by Australian troops. Many of these troops had watched the battle overhead and at least two groups of gunners fired Vickers and Lewis bursts at the low-flying triplane.

Australian infantry found a dead German pilot frozen to the controls. Blood trickled from the open mouth and there was an exit wound in the left breast. Von Richthofen was dead. Bullets from Brown's guns and from the ground undoubtedly struck Richthofen's aircraft but the wreck was effectively stripped of its fabric by eager souvenir hunters, destroying the interpretable evidence. The bullets which killed von Richthofen could have come from the ground or the air depending on the angle of the rapidly manoeuvring triplane when the fatal bullets struck.

The victory was semi-officially credited to Brown although in spite of extensive investigations mystery still remains as to who shot down von Richthofen.

In April 1918 however the outcome of the war was still in the balance. Richthofen was a statistic amongst millions, although a very important one—and *Jagdgeschwader 1* was still fighting for its life. At Cappy airfield *JG 1*'s adjutant *Oberleutnant* Bodenschatz opened the grey envelope Richthofen had handed him on 4 March to be opened in the event of his failing to return from a patrol—in effect the *Rittmeister's* will. Hauptmann Wilhelm Reinhard was to succeed him and the will of Richthofen was not to be denied.

His body lay first in a hangar of No 3 Squadron AFC and then was borne on a Crossley tender to a grave at Bertangles. A wreath from his so recent enemies bore the inscription 'To our gallant and worthy foe'.

The simple dignity of this wartime ceremony could not lay Richthofen's mortal remains or his legend to rest. In 1925, seven years after *JG 1*, renamed *JG Frhr von Richthofen Nr 1*, had gone down in defeat under the command of Hermann Göring, the *Rittmeister's* remains were borne by train to Berlin. Bells tolled and flags flew at half mast right across Germany. Richthofen was reburied at the *Invaliden* with President Hindenburg himself symbolically throwing the first handful of earth in the grave. Twelve years later Hermann Göring unveiled a much bigger memorial built on the same spot with the fullest National Socialist bombast. Once again the Richthofen legend became the property of a German propaganda machine, and once again German airpower was to go down in the ashes of defeat. The Richthofen legend endures.

from No 3 Squadron Australian Flying Corps flying at some 7000 feet busily photographing German activity west of Hamel. Four triplanes fell like hawks but the RE8s managed to scurry into the safety of a cloudbank their observers firing as they went. As the triplanes disengaged they were over British lines and the first white puffs of anti-aircraft began to crump and billow.

The mist which had delayed *JG 1* had also blanketed No 209 Squadron's airfield at Bertangles and they had got up late on a routine high offensive patrol at 12,000 feet. As the Camel pilots flew northeast to cross the Somme, Richthofen's formation had been joined by aircraft from *Jasta 5* and but for the engagement with the RE8s, the British and German patrols might have crossed unawares at widely differing altitudes. The Flight-Commander, Captain Arthur Royal Brown, led his Camels towards the gunfire and met the detached triplanes first disengaging from the RE8s. Almost simultaneously Richthofen spotted the threat and his formation turned to meet the attack.

Brown's fellow Canadian Second-Lieutenant W R May circled at 12,000 feet as ordered by his flight leader. Then he saw an opportunity and attacked an unwary triplane but managed to jam both his guns in the attempt. Again obeying orders he turned and ran for home. Richthofen saw it, an easy target, and put his triplane into a shallow dive. Brown saw it too and broke away to come to the rescue. As Brown dived in pursuit, Richthofen was catching up on the Camel following May's every evasive turn and waiting for the eighty-first opportunity to put in a short deadly burst from close range. The two aircraft were coming down very low, weaving some 200 feet above the tortured Somme Valley. Brown was still diving when the triplane filled his sight. The twin Vickers stitched holes in Richthofen's machine and in those adrenalin-surging seconds Brown saw the enemy pilot start round and then seem to slump in his cockpit.

# Francesco Baracca

W HEN Italy declared war on Austria-Hungary on 19 May 1915, the man who was destined to become Italy's leading fighter pilot of World War I was already a very experienced pilot. The Italian Army was not slow to see the potential of aircraft as a weapon of war. The first flying school in Italy had been set up early in 1910 at Centocelle near Rome, and in 1911–12 the Italians had conducted the first ever military operations using aircraft in Libya.

Francesco Baracca was born on 9 May 1888 at Ludo di Romagna near Ravenna and was educated in Lugo and Florence. He entered the *Scuola Militare* at Modena in October 1907, much against his parents' wishes, but by September he was a *Sottotenente* with a commission in the Royal Piedmont Cavalry proudly wearing his classical 'Minerva' helmet emblazoned with the cross of Savoy. In April 1912 he went to Reims in France for flight training with a small group of fellow cavalry officers and after two months spent on a 35 hp Hanriot he got his pilot's brevet. He missed the fighting in Libya but for three years he made an extensive tour of Italian airfields instructing and advising while extending his own knowledge of foreign types. When Italy at last declared war, he was in Paris on a military mission and was fully acquainted with the latest French aircraft and the progress of air fighting.

He was soon back in Italy, joining a squadron flying Nieuport two-seaters on the Udine Front. In September he had his first encounters with enemy aircraft but on three occasions he was frustrated by machine-gun stoppages. At last at the end of the year he got a single-seat Nieuport 11 *Bébé* but had to wait until 7 April 1916 for his first victory. With all the skill of a veteran he attacked an Austrian Aviatik from its blind spot and forced it to land with a well-aimed burst of fire. On 2 May he got another two-seater in his sight and pressed his trigger at some fifty yards' range but again the gun jammed and his prey slipped away.

On 16 May he was luckier. Fourteen Austrian aircraft crossed the Italian lines on a bombing mission at 4.00 am under cover of cloud and darkness but Baracca got up with fellow pilots of the *70ᵃ Squadriglia* and between them sent three enemy aircraft earthwards. Austrian two-seaters continued to fall before his guns throughout the late summer and autumn, the Italian getting his fifth victim on 25 November 1916. The newly fledged 'ace' commemorated his cavalry service by painting a prancing horse on the Nieuport 11 and this remained his personal symbol.

By early May 1917 his score stood at ten. On 1 May Baracca and a cadre of experienced pilots were detached to become the core of the new *91ᵃ Squadriglia* forming with Spad SVIIs newly-supplied by France and they were a formidable new arrival to the air war over Northern Italy. Baracca flying the Spad shot down three enemy aircraft in three weeks. Then at last he was given command of the squadron and on 6 June *91ᵃ Squadriglia* moved to

**Maggiore Francesco Baracca, 1917.**
Italian flying officers wore the uniform of their original regiment with the addition of a crowned flying eagle on both sleeves: Baracca wears the uniform of the 2nd Piedmont Cavalry, his original regiment, with these additions. Rank was indicated by the system of cuff stars and lace rings on the cap

*Right:* Typical of the opposition facing Baracca's squadron over the Piave—the Aviatik D I of 1917, the 'Berg Scout'
*Below:* Baracca's famous prancing horse insignia, given after the war by the ace's mother to Enzo Ferrari, the Italian racing driver and later founder of the Ferrari car company. It has become famous borne by all Ferrari's racing and road cars since

a new airfield at Istrana behind the Piave. By the end of September 1917 Baracca had nineteen confirmed victories. Then on 21 October he survived a running fight with five Albatros DIIIs, to shoot down a pair of two-seaters while making his escape.

On 24 October 1917 in driving snow and rain, Austrian storm-troops, backed by massive German reinforcements, fell on the Italian Second Army front of the Isonzo and tore it open at Caporetto. Strong German components were bolstering the Austrian effort in the air and the defending Italians found themselves dangerously close to being completely overwhelmed. On 25 October Baracca himself had no less than five separate engagements with enemy aircraft, shooting down an Albatros although being badly shot up himself. Two members of his squadron however, *Tenentes* Sabelli and Ferreri, were lost. The next day in revenge he personally despatched two German Aviatiks.

Meanwhile the Second Army front was crumpling up. Loaded on to carts and trucks and fighting their way along roads clogged with retreating troops, Baracca's *91ª Squadriglia* was evacuated wholesale to an airfield at Pordonone east of the Piave where new Spad SXIIIs were waiting for them. Immediately they were back in action staving off the onslaught of Godwin Brumowski's red Albatros DIIIs of *Flik 41J* who shot down one of Baracca's most promising protegés, *Sergente* Macchi, on 26 October. Baracca's revenge was swift and he shot down six more two-seaters throughout November bringing his score to thirty, his squadron destroying three aircraft on one day.

Baracca had begun his flying career a technical

expert and test pilot and now at the height of his fame he was withdrawn from the fighting to Turin to advise Ansaldo on the development of indigenous Italian fighter aircraft, and tested the Ansaldo A1 *Ballila* and later the more successful SVA5. Italy's greatest fighting airman was of greater use at the Front however and soon he was back with his squadron moving with it to a new airfield at Treviso covering the southern Piave. On 3 May 1918 he reopened his score when he attacked six Albatros DIIIs shooting one down and during the last Austrian effort to cross the last river line guarding Venice, the Piave, he shot down four more aircraft bringing his total to thirty-four.

By 18 June 1918 the Austrian offensive was faltering. General von Boroevic's troops were trapped on the wrong side of the flood swollen river and the Italians launched a counter-attack spearheaded by trench-strafing aircraft with strong support from the RAF. On 19 June Baracca took off with two others on a ground-attack mission near Montello, and the three poured fire into the enemy lines from as low as 100 feet in the face of fierce ground fire. His flight members lost sight of their leader and returned alone to report they had not seen Baracca during the last attacks. Baracca was dead. His Spad lay smashed on the banks of the Piave.

When the advancing Italians found the wreckage of his burnt-out aircraft, Baracca's body was found nearby with a bullet through his forehead—it may have been a lucky shot from the defending gunner of a two-seater but more likely a stray shot from the ground brought down Italy's ace of aces.

# Werner Voss

FOR the brave to honour the brave is high tribute. Major James McCudden wrote after he had seen the pilot of a green Fokker triplane put up the most courageous fight against his formation of SE5s—'I shall never forget my admiration for that German pilot, who single-handed fought seven of us for ten minutes and also put some bullets through all our machines. His flying was wonderful, his courage magnificent, and in my opinion he is the bravest German airman whom it has been my privilege to see fight.' The German pilot was called Werner Voss.

Werner Voss was at one point von Richthofen's closest rival but he came from a completely different background to the Prussian baron. Like Albert Ball, he grew up against a background of industry, and again like Ball his first love was machines and he was never happier than when tinkering with his motorcycle or an aero-engine. He was born in Krefeld, the son of a dye factory owner, on 13 April 1897. On the outbreak of war he was in a cavalry regiment, the 2nd Westphalian Hussars, enlisting while he was still under age. In August 1915 he transferred to the air service, then seen very much as an extension of the cavalry's military function. During the first weeks of the Battle of the Somme he flew as an observer where the highly dangerous routine of artillery observation brought him both a strong identification and sympathy for two-seater crews (he wrote later that of his original reconnaissance unit not one was still alive) and a desire to get behind the controls of an aircraft himself. He got his flight training in the late summer of 1916 and on 21 November he was transferred to *Jasta 2*, Oswald Boelcke's old command. Six days later he got his first victory when he forced down a BE2c. From then Voss's skill as a single-seater pilot cut a swathe through the Royal Flying Corps. In January and February 1917 Voss raised his score to twenty-two, trailing the Rittmeister himself by only five. During April 1917 he fought on the French Front during the disastrous Nivelle offensive on the Chemin des Dames which brought the French army close to cracking. Up to 31 July 1917 when Voss was posted back to the British sector to command *Jasta 10*, he shot down a total of thirty-four aircraft. Remembering his days on the Somme as an observer he wrote after shooting down a BE2, '*Verachtliken*—"Poor devils". I know how they felt. I have flown in such a type—they must be destroyed because they spy out our secrets but I would prefer to shoot down fighters.'

While flying an Albatros DV against the new British types that were arriving to avenge the disaster of April, Voss was called to Schwerin to test the latest product from the Fokker stable, the Fokker DrI, which it was hoped would maintain the German technical ascendancy. The qualities of the extraordinary new aircraft delighted the natural pilot in Voss. His triplane became an obsession and he would later endlessly tinker with his machine while wearing an old grey jacket. On 28 August at last the new operational triplanes arrived at Heule and Voss's *Jasta* used these superb offensive machines to their best ability, the RFC at first being taken completely off guard when the hitherto friendly shape of a Sopwith Triplane began to spit bullets at them. Voss's machine with its cowling marked with a face both ferocious and comic was the third machine from the factory, Fokker FI 103/17, the second FI 102/17 going to Richthofen himself. In the first ten days of August Voss shot down five aircraft from the cockpit of his DrI and four more before the end of the month. On 5 September he shot down a Sopwith Pup and a Caudron on the same day. On the 9th he attacked a formation of three Sopwith Camels, shot two down and drove away the third bringing down an FE2d on the same patrol.

By 23 September 1917, Voss's score stood at forty-seven. On his first patrol that day he shot down a DH4 to bring his score to just two short of the magic fifty. That afternoon his two brothers *Lt* Otto and *Uffz* Max Voss arrived at the airfield at Heule to accompany Werner on leave back home to Krefeld. What a present to bring home! For the twenty year old to have despatched fifty enemies of the Fatherland! At 6.05 therefore Werner Voss took off again in spite of failing light in his triplane Fok FI 103/17 looking for the enemy.

It was the day of the autumn equinox. That September evening a massive cloud formation at 10,000 feet effectively marked the operational ceiling. Patches of thin cloud at 1000 feet spotted the tortured and already darkening Flanders landscape below as Voss scanned the western horizon above the British lines looking for any stragglers from the afternoon's air battles running for home, silhouetted against the dying rays of the sun.

Then Voss saw a single SE5a scudding home and the Triplane fell in pursuit.

Unseen to Voss, above and to the east was a patrol of perhaps the best fighter pilots in the Royal Flying Corps. No 56 Squadron RFC with six of its most experienced pilots—A P F Rhys-Davids, R A Mayberry, V P Cronyn, R T C Hoidge and K K Muspratt led by James McCudden VC—were about to hunt the hunter. R Stuart-Wortley saw it from 1000 feet higher up. 'A red flare flickered from the leader of the SE5s. There was an enemy in sight! But search as I might I could see nothing. Then, of a sudden I espied the Hun . . . a solitary, lonely Hun in a Fokker triplane.'

Already the flight leader McCudden was building up a tactical trap to snare the triplane pilot with Rhys-Davids and McCudden at either side and Muspratt and Hoidge at top and bottom of an open mouthed box with the other two SE5s guarding any possible escape from the trawl. The leading SE5 pilots pressed their triggers together but at the first rattle of .303 gunfire Voss did the incredible. As Cronyn wrote 'he whipped round in an extraordinary way, using no bank at all but just throwing his tail behind him.' Pitching the aerobatic qualities

**Leutnant Werner Voss, 1917.**
Voss, originally in a reserve Hussar regiment, wears the uniform of the *Fliegertruppe* with an M.1910 tunic modified with breast pockets. Knee socks were a favourite of Voss's, whether for flying or riding his motorcycle. His *Pour le Mérite* was awarded in April 1917

of the rotary-engined triplane against the faster but heavier and slower-turning SE5s, Voss flew straight back towards his ambushers firing as he came. Another flick turn and the triplane was behind Hoidge and bullets tore into his aircraft. McCudden had taken the first burst of Voss's fire through his wings and had broken away sharply but now recovered. He wrote 'the pilot seemed to be firing at all of us simultaneously and although I got behind him a second time I could hardly stay there for a second. His movements were so quick and uncertain that none of us could hold him in sight at all for any decisive time.' Three times the SE5 pilots tried to use their advantage of speed and numbers to build a net to snare the snarling twisting triplane, and three times the Fokker escaped.

A formation of Albatros DVs flew above the fight but were held back by a cordon of Spads. One red-nosed DV got through and for a few desperate minutes the Albatros guarded Voss's tail until it was driven down. 'This left Voss alone in the middle of us', Capt G H Bowman recalled, 'which did not appear to deter him in the slightest.' Instead of breaking out and flying east into the safety of the gathering gloom Voss turned again and again into the attack. At last Rhys-Davids got on his tail in SE5a B585 with his propeller boss almost glued to the triplane's rudder and for a few seconds the Fokker filled his ring-sights. Rhys-Davids fired a long burst from both Lewis and Vickers raking the triplane from end to end.

After that Voss made no further attempt to turn. He was already dying in the cockpit of the triplane now slowing up and flying level. Then slowly down it went, gently gliding westwards. Rhys-Davids dived again, put a Vickers shot into Voss, reloaded and put another Lewis drum into the seemingly indestructible triplane. The Fokker turned right and its glide steepened and Rhys-Davids' diving SE overshot. McCudden however saw Voss's end. 'I noticed that the triplane's movements were very erratic, and then I saw him go into a fairly steep dive and so I continued to watch, and then saw the triplane hit the ground and disappear into a thousand fragments, for it seemed to me that it literally went to powder.'

British soldiers found the remains of the triplane and the body of the pilot and salvaged what they could. Voss had come down just north of St Julian some half mile behind the front line. The pilot's body was buried in a mass grave. Next morning No 56 squadron got a telegram from the RFC headquarters. The dead pilot had been found wearing the Boelcke collar and at his neck he wore the *Pour le Mérite*. His name was Werner Voss. As they counted the bullet holes in their own machines the pilots of No 56 Squadron knew they had faced one of the greatest air fighters of the war indeed many German and RFC pilots considered him a greater fighter pilot than von Richthofen. Rhys-Davids later said to McCudden 'If I could only have brought him down alive', a wish shared by McCudden.

**Fokker DrI Dreidecker**

Anthony Fokker had seen the Sopwith Triplane in action over the Western Front in April 1917, and like many other manufacturers in Germany and Austria his design department was urgently requested to design an 'answer'. The resulting triplane prototype numbered V3 designed by Reinhold Platz was even more unconventional than the Sopwith. The wings were three cantilever slabs based on deep-section hollow box spars and there were no orthodox interplane struts on the prototype. In spite of these components' strength and lightness, the next prototype V4 featured interplane struts to cure vibration and also improved controls. Manoeuvrability was outstanding and in virtually unchanged form two more prototypes were ordered plus 318 production aircraft.

The second and third aircraft FI 102/17 and 103/17 were given their service acceptance tests at Schwerin in mid-August 1917 and on the 21st they were delivered by Anthony Fokker himself to Courtrai. On the 29th Werner Voss commander of *Jasta 10* flew FI 103/17 for the first time and was delighted by its qualities. This was the aircraft with which he scored his ten victories between 3 September and fought his last fight on 23 September.

From mid-October deliveries of production DrIs (*Dreidecker*–Triplane) began to *JG 1* under the command of Manfred von Richthofen, but a series of fatal crashes caused them to be grounded and a special commission found defective wing construction. By the end of November the DrI was cleared but its career was to be brief. Its incredible agility appealed to the experienced pilots of *JG 1* although it was slower than its contemporaries and beginning to be outclassed by May 1918 when production ended.

Power unit was usually a 110-hp Le Rhône rotary licence-built by Thulin in Sweden (referred to euphemistically as 'captured'), or the Oberursel URII, a straight copy of the 110-hp Le Rhône, but pilots preferred the Swedish-built product.

Von Richthofen himself flew several triplanes from FI 102/17 in August 1917 until he was shot down and killed in DrI 425/17 on 21 April 1918.

| | |
|---|---|
| Manufacturer: Fokker Flugzeug-Werke GmbH | |
| Powerplant: Thulin-built Le Rhône 9-cyl rotary, 110-hp or Oberursel UR II 9-cyl rotary, 110-hp | |
| Span: 7.19 m (23 ft 7⅜ in) | |
| Length: 5.77 m (18 ft 11¼ in) | |
| Max. take-off weight: 586 kg (1289.2 lb) | |
| Max. speed: 165 kmh (103.12 mph) at 4000 m (13,120 ft) | |
| Ceiling: 6100 m (20,013 ft) | |
| Armament: 2 x Spandau 7.92-mm | |

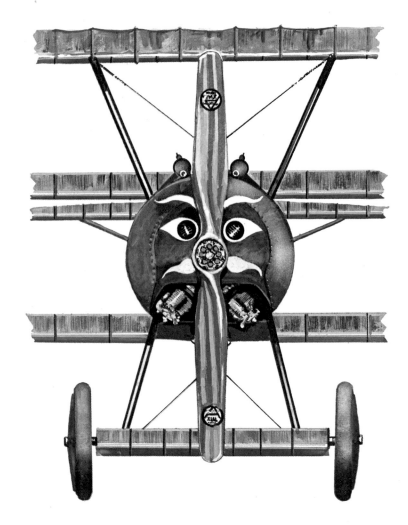

*Left:* The moments before take-off at a Fokker Dr I equipped *Jasta*. The rotary engines are run up and the pilots, like their machines, receive last minute attention.
*Above:* The tragi-comic face painted on the cowling of Voss' DrI. Individual German pilots often had their fighters doped in highly flamboyant colour schemes, much to the amusement of RFC pilots. Voss is reputed to have flown an all-black Triplane. However, the standard factory finish was light blue undersurfaces, and streaky brown or purple-brown upper surfaces

# Willy Coppens

Willy Coppens, created
*Chevalier* de Houthulst, was
Belgium's leading ace with
thirty-seven victories. Many
of his missions were flown on
Hanriot HD 1s. The aircraft
here is a Sopwith F1 Camel

WILLY Coppens was a slogging footsoldier in the 3rd Battalion of the 2nd Grenadiers when the German invasion of Belgium began on 4 August 1914. When at last a line was held and the Belgium Army was re-established to fight on the Yser covering Belgium's tiny slice of unoccupied territory, he joined a motor-cycle machine-gun detachment and was very nearly sent to North Russia in 1915 with the *Corps Expeditionnaire Belge des Auto-Canons-Mitrailleuses*. This obscure formation was finally to end up in China in 1918 after the Russian revolution, but there was another fate in store for Willy Coppens. He was to become Belgium's leading fighter ace of World War I.

He was born at Watermael near Brussels on 6 July 1892, the son of a painter. He was called up for National Service in 1912 and having escaped both the German invaders and a posting to Russia, paid his own way to learn to fly in the autumn of 1915 at the famous Ruffy-Baumann flying school at Hendon in England. He was then sent to the newly re-established *Aviation Militaire*'s own school at Etampes, flying old Maurice Farmans. At last in July 1916 he got his pilot's badge—the winged 'A' of King Albert.

At first the Belgian air arm had to make do with the cast-off of the French and British. Coppens started on the second hand and already battle-worn BE2cs and Farmans of *6ème Escadrille* at the end of 1916 conducting reconnaissance on the Belgian Army's tiny sector of front line round Dixmude. In April 1917 they received ex RNAS Sopwith 1½-Strutters and on 1 May, flying one of these Coppens, had his first aerial combat when he was attacked by four German fighters, escaping unharmed in a bullet-riddled aircraft. On 15 July he was posted to

the *1ère Escadrille* at Les Moeres, the premier single-seater squadron of Belgium's tiny air force, commanded by *Commandant* Fernand Jacquet and the home of de Meulemeester and Jan Olieslagers.

On 21 July 1917 Coppens fought his first single-seater action in a Nieuport 17 but without result. The frustration continued for Coppens throughout the autumn when he flew as de Meulemester's wingman in a Hanriot HD 1, but without luck.

In February 1918, the three Belgian scout *escadrilles* were grouped together and renumbered, *1ère* becoming *9ème* commanded by *Capitaine* Gallex, with Jacquet in command of the whole group based at Les Moeres. Coppens tried to shoot down several balloons before he at last opened his score on 25 April 1918, sending a German fighter crashing earthwards over Ramscapelle.

The Houthulst forest became a favourite hunting ground and Coppens became a specialist at shooting down observation balloons, all of which were included in his victory score. On 14 October Coppens set out from Les Moeres at dawn to answer an artillery request to force down a German balloon above Thoorout. Shooting down another balloon on the way Coppens found and attacked the Thoorout balloon already being frantically winched down. Up came a hail of anti-aircraft fire and shrapnel struck Coppens in the leg. Fighting the pain he corrected a spin and the Hanriot crashed heavily. He was pulled out of the wreckage alive, but the smashed leg was later amputated.

In spite of his disability, Coppens continued to fly after the war. He was knighted as a *Chevalier* by King Albert and took his title from the forest of Houthulst over which he had scored so many of his victories.

# James McCudden

JAMES Thomas Byford McCudden was with the Royal Flying Corps virtually right from its start. He was born at Gillingham in Kent on 25 March 1895 and joined the Royal Engineers as a boy bugler in 1910. In April 1913 he followed his elder brother, who had been in the original RE Balloon Company, in successfully applying for a transfer to the Military Wing of the RFC. On 15 June 1913 he joined No 3 squadron, which had formed a year earlier, as the first aeroplane squadron in the RFC. McCudden was an Air Mechanic First Class, swinging the props on Maurice Farmans and apparently enjoying every minute of it.

When the RFC went to France in August 1914, McCudden went with it, helping to keep the aircraft of No 3 squadron serviceable under extreme conditions as they hopped backwards from airfield to airfield in retreat.

By August 1915 he was promoted to Sergeant and had logged time as an observer and also some unofficial time as a pilot on the squadron's Morane Parasol. McCudden's first aerial combat was as an observer in December 1915 and in January 1916 he received the French *Croix de Guerre*. At the end of that month he was posted back to England at last to learn to fly and promoted Flight Sergeant.

His first official operational flight as a pilot was on 10 July in an FE2d of 20 Squadron. After a month of patrols and escort work over the Somme in these two-seaters McCudden was posted at the beginning of August to No 29 Squadron equipped with single-seater DH2s. A month after his first patrol, McCudden opened his score sending down a two-seater over Gheluve. On 1 October he was awarded the Military Medal—a commission followed on 1 January, and two more German aircraft fell to his DH2's Lewis gun before he was posted home as an instructor at Joyce Green and then Dover. A brief 'refresher course' on the Pups of No 66 Squadron in France followed but a revealing taste of the RFC's latest front-line aircraft came on 21 July when he flew an SE5a on patrol with No 56 squadron. The squadron's CO Major R G Blomfield applied for Captain McCudden to join the elite formation and on 15 August, with his score standing at eleven, he was posted to the squadron as a Flight-Commander.

McCudden's score shot up rapidly and the attention he paid to his guns and engine was matched

Britain's fourth highest scoring pilot, Major J T B McCudden, here in the cockpit of an SE5a of No 56 Squadron RFC. Before his death he was awarded the VC, DSO and Bar, MC and Bar, MM and *Croix de Guerre*

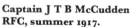

**Captain J T B McCudden RFC, summer 1917.**
McCudden had worn the distinctive RFC 'maternity jacket' uniform since transferring to the Military Wing from the Royal Engineers in 1913. Once an officer he wore a standard field service uniform officer's tunic plus a peaked cap with the addition of RFC badges. On this tunic rank was indicated by the standard army system on the cuffs:
*Top right:* Colonel
*Top centre:* Lt-Colonel
*Top left:* Major
*Upper left:* Captain
*Lower left:* Lieutenant
*Bottom left:* 2nd Lieutenant
On the 'maternity jacket' this system on shoulder straps indicated rank.
*Top far right:* SE5a construction, 1918. Potentially Britain's most effective fighter, SE5 production was at first badly hampered by problems with engines

by his careful study of enemy tactics. He became a practised stalker of two-seaters and forty-five of his eventual fifty-seven victories were of this type but he also excelled in duels with single-seaters. His mechanical and analytical mind, courage and exacting leadership made an outstanding fighter pilot.

By the end of 1917 his score was thirty-seven, four of his victories gained on one day, 23 December. Another day of quadruple victory occurred on the 25th and on 16 February his last victim fell, a Hannover CLIII. On 5 March he returned to England for another tour as flying instructor and on 6 April he was awarded the VC, the DSO and Bar and a Bar to his MC to make him the most decorated member of the RFC or RNAS at the age of twenty-two.

After four months instructing, McCudden was promoted to Major and given command of No 60 Squadron, another SE5 unit based at Boffles. He never got there—while taking off for his new command on 9 July from Auxi-le-Chateau his engine failed and McCudden tried to turn round and glide back to his airfield. As he turned the aircraft sideslipped and fell like a stone. A dazzling fighting career was extinguished by a mechanical failure and a tragically simple mistake.

**Royal Aircraft Factory SE5a**

When the 150-hp Hispano-Suiza in-line engine first became
available in summer 1915, the Royal Aircraft Factory began
design studies for single-seat fighters based on the powerful
new French engine. H P Folland's neat tractor biplane
proposal was selected for development and the first prototype
SE5, A4561, made its first flight on 22 November 1916. The
third prototype, A4563, was fitted with a 200-hp geared
Hispano and this machine became the prototype for the SE5a.

Performance was substantially better than the SE5, and the
SE5a was standardized for production after some 59 SE5s had
been built. The aircraft had all the inherent stability associated
with Royal Aircraft Factory machines, and while some scout
pilots like Albert Ball attuned to rotary engined machines
tended to deride it, other pilots found its speed in a dive and
its stability as a gun platform made it an excellent fighting
aircraft.

The SE5a went to Nos 56, 40 and 60 Squadrons from June
1917 and by the end of the year they also equipped Nos 24, 41,
68 and 84 Squadrons. By January however airframes were
stockpiling and deliveries of complete aircraft halted because
of a lack of engines.

British licence-built engines were constantly proving
defective but relief came with Wolseley's own development of
the original Hispano, the 200-hp Viper, and French engines
began to arrive again taken over from an Admiralty contract.
In spite of these difficulties, the SE5a quickly gained a
reputation for strength and performance and shared with the
Sopwith Camel chief credit for re-establishing air superiority
over the British sectors of the Front in 1918.

McCudden first flew a borrowed 56 Squadron SE5 on
21 July 1917 and remarked 'although it felt rather strange I
liked the machine immensely, as it was very fast after the
Sopwith Scout (Pup), and one could see out of it so thoroughly
well.' By August he was a Flight Commander of No 56

Squadron equipped with the aircraft and he could further
remark of SE5 B519 his Vickers-built machine, 'it was a most
warm, comfortable and easy machine to fly'.

He was less happy with his Royal Aircraft Factory built
SE5a, A4763, which needed a lot of tinkering to get working
properly but it was in this machine that he and his Flight had
their epic fight with Werner Voss on 23 September 1917.

He had a succession of SE5s after that, expressing a
preference for contract built machines over Royal Aircraft
Factory products. He fitted a spinner from a shot-down LVG
to his SE5a, A4891, which he claimed added another 3 mph
and made more modifications to squeeze extra performance at
height out of his '200-hp SE'.

| | |
|---|---|
| Manufacturers: Royal Aircraft Factory and subcontractors | |
| Powerplant: Wolseley Viper W.4a V-8, 200-hp | |
| Span: 26 ft 7$\frac{3}{8}$ in (8.11 m) | |
| Length: 20 ft 11 in (6.38 m) | |
| Max. take-off weight: 1988 lb (902 kg) | |
| Max. speed: 120 mph (193.1 kmh) at 15,000 ft (4572 m) | |
| Ceiling: 19,500 ft (5944 m) | |
| Armament: 1 x Vickers .303-in, 1 x Lewis .303-in | |

# 1918

THE successful German counter attack at Cambrai at the end of November 1917 demonstrated powerful portents of new tactical thinking within the German Army. Spearheaded by low-flying ground-attack aircraft, infantry using infiltration tactics recaptured ground lost to a new Allied weapon—tanks. During that fourth winter of the war, as the German and Austrian Home Fronts creaked, Ludendorff realised the only chance for winning the war lay in a decisive victory in the west in spring 1918 before American manpower could have an effect. These new tactics, used on a vast scale, must at last break the deadlock and win the war.

Ludendorff planned a series of mighty hammer blows, the first to fall on the British, designed to sunder the BEF from the French and destroy the British Armies in subsequent assaults as they fell back upon the Channel ports. The French, it was planned, would then collapse. The instrument was to be an army strengthened by forty-two divisions transferred from the east. Highly motivated groups of storm troops would lead the assault, trained in new tactics of infiltration. A finely orchestrated gas and artillery barrage would blast open their path and an umbrella of ground attack aircraft would keep it open.

In the first months of the new year, the *Luftstreitkrafte* intensively prepared for the part it would have to play in the coming great offensive. The provisions of the *Amerikaprogramm* stepping up fighter production and pilot training had increased the number of *Jagdstaffeln* to eighty-one by mid-February 1918 and two more *Jagdgeschwadern* (fighter wings—command groupings of four *Jastas*) were formed at the beginning of the month. The *Schusta* were renamed *Schlachtstaffeln* and a number of these units were grouped into larger formations (*Schlachtgruppen* and later *Schlachtgeschwadern*) following successful fighter practice. In addition 153 *Flieger Abteilungen* were included in the German order of battle on the eve of the offensive.

In Britain meanwhile on 2 January 1918 the Air Ministry was formed as a step towards the creation of the Royal Air Force with the newly-knighted Sir Hugh Trenchard as Chief of Air Staff. Major General J M Salmond took over as commander of the RFC in the field, and he continued to implement the Trenchard doctrine of the strategic air offensive. On 1 April 1918 the Royal Air Force formally came into existence (see appendix 2, page 142).

In the first winter weeks of the year while the air officers of the German Seventeenth, Second and Eighteenth Armies were conducting war games with infantry attacking enjoying full air support, RFC reconnaissance brought back a confusing pattern of the enemy's intentions. A usual precursor of an offensive was the construction of new airfields and a slackening of aerial activity on other sectors as a concentration was effected, but the Germans threw a carefully crafted cloak of deception over their aerial preparations. German photographic reconnaissance was done in machines familiar to the sector. Aircraft were moved at night and stored dismantled in farm buildings or hangars created in forest clearings. At zero hour minus two days the aircraft were assembled and test flown. With twenty-four hours to go they were brought to combat readiness on advance airfields and bad weather kept the secret.

The offensive opened with a paralyzing artillery bombardment before first light on 21 March. Behind it came the storm troops crashing into the British Third and Fifth Armies on a 60 mile front. Incorporated into the three attacking Armies were 49 *Flieger Abteilungen*, 27 *Schlastas*, 35 *Jastas*, and four *Bombengeschwadern*. The *Jastas* were equipped mainly with Albatros DV and DVas, the Fokker DrI, Pfalz DIII and a few Roland DIIIs. The *Schlastas* were equipped with the *Hannoveraner* CL II and the Halberstadt CL II.

Fog dashed the carefully laid plans for aircraft to assist the morning attack but by midday the first aircraft were taking off on both sides. The CL types came in low in ragged waves, attacking the British trenches, spraying the lines with machine-gun fire and dumping bundles of hand grenades. The *Infantrieflieger* machines, by pin-pointing the special white cloths laid out by the furthermost stormtroops, kept contact with the spearheads of the advance—eddying forward like the rivulets of an ink blot into the crumpling front of General Hubert Gough's Fifth Army. High above *Jagdgeschwarder I* flew top cover. On the second day the RFC managed to engage the fighters and on the third day they got through to the ground attack machines and engaged themselves in desperate ground attacks, leaving the fighters largely alone. Already the RFC's own airfields were coming under direct shellfire and Fifth Army's squadrons were ordered to retreat, taking off, flying their missions, and landing at airfields further back.

The weather showed a marked improvement on the 23rd and during the next five days the air fighting was intense and continuous. The British Fifth Army's front was sundered exposing Third Army's right and forcing a general retreat. Throughout the 24th, Third Army's aircraft desperately hurled themselves against the main Germany artery —the Bapaume-Péronne road. The crisis of the battle came on the morning of 25 March when Third Army's front began to crumble between Montauban and Urvilliers. Major-General Salmond got a call through to Trenchard at the Air Ministry in London and, after a brief discussion, Salmond ordered the three fighter squadrons of 9th Wing to attack with the words . . . 'These squadrons are to bomb and shoot up everything they see. Very low flying is essential. All risks to be taken. Urgent.'

By dawn on the 26th, 37 of the 60 RFC squadrons on the Western Front were flying ground attack or support missions for Third Army but more German blows were coming. British losses were very heavy and many aircraft were lost in crack ups on landing,

a sure sign of their pilot's fatigue. On the 27th *JG 1* patrolling over Albert shot down 13 British aircraft without loss to themselves.

By now however the pace of the German advance was slackening. The infantry had outrun its artillery and logistic support and even German airfields were becoming dangerously far back and commanders out of touch. As the offensive bludgeoned on to-wards Arras, aircraft were disengaged and switched north for another blow codenamed *Georgette* to fall on the British on the Lys. It began on 9 April on a narrower front and again German assault troops streamed through a gap torn in the line sweeping aside a Portuguese division. Fog restricted fighting in the air to some degree although the patterns of the Somme—desperate ground attack flying and huge wheeling dog-fights were repeated when the weather cleared.

The Germans had first established the concen-tration of fighter power called the *Jagdgeschwader* in July 1917. By March 1918 two more had been formed, able to be switched from sector to sector of front to achieve overwhelming local superiority. With the flamboyant colour schemes of their air-craft and frequent wanderings, the Allied pilots dubbed them 'Flying Circuses'. The greatest circus ringmaster, von Richthofen, fell over the Somme on 21 April.

*JG 3* with fourteen *Jagdstaffeln* under the com-mand of Bruno Lörzer covered the assault on Kemmel Hill on the Lys front on 25 April, the attack itself preceded by waves of battle aircraft from 16 *Schlachtstaffeln*. The fighters of *JG 3* retained complete air superiority over the Kemmel battle-field sustaining only one Fourth Army aircraft lost during the day.

By mid-May the attacks on the British fronts had been held but at great cost. Now the *Jagdge-schwadern* were switched south to Seventh Army's front, its troops poised to fall on the French on the Aisne. There *JG 1* (redesignated on 20 May *Jagdgeschwader Fhrh v Richthofen Nr 1*) commanded by Hauptmann Wilhelm Reinhard was joined by Lörzer's *JG 3*, five more *Jastas* and 3 *Gruppen* of battle aircraft.

On 27 May this combined strength fell on the front of Sixth Army on the Chemin des Dames. The *Schlachtstaffeln* flew in Group strength attacking the twelve retreating British and French divisions as they streamed back. By the 30th the Germans had reached the Marne.

Two more German blows were to fall on 9 June between Noyon and Montdidier and a month later again in Champagne when on 15 July fourteen German divisions crossed the Marne but it was the German's last offensive.

A scene in a German back area during the advance of March 1918. A wingless Halberstadt CL ground-attack type is taken forward by a truck which is also towing the fuselage of a captured French Salmson 2A.2 reconnaissance air-craft. By the last year of the war a wide range of fighting aircraft had been evolved by both sides to fill a great variety of tactical battlefield roles

*Skat* was the great game of the German and Austrian armies, played in the trenches from Bapaume to Lemberg. This pack, totalling 36 cards, was manufactured in Germany in 1917 and sold in aid of pilot's charities and shows scenes of the war in the air and its new heroes or background personalities.

*This page,* from top, left to right: Anti-aircraft gun mounted on a truck; Zeppelin crossing the English coast; Marine Naval Observer's breast badge; *Fregattenkäpitan* Strasser, naval airship commander; Aerial photo-reconnaissance; The *Pour le Mérite*; Prince Albrecht; *Direktor* Fokker, 'inventor of the first single-seat fighting aircraft'; Rear-defence machine-gun; Manfred von Richthofen; *Graf* Zeppelin; Albatros fighter; AEG bomber sets off for London; Army pilot's breast badge; Prince Leopold of Bavaria; Crownprince Wilhelm.

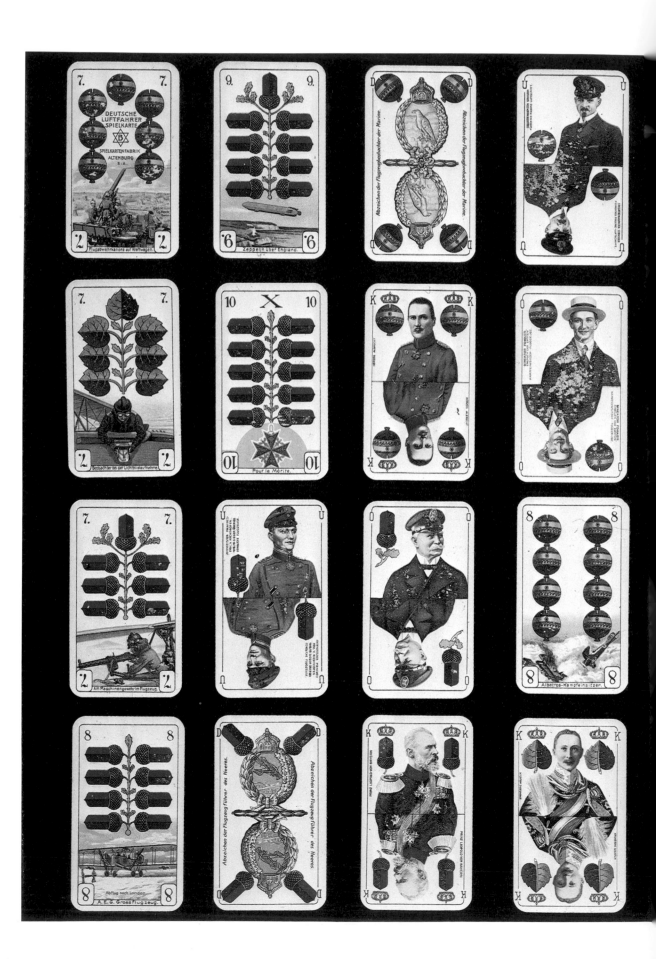

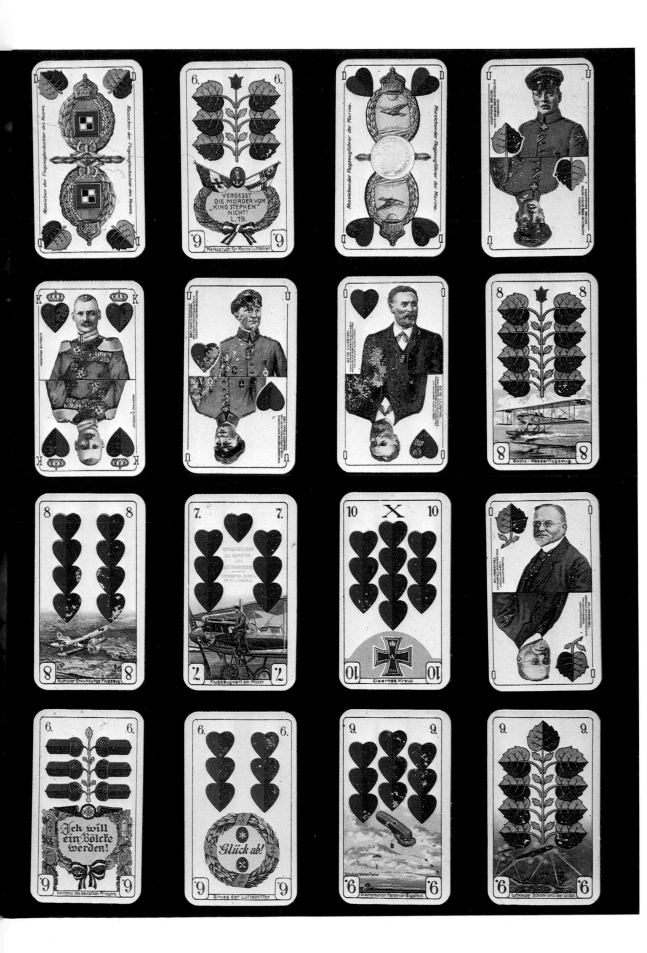

*This page,* from top, left to right: Army observer's breast badge; Naval airship crew's motto: 'Don't forget the murder of *L19* by the *King Stephen*' (recalling an incident in 1916 when a British steamer allowed a ditched airship crew to drown in the North Sea); Naval pilot's breast badge; Hauptmann Boelcke; Crownprince Rupprecht of Bavaria; *Oblt Frhr* von Pechmann, the first observer to win the *Pour le Mérite*; Otto Lilienthal, the German glider pioneer killed in 1896; Gotha seaplane; Rumpler reconnaissance aircraft; Engine maintenance; the Prussian *Eisernes Kreuz*; Dr Parseval, inventor of the *Drachen* observation balloon and airship pioneer; Motto of German pilots 'I will be like Boelcke'; Greeting of airship crews; *Drachen* balloon with a Paulus parachute for the observer; Schutte-Lanz airship over London

At various stages in the war the Germans sent squadrons, pilots and technical advisers to bolster the air efforts of their Turkish allies. Here German pilots show a range of bombs and fuses to Turkish staff officers at a demonstration in Syria in 1918. The officer fourth from right wears the Turkish pilot's badge below his Iron Cross

A French Salmson 2A.2 reconnaissance two-seater flies over the shell-pocked 1918 battlefields of the Aisne

By July there were 25 American divisions in France, seven of them at the front, and 300,000 troops arriving every month. Resisting French and British attempts to incorporate US troops into their own commands, Pershing strove to keep his troops, his equipment and his air power as an intact American Expeditionary Force. Following the American declaration of war, an enormous expansion programme was instigated with largely French technical advice. It called for the production of 22,625 aeroplanes, plus 80 per cent spares and 44,000 engines. In fact in spite of American mass-production techniques and massive Congressional funding very little of US manufacture reached the front line before the end of the war. Some DH4s and Liberty aero-engines arrived in numbers but the front-line USAAS itself was equipped almost exclusively with British and French aircraft.

Primary training fields were established across America with advance training being completed in France and Italy. The largest of these Aviation Instruction Centres was established at Issoudun in France with no less than eleven satellite fields and a main base with complete repair and testing facilities.

In February 1918 the build up of concentrated American air strength began in the relatively quiet Toul sector in the Vosges with the arrival of the 94th Pursuit Squadron followed in March by the 95th. By June this force constituted an Observation Group and a Pursuit Group, and moved to Château Thiêrry as the 1st Brigade commanded by Colonel William Mitchell. Here the eager Americans met German aircraft in numbers flown by highly experienced pilots for the first time and were taught a painful lesson.

In August 1918 General Mason M Patrick commanding the Air Service organized this relentlessly building American air strength into a First Army Air Force of some 600 aircraft, including French, British, Italian and Portuguese units to cover an offensive designed to pinch out the St Mihiel salient. In the air and on the ground the operation was a complete success, repeated in the American Meuse-Argonne offensive of September-

November. By the Armistice there were forty-five American combat squadrons at the front operating 740 aircraft. The total strength stretching from Texan flying training fields to the front line was 14,000 aircraft and still rising with American industry and training structures in high gear to continue their expansion from almost nothing.

Ludendorff's five offensives had spent the power of the German Army and failed to break the Allied line. Still the officers of *Kogenluft* were preparing expansion plans endorsed by Ludendorff aimed at sustaining German airpower into 1919 by promoting advanced technical development in the face of overwhelming Allied numbers. By August 1918 however shortages of raw materials and trained aircrew were becoming critical. There were choking shortages of rubber and castor oil lubricant for rotary engines. *Jasta* and *Schlachtstaffeln* were allowed 150 litres of fuel per aircraft per day from mid-August and one seventh of front line pilot strength had to be replaced monthly, a total of over 360 pilots.

On 8 August the French and British counter-attack at Amiens covered by a huge concentration of air strength spun the German armies round in retreat. Now the Germans were on the defensive, the *Schlastas* hurling themselves at the advancing infantry and tanks and lashing the British supply columns. The *Jagdgeschwadern* and *Jagdgruppen* offered a spirited defence throughout August breaking up the large Allied formations that came over up to five squadrons strong. Up to 100 fighters could be involved in huge dog fights spanning miles of sky, but week by week British, French and American air power claimed the upper hand.

As the German Army tottered on the brink of defeat and its Allies progressively collapsed, German airmen could still give a bloody nose. From September 12-19 the aircraft of *JG 2* shot down 81 enemy aircraft for the loss of only two of its own. On 30 October, a day of intense air fighting, 67 German fighters were shot down for 41 British. Right up to the eve of the Armistice, German bombers attacked objectives behind Allied lines and the last generation of very high altitude reconnaissance aircraft were flying deep over the Allied rear areas.

The Armistice of 11 November 1918 ended the fighting on the Western Front. Fighting ended on the Italian Front on 3 November after the collapse of Austrian resistance at Vittorio Veneto.

The German Army turned round and slouched home. The Armistice demanded the immediate surrender of 2000 fighter and bomber aircraft and some were flown to specially allocated landing grounds. Others were burned on their airfields, had their engines run with empty sumps until they seized up and some were simply flown home.

The first war in the air did not end with a cataclysmic final battle but puttered out as the German air forces ran out of fuel, lubricants and pilots until they could no longer effectively defend the German armies in the field or its industries at home.

# Eduard *Ritter* von Schleich

THE kingdom of Bavaria retained more than nominal control over its armed forces. Even after the formation of *Kogenluft* in 1916, Bavaria kept its own aircraft inspectorate with a highly complex system of interlocking responsibility for tactical deployment, operational orders, supply and discipline with the Prussian command. Bavaria also had had a virtual state aircraft factory since 1913 in the Pfalz Flugzeug-werke. As far as possible Bavarian units would have Bavarian equipment, Bavarian officers, Bavarian pilots and would fight with Bavarian Armies in the field.

Eduard Schleich was a Bavarian who rose to command a Prussian fighter *Staffel* only to have it taken away due to this Bavarian particularity. He was born on 9 August 1888 and started his career in the air flying unarmed B-types in 1915, became the commander of Bavarian escort unit, *Schützstaffeln 28*, and then briefly a flying instructor at Schleissheim near Munich, the site of Bavaria's first air formation the *Fliegerkommando-München* of 1913. After two uneventful years, in early 1917 Schleich was ordered to the Valenciennes *Jastaschule* where he was taught the arts of single-seater fighting by Erwin Böhme in two weeks. Without a single victory to his name he was posted to command the Prussian *Jasta 21* in March, and, after an inauspicious start, Schleich flying an Albatros DV managed to bring down the French ace René Dorme on 25 May. Schleich's score climbed quickly. Flying a black-painted Albatros DVa Schleich scored seventeen of his command's total of forty-one in six months over the, at the time, relatively quiet Verdun sector.

*Above:* Two German aces who would survive the war, von Schleich (left) and Ernst Udet, meet at the Johannistal fighter competition in January 1918

**Hauptmann Eduard Ritter von Schleich, late summer 1918.**
Schleich was enobled by the Bavarian *Militär Max-Josefs Ordern* in May 1918. The Prussian *Pour le Mérite* was awarded on 2 December 1917.

Schleich favoured captured British flying clothing, often being photographed in the chrome-leather knee-length RFC coat. Here he is depicted wearing the latest in flying clothing, the Sidcot suit.

The Sidcot suit story began in May 1917 when the Director of Aircraft Equipment received proposals from the RFC's Quartermaster in the field for the provision of effective winter flying clothing. 'Every effort should be made to produce some form of clothing that should be very warm, as light as possible and allow free movement of the upper part of the pilot's body', he suggested.

Lt Sidney Cotton of the RNAS with the help of the firm of Robinson and Cleaver meanwhile proposed a one-piece suit that retained the double-breasted front of the 'maternity jacket' and the chest slant pocket of the leather coat. With a twill cover, a lining of mohair and an inter-lining of 'Racobine', a patent wind- and water-proof material, the experimental suit proved wind and cold proof at 20,000 feet, and after tests against four 'Racobal' asbestos fire-proof suits, the Sidcot Flying Suit No 5 (No 5 in these tests) was ordered into large scale production, the first suit being despatched to France on 26 October, 1917.

The Germans meanwhile were developing the technology of the parachute and by mid-1918 the Heinecke type was in large scale service. Schleich has one here. Udet was probably first to use one in action on 29 June 1918.
*Top:* The personal insignia of Schleich borne adjacent to the national markings

Taken ill with dysentery after his twenty-fifth victory the Bavarian was relieved of the command of his Prussian unit. A new command the Bavarian *Jasta 32* followed in August and Schleich marked his aircraft with the black and white of Prussia next to the rampant crowned Lion on a blue and white field of Bavaria.

On 2 December 1917 Schleich was awarded the *Pour le Mérite* and promptly fell ill again. By the eve of March 1918 offensive he had completely re-covered and was now in command as a *Hauptmann* of *Jagdgruppe Nr 8*, a grouping of three *Jastas, 16, 32* and *34* stationed first at Favreuil near Bapaume and later Epinoy. In June 1918 after a period of intense action against the Royal Air Force, came the award of the Bavarian *Militär Max Josef Ordern*, making him in effect a Bavarian Knight.

After a brief period based in the Saar to defend southern Germany from French bombing attacks, Schleich's command was upgraded to *Jagdge-schwader* on 14 October 1918, *Nr 4* containing the Bavarian *Jastas 23b, 32b, 34b* and *35b* being the last to be formed of the war. *JG 4* moved back to the front at Fleueres near Charleroi.

Meanwhile in October Schleich attended the third and last of the D-type competitions held at Adlershof near Berlin. Since the first *Flugzeug Wettbewerb* or aircraft trial in January, the élite of Germany's air force had gathered at Adlershof to fly and evaluate new fighter designs. Now here with

Schleich were gathered Udet, Lörzer, Baumer and Lothar von Richthofen amongst other famous names come to test the last generation of Germany's wartime aircraft. The competition was restricted nominally to aircraft powered by the BMW IIIa liquid-cooled in-line engine but Schleich flew and reported favourably on the parasol monoplane Oberursel rotary-powered Kondor EIII.

Schleich returned to Fleures waiting for the EIII to follow him from Germany for a front line test. It never arrived. While the discipline of the air units still held, the German army was buckling in defeat and the will to wage war was evaporating at home.

*Jagdgeschwader 4* fought its last action on 8 November, three days before the Armistice. On the 11th the unserviceable aircraft were burnt and the Bavarians flew their Fokker DVIIs to Germany.

Bavaria was the centre of political ferment, first the Munich Soviet of 1919 and then Hitler's 'Beer Hall putsch' of 1923. The embittered Schleich became a very early member of the *NSDAP* and then of the *Allgemeine-SS*. He was an important figure in Lufthansa and the NSFK, the National Socialist Flying Corps, and when Germany's reborn air force came out into the open he joined the *Luftwaffe* in 1938, first leading a divebomber unit, then commanding *JG 131 Schlageter*. He became a *General der Flieger* in 1941 commanding the Luftwaffe in Denmark. He died in November 1947.

Eduard *Ritter* von Schleich (second right), wearing the *Pour le Mérite*, nicknamed the 'Blue Max' after Max Immelmann, at his neck, seen with members of his unit, with an Albatros scout in the background

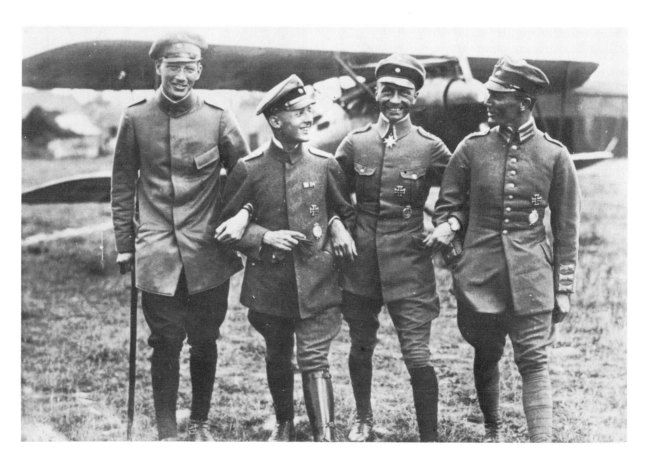

# Friedrich Christiansen

WHEN the trench lines snaking through France and Flanders reached the sea in the dunes of Nieuport beach, the combat zone did not stop there. The North Sea was the enormous flank to a front line which could not be turned by repeated frontal assaults. The North Sea was the exit route for U-boats and the entrance for blockade runners. It was the disputed battlefield of the Grand and High Seas Fleets in 1916 and the transit route for marauding Zeppelins. For five years its stormy waters were sewn with mines, blasted by depth charges, and churned by 16-in. shells. Throughout the war command of the North Sea was of supreme strategic importance and more and more that meant command of the skies above it.

The war fought by the Royal Naval Air Service's North Sea and Flanders Air Stations and their German counterparts at Zeebrugge, Ostend and at stations strung along the Frisian Islands was as bitter and determined as anything on land (although there was still room for occasional chivalry), and throughout the war specialist aircraft were evolved on both sides to meet this battle's needs.

When the German Armies overran Belgium, it was the possession of the Flanders coastline and its potential for launching U-Boat operations which most alarmed the British High Command. Indeed before the first year of the war was over, U-Boats were being assembled at Bruges and seaplane stations were being established at Zeebrugge and Ostend; both exits for canals from the inland port of Bruges itself 300 miles nearer to Dover than any of the German ports. If you account for the repeated and bloody Flanders offensives launched by the British to win back possession of the coastline, the toll of lives taken by the fact of its possession by the German Navy was enormous.

The Zeebrugge naval air station was always in the front line. It was at the end of the Bruges ship canal used by at least two U-Boats a day and only some thirty miles from the big RNAS base at Dunkirk. Ostend was even nearer. A seaplane unit was established on the Zeebrugge Mole (breakwater) soon after the German occupation and it was to become one of the most famous naval flying stations of the war, repeatedly bombed and bombarded, and finally on St George's Day 1918, the scene of a large-scale British assault landing. Zeebrugge's most famous pilot, *Oblt d R* Friedrich Christiansen, who rarely flew a single-seater in action yet shot down 21 enemy aircraft, had his extraordinary career largely because Zeebrugge was so much in the front line.

He was born on 12 December 1879 at the little town of Wyk on the island of Föhr, off the coast of North Friesland. The island tradition was the sea, and Christiansen's family was no exception—and the sailor's son went to sea. However at the age of thirty-five Friedrich decided to learn to fly and quickly got his pilot's certificate.

Beach huts and children bathing on a Flanders beach contrast oddly with barbed wire, sailors of the *Marinekorps Flandern* and a Hansa-Brandenburg WL29 from Zeebrugge air station making a low pass along the shore

**Oberleutnant Friedrich Christiansen.** Called the 'Fighter of Zeebrugge', Christiansen's *Pour le Mérite* was awarded on 12 December 1917

By 1915 he was at Zeebrugge where naval flying at the time was very much a question of unarmed reconnaissance and avoiding combat wherever possible, especially with landplane types. Seaplanes formed the bulk of equipment of the *Flieger der Hochseestreitkrafte*, and the German Navy had a strong preference for floatplane types. Nevertheless Christiansen did fly a Hansa-Brandenburg FB three-seat flying boat Nr 512 successfully in 1916 carrying his personal marking *Klar Klimming*, or 'clear gunsight' on the nose.

The chance for more aggressive action came in early 1917 with the arrival of the first of the single-seat seaplane fighting scouts (*Jagdeinsitzer Wasser*) to combat the aggressive RNAS. The Albatros W 4 had arrived in September 1916 and the Brandenburg KDW (*Kampf Doppeldecker Wasser*) soon afterwards but both were adaptations of existing landplane types. Much more effective aircraft were coming however from Ernst Heinkel at Hansa-Brandenburg who had been briefed to design a two-seat floatplane for station defence.

On 15 September 1917 Christiansen took command of Zeebrugge Naval Air Station. With the expansion and reorganization of German naval flying, Zeebrugge was now primarily a fighter station and by the beginning of 1918 equipment included Rumpler 6B1, Albatros, W4, Friedrichshafen FF33 and Brandenburg W12, W19, W29 and W33 fighter-reconnaissance types. Zeebrugge and Ostend seaplane stations at that time came under the overall command of the *Kommandeur der Flieger beim Marinekorps Flandern* and the *Gruppenkommandeur der Seeflieger* while the remaining three groups of Marine aviation in Flanders were the coastal reconnaissance group and support group for the Marine Corps holding the coastal trench line and the *Marine Jagdflieger* or landplane naval fighters.

The new equipment represented a big step forward in the station's offensive capacity and especially the new Heinkel-designed Brandenburgs. The arrival of the W 12 at the end of 1917 gave the Zeebrugge pilots a chance to hit back at the large well defended RNAS flying-boats such as the Felixstowe F2A. Christiansen soon proved himself a highly capable exponent of the type. On 17 December 1917 flying a Brandenburg W12 he shot down the British Coastal Class airship C27 which crashed in flames over the East Anglian coast. Later he forced down an F2A with a broken fuel pipe. The pilot taxied it to Dutch waters, beached the large aircraft and set it on fire.

With some operational advice from Christiansen, Ernst Heinkel began design work at the end of 1917 on a new floatplane reconnaissance fighter to keep the technical edge over new British types and tactics being encountered over the North Sea. The result was the W29, virtually a monoplane version of the W12, yet still an advanced and potent design. Christiansen tested the prototype on the Havel at Brandenburg and was so delighted he flew it to Zeebrugge the next day. The W29 was short on range but was an excellent fighting machine and the Zeebrugge aircraft were used for duties ranging from intercepting and capturing merchantmen to interdiction patrols against British reconnaissance aircraft. When the sea was not too rough, the W29s could alight upon the water while aircraft with longer range (W19s for example) scouted ahead and then could return for or call up by wireless the W29s if an action developed.

On the night of 22 April 1918, Royal Navy and Royal Marine assault troops made a large scale attack on Ostend and Zeebrugge with five old cruisers full of concrete and an elderly submarine stuffed with Amatol in an heroic attempt to block the canals from which the Bruges U-Boats emerged into the North Sea. The seaplane station was on the Mole itself, and after three years of attack was now protected by a bomb-proof roof of reinforced concrete. A railway ran out along the Mole and the aircraft themselves were hangared standing on railway flat-cars with a locomotive kept constantly in steam. When the whistle blew, the aircraft were calmly shunted on to the mainland and not one of the 55 machines was lost in the assault on the Mole.

Christiansen's revenge was swift. Two days later on 23 April he led a flight of seven W29s when they encountered and attacked two F2a flying-boats from Felixstowe. A German pilot related. . . .

'*Oberleutnant* Christiansen shot down a Curtiss flying-boat in 133a [a patrol grid square] after a long combat. After fire had been opened on the flying-boat from aft by the fixed machine-gun, and the machine-gunner in the stern of the flying boat killed, Christiansen flew parallel with the boat and

**Hansa-Brandenburg W29**

Whatever part Christiansen may have played in urging the development of the W29 on Ernst Heinkel at Brandenburg, it arrived in April 1918, just in time to keep the German Air Stations' edge against stiffening competition in the North Sea. The biplane W12 and W19s were tough and well armed opponents but slow and clumsy in a fight with landplane fighters. To save time, Heinkel's solution was virtually a monoplane version of the successful W12 of which Christiansen was already a capable exponent.

Floats and fuselage were largely the same with a new monoplane wing increased in span and chord almost to the same area of the W12's two wings. The inverted tail assembly carried on the upswept rear fuselage was repeated with detail modification affording the gunner an unobstructed field of fire with no blind spot dead astern. The power plant was the Benz Bz III of 150-hp and later versions were built with 175-hp Benz IIIas. Armament varied, twin forward-firing Spandaus and a flexible Parabellum or single forward Spandau when carrying radio equipment. As such the W29 could be regarded as a two-seat fighter being fast (faster in fact than a Fokker Triplane), manoeuvrable and well armed.

They were used extensively to escort reconnaissance machines and to escort U-boats through the Allied minefields, or cover surface mine-sweeping patrols. They attacked and even captured enemy merchantmen on the surface and attacked sometimes successfully, light enemy naval craft. Their doughtiest opponents were the big well-defended F2a flying boats from RNAS bases in East Anglia with which Christiansen himself fought several dramatic actions from the cockpit of a W29.

The weakness on choppy sea caused them to be accompanied by larger stronger types in bad weather which handicapped the formation's speed but the biplanes could alight and rescue the crew of a W29 if it were shot down. When the sea was not too rough, the W29s could alight upon the water while aircraft with longer range (W19s for example) scouted ahead and then could call up the W29s by radio if an action developed. In spite of being a compromise design rushed through to meet an urgent need, Heinkel's W29 strongly influenced several subsequent designs from other manufacturers. A larger version, the W33 with a 245-hp Maybach engine was just reaching the North Sea stations at the time of the Armistice and a later and still larger version the W34 was used by the Finnish and Latvian Air Forces after the war. (Data for W29.)

| | |
|---|---|
| Manufacturer: Hansa und Brandenburgische Flugzeug-Werke GmbH | |
| Powerplant: Benz BzIII 6-cyl in-line, 150-hp | |
| Span: 13.5 m (44 ft 3½ in) | |
| Length: 9.36 m (30 ft 8½ in) | |
| Max take-off weight: 1,494 kg (3,286 lb) | |
| Max speed: 175 kmh (109.3 mph) | |
| Ceiling: 5000 m (16,400 ft) | |
| Armament: 2/1 x Spandau, 1 x Parabellum 7.92-mm | |

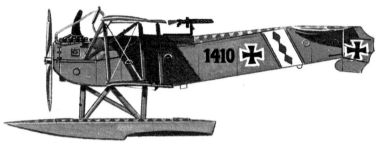

*Above:* the Hansa-Brandenburg W12 entered service in April 1917 and proved an effective station-defence fighter. It provided the basis for the monoplane W29

A contemporary drawing of a German Friedrichshafen seaplane crew. Note the naval breast badge and the sleeve badge of a *Flug-Obermaat*

*Above:* The British submarine C-25 under attack by Christiansen's Brandenburg W29. The disabled submarine was accredited to his victory total.
*Below:* Officer and NCO pilots relax at a German North Sea air station in 1917. The aircraft is a Rumpler 6B1 single-seater employed for station defence

his observer opened fire with his machine-gun at the oil tank at the rear of the port engine, setting the tank alight. The pilot of the flying boat then tried to alight, but as his machine was only ten feet from the water, he could not turn her into the wind, so that she crashed on alighting and burst into flames.' So perished F2a N8677 and its US Navy crew, Captain Magor and Ensign Potter.

On 6 July, Christiansen attacked the British submarine C-25 off Harwich, just as she was diving. Machine-gun bullets pierced the pressure-hull and the Commander Lt Bell RN was killed along with five crew. The helpless submarine was towed into harbour and Christiansen counted C-25 in his victory score. When the first red flags were raised on German warships at Kiel on 28 October 1918, it signalled the end of the naval war in the North Sea. Christiansen, like so many other embittered ex-pilots, drifted into the grip of Nazism after taking various positions including being Captain of a Hamburg-America line steamer. He became chief of the *National Sozialistische Flieger Korps*, a gliding and sport flying organization which was in fact a shadow for the new *Luftwaffe*. On the outbreak of war he was a high-ranking officer of Germany's new air force. During the war he was military governor of the Netherlands under the notorious regime of *Reichskommissar* Artur Seyss-Inquart. Christiansen was imprisoned for war crimes, later released and he retired in West Germany.

# Theodore Osterkamp

THEODORE Osterkamp was rejected for service with the Prussian army on the grounds of ill-health on the outbreak of war when he was twenty-two. He went on to become the German Navy's greatest fighter ace and amazingly an ace of World War II as well before being ordered off combat flying at the age of 48. His early career was intimately linked to that of Gotthard Sachsenberg, one year his elder and the man who was to become his teacher, later his commander—and who formed the German Navy's first true fighter unit which fought on the Western Front as determinedly as did the squadrons of the Royal Naval Air Service.

Sachsenberg was born on 6 December 1891 at Rosslau, a suburb of Dessau on the north bank of the Elbe. A class-mate at the Dessau *Gymnasium* was one Oswald Boelcke. Osterkamp was born in Aschersleben in Prussian Saxony on 15 April 1892 and like Sachsenberg joined the Voluntary Naval Flying Service, the *Freiwilliges Marine Flieger Corps* soon after the outbreak of war and was taught the rudiments of flying on the famous field of Johannistal at Berlin. Osterkamp was posted to *2 Marine Fliegerabteilung*, then using unarmed Albatros BIs for coastal reconnaissance. Osterkamp felt highly uncomfortable in the observer's cockpit of a slow unarmed aircraft especially with French armed opposition around, but relief came when the unit was re-equipped with Albatros CIs with the comparative security of a flexible Parabellum machine gun for the observer.

In June 1916 Osterkamp was promoted *Leutnant* and received the Iron Cross First Class for his excellent reconnaissance work. Sachsenberg followed the same route, the volunteer naval fliers, service as an observer, then pilot training and service with *2 Marine Fl Abt.* In May 1917 Sachsenberg had formed the first true naval fighter unit the *Marine-Feld-Jagdstaffel* and by the end of the year this had grown to a full naval fighter wing, the *Marine Feld Geschwader* with four *Jagdstaffeln* and a fifth cadre *Jasta* under its command.

Meanwhile on 21 March 1917, Osterkamp made his first solo flight learning the art of a fighter pilot on elderly Fokker EIVs retired from the front to the Navy Flying School at Putzig on the Baltic. By the end of the month he had his pilot's certificate and in mid-April was posted to Sachsenberg's unit at Aertryke on the Flanders coast. Osterkamp crashed an Albatros CI on one of his first landings and his commander was furious. He was grounded but Theo took off again in a new aircraft against orders and promptly shot down an SE5 near Dixmude. That first victory precluded any further disciplinary measures and the commander and his new pilot were about to start a famous partnership.

Osterkamp and Sachsenberg went on to score almost alternately. The unit moved to Steenbrugge near Bruges but the rate of scoring did not slacken. In an action with the great Guynemer, Osterkamp took some bullets in his aircraft and was driven down. Within an hour however he was up in a new mount and added another victory to his steadily growing score.

With the formation of the *Marine-Feld-Geschwader* Osterkamp was given command of its second *Jasta*. By April of 1918 Sachsenberg was in command of the whole formation and in August he received the *Pour le Mérite*. Proudly wearing his Blue Max he went home on leave and Osterkamp took over temporary command of the *Geschwader*. It was anything but black August for the naval pilots and on the 12th with Osterkamp leading a formation of Fokker DVIIs the *Geschwader* shot down nineteen British aircraft without loss. In mid-1918 the *Marine Jagdgeschwader* was one of the first formations to be equipped with the latest Fokker product, the elegant parasol monoplane first designated EV. This potent fighter had little time remaining to show off its qualities (like the DrI it was briefly withdrawn for structural strengthening) but Osterkamp scored his 25th and 26th victories on this machine when he jumped two Camels of an American squadron who promptly collided. A few days later Osterkamp himself was shot down by three French Spads but he managed to come down uninjured in his own lines. By this stage of the war the *Jagdstaffeln* were desperately fighting on the defensive and Osterkamp was back in action within hours. Taking off that same evening Osterkamp shot down a French Breguet bomber and machine-gunned and destroyed a British tank for good measure. He had thirty-two victories and Sachsenberg had thirty-one. Osterkamp received the *Pour le Mérite* just before being

The Fokker D VIII was the winner of the April 1918 fighter competition. The old designation of *Eindecker* was at first revived for the cantilever monoplane but after a series of disastrous crashes in squadron service, the 'Fokker E V' became the 'D VIII' the eighth service fighter from Fokker, in an attempt to allay lingering suspicions of monoplanes' weakness.

Some 85 of these fast and potent fighters reached the front in the last months of the war. *Jagdstaffeln 4, 6, 10* and *11* of the *Richthofen Geschwader* flew the type, as did *Jagdstaffeln 23* and *35* and the *Marine-Jagdgeschwader* although no units became completely equipped with the type.

Flying E V 156/18, Theo Osterkamp scored his twenty-fifth and twenty-sixth victories

**Oberleutnant zur See
Theodore Osterkamp,
1918.**
Like the RNAS and the
Royal Naval Division who
went into khaki, the men of
the *Marinekorps Flandern*
went into field-grey early in
the war. The flying units did
the same—Osterkamp
wears a version of the Army's
M.1915 tunic and a field-
grey crown to the naval cap,
which retained its black
band. The naval aviator's
badge is illustrated on
page 119

hospitalized with influenza. He got back to his unit
on 9 November—it was just two days before the
Armistice put an end to all he had fought so long to
defend.

The naval fliers were particularly embittered.
Since Jutland it seemed the sailors of all but the
U-Boat arm had ridden out the war at anchor in
Kiel harbour and it was here that the naval mutiny
had signalled the end of the German armed forces'
ability to continue fighting. For these naval fliers,
veterans at twenty-six who knew no other trade than
flying and fighting, defeat was particularly ignomin-
ious. Both Sachsenberg and Osterkamp went East
to join the swirling inchoate war in the Baltic being
fought by virtual private armies against the Bolsheviks. They both continued fighting throughout 1919,
flying such types as the Junkers DI and Junkers CLI,
ironically fighting the same enemy as Britain's
greatest naval ace Raymond Collishaw. At last the
German Republic managed to assert its slender
authority and the legions in the Baltic were called
home. *Kampfgeschwader Sachsenberg* was disbanded at
Riga in October 1919. It was too much for Osterkamp. The years of hard fighting and this second
ignominy led to a mental breakdown and he was
hospitalized for some time.

Sachsenberg was happier. He joined Junkers
now established as a manufacturer of civil aircraft
in his home town of Dessau and embarked upon
ambitious plans for a 'European Air Union'—flying
Junkers aircraft. He became a *Reichstag* deputy and
in the fateful year 1933 became head of his own aircraft concern. In World War II he had an administrative job in the Navy.

The extraordinary Theo Osterkamp however
was to have a third fighting career in the air. When
the *Luftwaffe* came into the open in 1935 he was
already forty-three years old but donned the new
blue-grey uniform as commander of the *Jagdgeschwader Horst Wessel*. He then went to Werneuchen
east of Berlin as head of the new fighter school but
by the time of the Battle of France he had a combat
command—*Jagdgeschwader 51*. 'Onkel Theo' as a
new generation of fighter pilots called him, went
into action all over again. At the height of the Battle
of Britain he was ordered off combat flying (he
scored six victories) and handed over command of
JG51 to Werner Mölders, one of the oldest *Kommo-
dore*s in the *Luftwaffe* handing over to the youngest,
and 'Onkel Theo' became *Jafü 2*, commander of all
the fighter aircraft in *Luftflotte 2*, with several of the
greatest aces of German's second war in the air under
his command. *Generalmajor* Osterkamp filed realis-
tically pessimistic reports from the Channel Front.
For this he was severely rebuked by Erhard Milch,
second most powerful man in the *Luftwaffe* after
Göring himself. Nevertheless he was promoted
*Generalleutnant* and went on to be Fighter Commander in Italy. He was awarded the *Ritterkreuz*,
the highest award for valour in Hitler's war worn at
the neck with the *Pour le Mèrite*, the highest award
for valour in the Kaiser's.

# Elliott White Springs

THE enormous expansion of the American Air Force after the declaration of war was a masterpiece of improvised organization which extended from brilliant production engineering in the factories to the production of the most important raw material of all—trained pilots. For advanced training pilots had to go to Europe, either France, Italy or Great Britain. One such young man was Elliott White Springs who not only trained in Britain but flew wearing American uniform with No 85 Squadron of the RAF commanded by Billy Bishop.

He was born in South Carolina in 1896 and educated at a fashionable military academy followed by Princeton. Shortly after America came into the war Springs left university before graduating to enlist at the newly established Princeton aviation ground school. By September he was in England along with 209 other American cadets for the completion of their flying training. It did not come easily. For six months Springs attended flying schools at Stamford, Hounslow, Thetford, London, Colney and Ayr. After three years of war the hardened British instructors looked on these keen young men with a kind of awe. They were superbly fit and desperately eager to get to the front—but first they had to learn the harsh lessons of combat.

Springs came to the attention of Major W A Bishop commanding the school of aerial gunnery at Turnberry, and on the Canadian's appointment to command No 85 Squadron Springs went with it to France on 22 May 1918 to its new base behind Dunkirk. The months of training paid off and on 25 June flying an SE5a he scored his first victory. Before the end of the month he had three more but on the 27th he was shot down himself. After a week in hospital he was transferred to the 148th Aero Squadron. Flying Sopwith Camels and under the nominal control of the 65th Wing RAF, Springs had by no means yet broken his British connections. On 3 August he won his fifth victory to become an ace and ended the war as squadron commander with a score of twelve and the British DFC and DSC.

Springs was a rich young man, a squadron commander and an ace of two air forces. He was only twenty-two years old.

**Captain Elliot White Springs, 1918.**
Springs flew with the RAF in 1918, transferring to the US 148th Aero Squadron in July. He wears the standard US 1902 officers' tunic, bronze aviation badges and Military Aviator wings. He retains his RFC cap.
*Below left, top to bottom:*
The first US badge for military aviators, an eagle holding in its beak the crossed flags of the Signal Corps, instituted on 27 May 1913.
US military aviators Qualification 'wings' instituted on 15 August 1917.
The Qualification wings pattern instituted in October 1917; the earlier pattern was given to Junior and Reserve Military Aviators

# Douglas Campbell

**Lieutenant Douglas Campbell, March 1918.**
The first badge of a US Military Aviator was instituted in May 1914 showing an eagle clutching the crossed flags of the US Signal Corps. The pilots who came to France in 1917-18 continued to wear the uniform and collar badges of the Signal Corps. In April 1918 an official collar badge was introduced, the flags and torch of the signal corps with a winged hemisphere superimposed on its centre; then in July the definitive winged propeller badge was introduced.

Qualification wings were introduced in August 1917. Qualified aviators wore the winged US shield, with only one wing for Junior and reserve aviators, although this was soon changed to a two-winged shield with star above and a two-winged shield without star for the two grades of pilot.
*Below far right:* Lt Alan Winslow, a fellow member of the 94th Aero Squadron, who accompanied Campbell on his first victory mission, flying Nieuport Nie 28s

DOUGLAS Campbell was the first pilot trained in America to score a victory. He was also the first American pilot trained in the United States to become an ace, shooting down his fifth enemy aircraft to qualify on 31 May 1918. American aces did not have long to prove their mettle but their arrival at the front coincided with the last great German offensive effort to win the war, an effort matched in the air, and the build-up of American airpower itself was astonishingly rapid. Campbell saw it from the beginning—he flew with Lufbery and Rickenbacker on the first US offensive patrol on 19 March and fought hard for three months until he was severely wounded on 6 June having shot down six enemy aircraft.

His father was head of the famous Mount Wilson Observatory in California, and Douglas was born in San Francisco on 7 June 1896. He was at Harvard when America entered the war but left college to enlist. In 1917-18 an astonishing twenty-seven airfields were established across America largely equipped with Curtiss JN4 Jenny trainers and it was on these that Campbell learned to fly. On 1 March 1918 he arrived at the 94th Aero Squadron at Villeneuve-les-Vertus on the Marne, still waiting for their aircraft. On 19 March, flying Nieuport 28s, they crossed German lines for the first time. Less than a month later Campbell and Lieutenant Alan Winslow were on alert when two low-flying aircraft were reported. Within four minutes both had been brought down in flames near to the squadron's new airfield at Toul. Campbell was first and Winslow only seconds later but here was real proof that American air power had arrived.

On 6 June Campbell attacked a Rumpler and a bullet from the observer's machine-gun struck his cockpit fairing, fragmented and ripped into his back. Campbell managed to get back within French lines but he was out of the fighting. He returned to the 94th just a few days before the Armistice after a long stay in hospitals. He was promoted Captain and stayed on in the Air Service until early 1919, leaving to join a famous shipping line. From there he built a distinguished career in civil aviation.

# Edward Vernon Rickenbacker

FLYING a fighter aircraft of World War I demanded a great affinity between man and machine. To become an ace or even to survive at all, this affinity had to become almost instinctive. From all over Europe young men with a delight in things mechanical were drawn towards the war in the air but some very successful wartime pilots such as Charles Nungesser and the Belgian Jan Olieslagers had already proved their affinity with speed and power as champion racing drivers.

Edward Vernon Rickenbacker had all the right qualifications. In 1912 he resigned his job as salesman for the staid Columbus Buggy Company and was hired by the Mason Automobile Company of Des Moines. The chief engineer was another young man with a genius for machinery named Frederick Deusenberg. From mechanic Rickenbacker became Deusenberg's star driver and soon he was making a dazzling reputation on the track for himself and the cars. His rise to fame was rapid and when he switched leading a team of Maxwell Specials, their success was making him a rich man. In 1916 Louis Coatalen the director of the British Sunbeam Motor Works approached him with a proposition to test Sunbeam cars on US circuits.

In late 1916 Rickenbacker stepped ashore at Liverpool and was promptly put back on board the ship, prohibited entry as a suspected German spy (an over-eager journalist had floated a story that the dashing racing driver was in fact the remittance-man son of a Prussian baron). Coatalen at last got

him out and a sojourn at the Savoy Hotel erased the memory of his interrogation. The serious business began at the famous racing track at Brooklands. There in his own words he 'strolled round and looked with admiration and envy at the airplanes and the young men—actually youths just out of school—who were learning to fly them'.

On the American declaration of war Rickenbacker proposed an élite squadron along the lines of the French *escadrille sportif*, but to be composed entirely of racing drivers. The United States had enough problems organizing an Air Service at all, without such melodramatic gestures, and Rickenbacker's suggestion was shelved. Once in France Colonel Billy Mitchell took Rickenbacker on as his personal chauffeur. Driving Mitchell's 'flashy Packard' even at thunderous speeds down narrow French roads was not Rickenbacker's idea of fighting and in August 1917 he successfully applied to be transferred to one of the first Aviation Instruction Centres of the AEF established in France at Tours, but with his expert knowledge of engines he was then posted to the 3rd AIC at Issoudon as Chief Engineering Officer. Meanwhile he managed to obtain advanced flying training and take an aerial gunnery course at Cazeau. He took to flying easily, in spite of cracking up the undercarriage on his first solo.

Meanwhile the USAAS was experiencing immense difficulties in getting trained pilots in new machines actually into action. Their first airfields were wretched quagmires of churned-up mud and

The United States had to build an operational air force in Europe from a standing start. Here riggers train on old Nieuport airframes. Rickenbacker began his service career as Chief Engineering Officer at the vast 3rd Aviation Instruction Centre at Issoudun

**Captain Edward Vernon
Rickenbacker, October
1918**

their training aircraft antique. France and Britain could barely spare enough aircraft and America's own aviation industry was not yet even in first gear. At last the first American air combat units began to be organized in early 1918. The veterans of the *Lafayette Escadrille* were belatedly commissioned into the US Army and from their ranks three out of the four Pursuit Groups that saw service found commanders.

On 4 March 1918 Lieutenant Rickenbacker reported to the newly formed 94th Aero Squadron commanded by *Escadrille SPA 65* veteran John W Huffer and soon to be commanded by *Lafayette*-veteran Raoul Lufbery. Their Nieuport 28s arrived soon afterwards, but their neighbours, the 95th Aero Squadron, had their aircraft delivered minus machine-guns, and US-built Marlins had to be rapidly made available.

On 18 March 1918 in the Toul sector Rickenbacker in company with Major Lufbery and Lieutenant Douglas Campbell made the first American patrol over enemy lines. Rickenbacker was older than the bulk of his fellow pilots and fought his war in a cool calculating way that paid off handsomely. Within six weeks he had his first victory shooting down an Albatros two-seater over Pont-à-Mousson on 29 April. By 30 May he had shot down his fifth enemy aircraft making him an ace. Rickenbacker was made a Flight Commander but in June he developed an ear infection which it seemed would end his flying career. He spent July and August recovering from an operation in a Paris hospital and was grounded until 14 September.

Meanwhile by the end of June the First Pursuit Group was gathered south of Château-Thierry and the squadron was re-equipped with Spads. Rickenbacker took to the aircraft with delight. With its V-8 water-cooled engine, speed and rate of climb, the Spad was like a racing car with wings. It was something he could understand. On the 12th Rickenbacker re-opened his score and on the 15th shot down two aircraft on the same patrol. His score began to rise steadily and by the end of October he had twenty-six confirmed victories, not just two-seaters but including Fokker DVIIs. He ended the war on that score and returned to the United States as a national hero. He had two loves—automobiles and aircraft—and he split his subsequent career between the two. In 1921 he launched the Rickenbacker Motor Company and its first product the Rickenbacker sports sedan featured the Hat in the Ring of the 94th Aero Squadron as its radiator mascot. The Rickenbacker marque however was soon to join other names like Templar and Jordan Speedboy in automotive obscurity; Rickenbacker himself counted 1600 defunct US-marques in his 1967 autobiography. In 1928 he joined General Motors. In 1935 he was appointed General Manager of Eastern Airlines and continued to combine a distinguished business and public life with a native American genius for machines throughout his subsequent career.

## Spad SXIII

When the US Army Air Service came to France it had more pilots than aircraft and had to go shopping for whatever was available. Two hundred and ninety-seven of the troublesome Nieuport Nie 28s were purchased, a type which the French would not accept into service and these formed the main equipment when the Americans began combat patrols proper in March 1918. Those pilots who had flown Spad SVIIIs, also in USAAS service, knew which was the better aircraft but in February 1918 the US Purchasing Commission had already ordered eight hundred and ninety-three of a type which was truly in the first rank of contemporary fighters—the new Spad SXIII.

It was a development by Louis Bêchereau of the Spad SVII, via the unsuccessful Spad SXII, armed with a cannon mounted between the cylinder blocks of the Hispano-Suiza V-8 engine. Armed with two .303-in Vickers machine-guns and with an excellent rate of speed and climb, the fast and hard-hitting Spad SXIII was immensely popular with American pilots from July when they began reaching the Pursuit Squadrons. Two models of Spad SXIII were built, the first, powered by the 200-hp Hispano-Suiza 8BEa, reached over 134 mph, and the second, 235-hp 8BEc-powered model, reached 138.5 mph, very high speeds for their day.

Marc Birkigt's masterpiece, the Hispano-Suiza *monobloc* V-8

| | |
|---|---|
| Manufacturer: | Société Pour Aviation et ses Derivées |
| Powerplant: | Hispano-Suiza 8BEa V-12, 200-hp |
| Span: | 8.08 m (26 ft 4⅜ in) |
| Length: | 6.22 m (20 ft 4⅞ in) |
| Max. take-off weight: | 820 kg (1808 lb) |
| Max. speed: | 215 kmh (134 mph) at 2000 m (6562 ft) |
| Ceiling: | 6650 m (21,818 ft) |
| Armament: | 2 x Vickers .303-in |

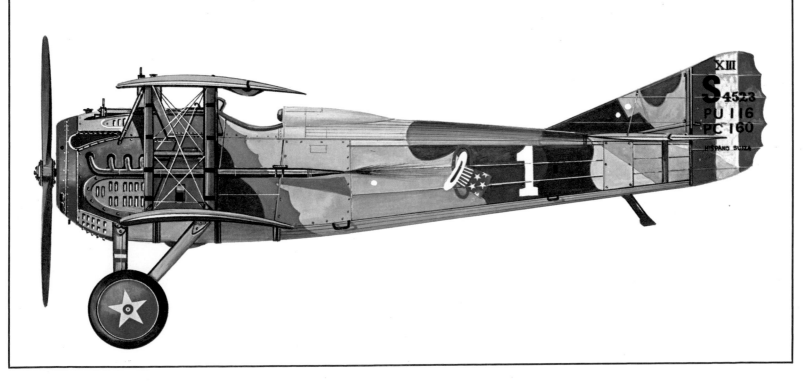

# William George Barker

WILLIAM Barker was a survivor. He survived the Flanders trenches of 1915, and even survived serving as an aerial gunner in the back seat of a BE2d. In October 1918, with the Armistice only two weeks away, he survived an attack by a complete *Jagdgeschwader* of Fokker DVIIs before crashing severely wounded into the British lines. He was to be claimed at last in an air crash on 12 March 1930 at Uplands Field outside Ottawa in his native Canada.

He was born at Dauphin, Manitoba on 3 November 1894 and joined the Canadian Mounted Rifles on the outbreak of war and became a machine-gunner. From Shorncliffe Camp in September 1915 they were despatched to France in time for the Second Battle of Ypres where this nominal cavalry regiment fought as infantry. Like many other trench-bound Canadians he successfully applied for a transfer to the RFC and was accepted as an Air Mechanic, posted to No 9 Squadron RFC at Allonville. His first combat flight was as a Lewis-gunner in a BE2d and, in contrast to the usual practice during the 'Fokker scourge', he sent an enemy single-seater down in flames in March 1916 during the Battle of Neuve-Chapelle. By 2 April he was commissioned as a Second Lieutenant and came back from leave as an observer to No 4 Squadron on the Somme where his skill and pugnaciousness with a machine-gun still in the back seat of a BE2d once again showed themselves.

Late in 1916 he was sent back to England for pilot training and again showed an exceptional aptitude, soloing after only fifty-five minutes of dual instruction and getting his wings in January 1917.

The same month he was back in France as a Captain flying RE8s and even managing to shoot down an enemy aircraft with this unforgiving machine. Later he was nearly killed when his badly combat-damaged RE8, A3598, stood on its nose in a crash-landing. He had survived months of intense and deadly air fighting flying aircraft on which the crew casualty rate was very high. In September 1917 he was called back to England to impart some of this invaluable experience as an instructor.

Barker was not pleased. He applied for a transfer to a scout squadron and found himself doing more flight training but this time on Sopwith Camels. The qualities of this aircraft came to the experienced Canadian as a revelation. In late September he was posted to No 28 Squadron forming at Yatesbury with Camels and by 2 October they were in France ending up at Droglandt. Two weeks later while attacking troop concentrations on the Ypres-Menin road, his 'A' Flight was attacked by ten Albatros DVs. Barker shot down two, but narrowly escaped himself and two of his flight were lost.

His score of enemy aircraft destroyed stood at five, when No 28 Squadron was transferred to join VII Brigade RFC in Northern Italy as part of Sir Hubert Plumer's British Expeditionary Forces bolstering the sagging Italian forces still reeling from the great Austro-German victory of Caporetto in October 1917. As a measure of this Front's importance Camel squadrons 28, 45 and 66 were sent.

The Italian Front was no sideshow and Barker took his war right to the enemy, attacking balloons, forward trenches, and even the Austrian Army HQ at San Vito. Early in 1918 Barker was disappointed when he was not given command of 28 Squadron on the posting of its old CO and he applied for a transfer back to the Western Front. Instead he went to No 66 Squadron, still in Italy, but this 'artist with a pair of Vickers' as a contemporary described him took his Camel, B6313, with him. There was no shortage of missions including piloting a Caproni bomber behind the Austrian lines to drop an Italian *informatori* by Salvatore parachute. His score painted in white stripes on the Camel like a sniper notching his rifle stock climbed higher throughout the summer. Between 17 April and 13 July while the Battle of the Piave was at its height he shot down 16 enemy aircraft.

In July 1918 Barker was promoted Major and he was at last given command of a squadron. His decorations by now included the DSO and Bar, MC and two Bars, *Croix de Guerre* and the Italian *Valore Militare*. He was twenty-four years old. 139 Squadron flew Bristol Fighters and Barker was forbidden to take his Camel with him, however by having his beloved B6313 sent back to 'Z' Flight's Aircraft Depot and then 'temporarily attached' to 139 squadron he kept his single-seater and only rarely flew 'Brisfits' himself. In March 1918 the German squadrons were withdrawn from the Italian Front for their last offensive effort in the West. The Austro-Hungarian *Jagdkompanien* were worn down during June and July and the loss of Frank Linke-Crawford (mis-reportedly to Barker himself) was a severe blow to morale. By the autumn the Italians had recovered and the Austrians were finished.

In September 1918 he was recalled to command a school of air fighting at Hounslow, west of London, but before taking over he requested a tour of duty of the Western Front arguing that he would be better qualified to teach the tactics of air fighting if he had experience of the newest generation of German front-line opposition. He got his way and was attached to No 201 Squadron flying Camels, although Barker himself was given a brand-new Sopwith Snipe, a formidable fighting machine powered by a 230-hp Bentley BR2 rotary. In its short time at the front-line the Snipe fulfilled its

*Left:* Major Barker in Italy in the cockpit of his Sopwith F1 Camel. Like a sniper notching his rifle stock, Barker added a white flash to the struts to tally his rising score.
*Above:* Barker's bullet-ridden Sopwith Snipe, reassembled after his epic fight with over sixty German aircraft

**Major William George Barker RAF, Italy, summer 1918.**
In March 1918 dress regulations for the RAF were announced in Air Force Memorandum No 2 (*see* Appendix 2). This was prefaced with the words: 'The uniform for Officers, Warrant Officers, NCOs and men of the Air Force has now been approved. Khaki will be worn as Service Dress for the period of the war, after which uniform of the same pattern, but of light blue cloth, will be substituted as early as possible.

'This blue uniform may be worn by Officers during the war as Mess Kit. This is purely optional'

design function of air superiority most efficiently. Barker was delighted with it but at last on 27 October he set out to fly Snipe E8102 to Hounslow.

Over the Forêt de Mormal he spotted a Rumpler CVII reconnaissance aircraft above him and, with the Bentley puffing at its maximum ceiling, he climbed to 20,000 feet. After three passes the two-seater's observer was dead. The pilot got out by parachute as the aircraft began to break up. As Barker followed the Rumpler down an unseen Fokker DrI had locked on to his tail and put a spurt of bullets into the Snipe, one piercing Barker's thigh. The Canadian corrected a spin by instinct and as the Fokker overshot, the Snipe's two Vickers replied and the DrI went down in flames. His right leg was useless and the Snipe banked on full left rudder to put the wounded Barker flying head-on into the full strength of *Jagdgeschwader* 3 whose four *Jagdstaffeln* were in a stepped formation of over 60 Fokker DVIIs ranged from 8000 feet. For Barker who had fought and survived so long, there seemed no escape.

Barker flew straight through the huge formation but fifteen Fokkers attacked him in clusters of five. Barker kept the Snipe turning and firing and got a DVII as his forty-ninth victim. After a few minutes of this flailing mêlée the Snipe had taken over 300 bullets and Barker took another bullet in the left leg making it almost impossible for him to operate the rudder. Still he hung on but at last fainted from loss of blood, the Snipe going into a falling-leaf spin for 6000 feet. The rush of cold air revived him but he awoke in the blood-spattered cockpit to find himself in the midst of the lowest of the four *Jastas*, with his original tormentors still on his tail.

There could be no way out but, almost by instinct, he went into his fighting circle, cocked the twin Vickers again and took another Fokker DVII before he was hit in the elbow and again fainted. He went into another spin which the swarming frustrated Fokkers could not follow. Once more he came out of it to find a black-crossed aircraft in his sight and shot it out of the sky. The enraged *Jagdgeschwader* withdrew to lick its wounds and Barker's bullet riddled Snipe flew earthwards with its terribly wounded pilot just keeping control with his left arm and barely conscious.

Skimming the ravaged ground at 90 mph, the Snipe's undercarriage at last hit the earth, tore away and the remains of wing and fuselage went bounding on for a further two hundred yards. Miraculously the aircraft did not explode and men of the Highland Light Infantry who had witnessed the epic fight from the ground pulled the half-dead Barker from the cockpit. In the crash itself he sustained nothing more than a broken nose.

For ten days he lay unconscious in hospital in Rouen. When he finally regained consciousness he was told that he had accounted for four aircraft officially and two more listed as probables going down out of control. He was also told that he had won the Victoria Cross.

## Sopwith Camel

Where the Sopwith Pup was a pilot's delight, the Camel was a very different proposition. With its high-powered rotary engine, and its forward-placed centre of gravity, it was tricky to fly—but in the hands of an experienced pilot it was unbeatably manoeuvrable and the Camel accounted for more enemy aircraft destroyed than any other Allied type.

The prototype nurtured from Herbert Smith's drawing board was passed by the Sopwith's experimental department on 22 December 1916 and like many of Sopwith's products it was built first for the Admiralty. The prototype had a 110-hp Clerget 9Z rotary and was tested at Brooklands on 26 February 1917, and a small experimental batch of test aircraft soon followed, as did RNAS and RFC production orders.

The FI/3 was the first true production prototype powered by a 130-hp Clerget 9B. First deliveries were for the RNAS, and Naval Squadrons 3, 4, 6, 9 and 10 were equipped with the Camel by the end of the summer No 4 becoming the first operational Camel squadron in July 1917. The RFC placed concurrent orders, No 70 Squadron being the first RFC recipient with many more following.

Camels were built with a range of engines including Clerget 9B, Bentley BRI, Gnome Monosoupape, and Le Rhône 9J and were fitted with twin Vickers machine-guns and synchronizing gear according to engine type.

By the end of 1917 well over a thousand Sopwith Camels had been delivered and sub-variants were being tested for shipboard use (2FI) and as armoured trench fighters (TFI) and others were impressed for Home Defence duties with twin Lewis guns above the upper wing centre section replacing the standard twin Vickers.

When William Barker was posted to No 28 Squadron equipping with Camels in September 1917, he was then used only to lumbering RE8s. Capt J Mitchell who commanded another Flight in the same squadron wrote, 'He had no experience with rotary engines and was a little ham-fisted on the Camel controls. Whilst one could not say he was a good pilot he certainly made up for this in his shooting.' It was a typical pilot's introduction to the unforgiving machine but once he understood the Camel's vices, Barker became a brilliant exponent of its qualities. The Camel spun very quickly, had a very sensitive elevator control and was very fast on right-hand turns due to the gyroscopic effects of the heavy rotary-engine and the short fuselage. Barker took Camel B6313 with him to Italy and scored the first British victory on the Italian Front with this machine on 29 November 1917.

| | |
|---|---|
| Manufacturer: | The Sopwith Aviation Co and sub-contractors |
| Powerplant: | 110-hp Clerget 9Z, 110-hp Clerget 9B, 130-hp Clerget 9Bf, 140-hp Gnome Monosoupape, 100-hp Bentley BRI, 150-hp Gnome Monosoupape, 150-hp Le Rhône 9R, 9-cyl rotary engines |
| Span: | 28 ft (8.5 m) |
| Length: | 18 ft 9 in (5.68 m) |
| Max. take-off weight: | 1482 lb (Clerget) (672 kg) |
| Max. speed: | 104.5 mph at 10,000 ft (130-hp Clerget) (158 kmh) |
| Ceiling: | 19,000 ft (5791 m) |
| Armament: | 2 x Vickers .303-in |

# Appendix 1 : Fighter Armament

*Right:* Overwing Lewis on an SE5a's Foster mount. Changing drums in a slipstream required tremendous exertion by the pilot

Stripped air-cooled Austrian Schwarzlose on an experimental test ring mounting

Parabellum lMG '14, standard rear defence for German two-seaters

By 1914 the water-cooled machine-gun based on the mechanically-actuated Maxim principle was a comparatively reliable and sophisticated weapon (at least compared with contemporary aircraft). The Vickers Mk VI of 1912 was not declared obsolete in British Army service until 1968 and the German Maxim M '08 was equally long-lived. The problem of using these weapons in the air was their weight.

The brass-jacketed Vickers-Maxim of 1913 weighed 57 lb. The Vickers experimental pintle-mount for aircraft of the same year weighed 50 lb. The spare parts case weighed another 15 lb, ammunition 30 lb and water coolant 10 lb, the whole adding up to more than the weight of a third crew member. This weapon which armed some early Vickers FB5s only fired at 380 rpm and delivered a weight of fire of 9.5 lb per minute. Furthermore low-powered engines meant that early 'fighting aircraft' carrying this weight penalty and of necessity a crew of two had little chance of catching an unarmed fast 'scout' single-seater, which for a period enjoyed the kind of immunity later exemplified by the fast unarmed wooden DH Mosquito of World War II.

On the eve of war the newly developed gas operated machine-gun seemed to offer the ideal lightweight aircraft weapon. The Lewis gun weighed only 27 lb and was first used in successful air-firing tests in America in 1912. In September two Belgians successfully flew a Lewis armed Farman at Brasschaet and in November 1913 the same Belgians demonstrated their techniques to the RFC at Aldershot who were suitably impressed. By 1915 BSA in Britain were building large quantities of the US-designed weapon and the Lewis was easily adapted for airborne use by replacing the stock with a spade-grip and later by deleting the aluminium cooling fins and jacket altogether, the gun certainly functioning better in the dust-free aerial environment than in the trenches, cooled by the force-draught of the slipstream.

In late summer 1916 the two tier 47 round drum was supplemented by a four-tier 97 round drum and combined with the fast slewing Scarff No 2 Ring Mount of the same year the Lewis became the standard weapon for protecting the tails of British, French and later American two-seaters.

The French Hotchkiss was also air-cooled but its strip feed and the integral breech block and firing pin made it unsuitable for airborne use or synchronization, factors which hampered the first Garros/Saulnier synchronization experiments. The Model 1908 was however successfully modified as a flexible observer's weapon with a drum feed.

By 1915 the tractor aircraft with the propeller in front, whether monoplane or biplane, was certainly the fastest and most manoeuvrable style of airframe. Equally important it was now being recognized that these were the very qualities necessary for a military aircraft to survive in an increasingly hostile environment—and undependable stability. But without higher-powered engines to lift a greater useful load and without an effective method of firing a machine-gun along the line of flight, 'fighting duties' still devolved on clumsy two-seat pusher types like the FB5 or the more conventional German C-type two-seaters ordered early in 1915 with a Parabellum machine-gun for the observer.

Designers meanwhile experimented frantically with unconventional airframe layouts, including bizzare 'pulpit' fighters such as the Spad A2 and BE9 and multi-engined 'battle aircraft' but weapon research was progressing along two lines to put them out of their agony. The first was modification of the sustained fire belt-fed Maxim machine-gun to achieve lighter weight. The second was the perfection of interrupter or synchronizing gear enabling these weapons to fire through the rotating blades of a tractor airscrew, as fixed line of flight weapons, yet be positioned so that a single-seater pilot could tend them in action.

The Deutsche Waffen and Munitionsfabrik of Berlin had been working on a lightweight machine-gun based on the

Maxim principle since 1909. In 1911 their 7.92-mm 'Parabellum' appeared which dispensed with the water jacket replacing it with a perforated casing allowing a free flow of slipstreaming air. As an observer's weapon, the *leichte* MG '14 as it was standardized had a pistol grip and stock, a drum magazine and was compact and wieldy weighing some 18 lb less than the standard Maxim.

The same principle of stripping down a standard water-cooled Maxim type was applied successfully to the German MG '08 manufactured at the Spandau arsenal (lMG '08/15) and the Vickers Mk VI (Vickers Mk I), both guns with their mechanical actuation and belt feeds being suitable for adaptation as synchronized sustained-fire weapons.

The story of the 'Garros wedges' has been told on page 23. When the remains of Garros's device were reassembled and both its crudity and importance were made obvious, Anthony Fokker had a better weapon to work with (the air-cooled belt-fed Parabellum, lMG '14 and later the lMG '08/15) and almost certainly knowledge of previous unsuccessful attempts to make an operable interrupter gear from which to draw conclusions. He was also amply assisted by the engineers Heber, Leimberger and the ex-watchmaker Luebbe on the Schwerin staff to get his system working.

The first proposal to mount a rigid machine-gun firing along the line of flight of an aircraft (in this case a pusher) was made by the German August Euler and patented on 23 July 1910. In 1912 the Swiss engineer Franz Schneider conducted ambitious but unsuccessful aircraft armament experiments featuring hollow airscrew shafts and offset gearing of engine and tractor airscrew. In 1913 he patented a synchronizing gear in the name of LVG and in the first month of the war his proposals were published in a German aviation magazine.

In early 1915 Schneider designed LVG's own *Eindecker I*, a two-seater with a fixed forward firing weapon and a ring mounted flexible machine-gun for the observer. The LVGEI prototype was wrecked on its way to the front for operational trials when the badly fitted lower wing struts collapsed.

In January 1914 the receiver for the bankrupt Deperdussin concern filed a broad outline proposal for a synchronizing device including the notion of armouring the airscrew. Nieuport-Macchi in Italy filed a more specific patent for such a device in February 1914 and Robert Esnault-Petrie again in France patented an *Avion de Guerre* proposal in March 1914 featuring an armoured crew cabin, flexible rear firing weapon and a fixed machine-gun firing forward through the airscrew arc.

Morane-Saulnier were granted a patent for the armoured airscrew system on 5 February 1915.

A Russian naval lieutenant named Poplavko reportedly designed a synchronizing gear as early as 1913 and later fitted it to a Maxim-armed Sikorsky S.16. In November 1914 Engineer Smyslov and Lt Cdr Dybovski of the Imperial Russian Navy built an improved version, and, in late 1915 Dybovski brought his ideas to Britain on a technical mission and together with W/O F W Scarff of the Admiralty Air Department they produced the Scarff-Dibovski gear ordered into production by the Admiralty and fitted first to RNAS Sopwith 1½-Strutters, later handed over to RFC. The Sopwiths of the Third Flight of No 70 Squadron had the gear fitted before they went to France on 30 July 1916.

The first British aircraft equipped with a synchronizing gear to arrive in France was a Bristol Scout operational on 25 March 1916 (two weeks *before* an E-type was captured intact and its secret revealed). The Scout was equipped with the Vickers-Challenger gear patented in December 1915 and ordered by the War Office for RFC aircraft. Other British developed synchronizing gears of 1916 were the Sopwith-Kauper and Arsiad gears (devised in the field by Maj A V Bettington OC Aeroplane Repair Section No 1 Aircraft Depot —hence the acronym), and the Ross gear which worked on the Fokker 'interrupter' principle.

These British 'synchronizing' gears worked by cam and push rod like Fokker's with all the concomitant necessary fine-tuning and tendency to jam but differed in allowing the gun to fire when the bullet's path was clear rather than preventing the gun from firing when the line of fire was blocked by the passing airscrew blade. All these devices cut down the firepower. The Vickers Mk I had a theoretical rate of fire of 800 rpm and a weight of fire at 2 lb in a six second burst—enough severely to damage an opponent's wood and canvas airframe—but the Ross gear for example brought the rpm down to a leisurely 300. Collishaw described the sound of a mechanically synchronized single Vickers as like the 'put-put of a worn out motorcycle engine', and many an enemy pilot caught in a British or French gunsight escaped when the trigger was squeezed either because the guns failed to deliver a fatal weight of fire or the cams, rods and bell-cranks simply jammed.

Malfunctioning interrupter gear was said to have caused Max Immelmann's fatal crash and, in May 1916, Albert Ball nearly repeated the experience in a Vickers-Challenger equipped Bristol Scout. Like several other British pilots and French pilots Ball preferred an overwing mounted Lewis on its curved Foster mount not just because it suited his method of attack from below but it could deliver 2 lb of fire in a 97 round eight second burst without interruption—its only drawback being the drum feed.

A synchronization gear was developed early in 1916 for the Lewis in France, by *Sergent-Mecanicien* Alkan intended to equip RFC Morane Type Ns although hardly used operationally. Another forward-firing Lewis device was the Cadroy-Cordonnier gear of late 1915 which featured a small bar rotating in front of the gun at the same time as the airscrew and acting in the same way as the armoured deflectors of the Garros device yet permitting an airscrew of much greater efficiency but the arrival of true synchronizing gears ended its development.

A far improved British synchronizing gear was demonstrated on a BE2c in August 1916. It was developed by a Rumanian mining engineer named Georges Constantinesco in partnership with a British artillery officer, Major G C Colley, and put into production by Vickers. It worked hydraulically, like a car's braking system, and improved the rate of fire, eliminated much maintenance and was adaptable to any engine, gun or number of guns. It was manufactured and fitted to Allied aircraft as quickly as possible—6000 sets were manufactured between March and December 1917 and 20,000 in 1918, the first Constantinesco-equipped aircraft, DH4s of No 55 Squadron RFC arriving in France in March 1917.

Parallel development was taking place in ammunition technology—incendiary, tracer, explosive and armour piercing rounds all being developed in rifle calibre. The specialist demands of anti-Zeppelin and anti-balloon warfare produced several ingenious ammunition types and the spectacular if short range Le Prieur rocket, used with considerable success to knock out German observation balloons on the eve of the Somme offensive. Armour plate began to appear on ground attack machines on both sides as did an increasingly lethal range of air to ground attack devices.

Gun sights progressively improved and detail developments such as disintegrating link belts, muzzle boosters and electrical breech heaters much improved the Vickers performance and rate of fire while the Germans incorporated low ammunition indicators, and remote operating levers on twin Spandau installations facilitating reloading and the clearing of jams or ammunition failures. Accessibility of the guns remained a prime design consideration. Norman Macmillan recalled the 'Feroto' patent jam-clearer issued with the Sopwith Camel's twin Vickers—but added sardonically that a hammer was more effective.

Fighters of the 1916 generation such as the Sopwith Pup and Fokker DIII with their single mechanically synchronized machine-gun, sacrificed firepower for manoeuvrability. With the development of higher powered engines, the two-gun fighter could now hold its own. The Albatros DI of autumn 1916 employed a 150-hp Benz BzIII water-cooled engine of unprecedented power, and carried the load of two Spandau machine-guns without loss of performance. Because of the high wing loading manoeuvrability suffered marginally but it could attack, put in a fatal burst of fire, and escape at a speed which gave it a crucial edge in combat.

The Albatros DI set a pattern followed in an upward curve of engine-power and firepower until the aircraft of 1918 were true multi-gun fighters as manoeuvrable and fast as their much lighter predecessors. The 80-hp Le Rhône powered Sopwith Pup of 1916 weighed only 787 lb empty and its single Vickers had a theoretical weight of fire of 20 lb per minute. The 200-hp Hispano-Suiza powered Sopwith Dolphin of 1918 had a loaded weight of over 2000 lb and its twin Vickers and two upward firing Lewises had a theoretical weight of fire of 75 lb per minute.

With such fragile targets batteries of rifle calibre machine-guns were normally considered adequate for air fighting but the installation of large calibre weapons, able to destroy an opponent in one shot, was pioneered in France before the war. The earliest installation of such weapons was a short barrelled Hotchkiss *Canon de 37-mm*, mounted in a Voisin pusher in 1913. The big Breguet BUC and BLC twin boom pushers of 1915-16 were designed specifically to carry the 37-mm weapon although these *Avions Canon* were really too slow to engage enemy aircraft, concentrating on ground attack work.

There were many other wartime schemes for cannon armament including the extraordinary Dufaux fighter reportedly built at the personal request of Charles Nungesser. It was a tractor biplane with two sideways mounted rotary engines driving a single common airscrew, with a 37-mm cannon lying between them and firing through the propeller boss. In Britain the Royal Aircraft Factory's FE6 of 1914 was designed from the outset as a carrier for the Coventry Ordnance Works 1-pdr quick-firer, and the FE2b from the same stable was modified to carry Vickers 1-pdr QFs or .45-in Maxims but again these were really ground attack weapons. Anti-Zeppelin defence spawned a variety of interesting weapons in Britain and special machines to carry them—the Davis recoilless gun and the Vickers Crayford rocket-gun being two, but much more success was gained with batteries of overwing Lewis guns firing incendiary ammunition.

A much more significant portent of future developments was the Spad SXII-Ca.1 with a 37-mm Hotchkiss cannon mounted in the Vee of the Hispano-Suiza engine. Three hundred were built but they were largely unsuccessful, the heavy recoil throwing the aircraft off balance and the fumes of the cordite propellant filling the cockpit.

Twin CC-synchronized Vickers on a Sopwith Camel of No 203 Squadron RAF. The breeches were enclosed in the aluminium hump which earned the Camel its name

# Appendix 2: Uniforms of the Royal Air Force 1918-19

On 29 November 1917 the Royal Air Force (Constitution) Bill received Royal Assent. On 1 April 1918, as the fighting in France was at its height, the world's first fully independent air force came formally into being. From that date all the old RNAS squadrons were renumbered—No 1 (Naval) Squadron became No 201 Squadron Royal Air Force, No 2 (Naval), No 202 and so on. Further all RNAS officers who transferred to the RAF received Army ranks.

The precious and hard won traditions of the Royal Flying Corps and Royal Naval Air Service had to be reconstituted in the new force. The question of uniforms was as delicate as it had been in 1912-13.

Air Force Memorandum No 2 published in March 1918 set out the regulations for the new service. Although a new light blue uniform had been approved, khaki would be worn as service dress for the duration and it would not be made compulsory until the existing RFC and RNAS uniforms had worn out.

The khaki service dress incorporated features from RFC and RNAS tradition but owed much more to the naval khaki uniform than the RFC maternity jacket. The cap was the RNAS khaki version with a new cap badge—the eagle surmounted by a Tudor crown between entwined laurel leaves. The tunic remained basically the same as the army pattern but without shoulder straps and incorporating a self-belt, to be worn with a khaki shirt and black tie.

For officers rank was indicated by . . .

| | |
|---|---|
| Second lieutenant | No lace, but bird and crown on both sleeves where lace would otherwise be. On the cap 1 upright bar on each side of the badge.[1] |
| Lieutenant | 1 row of distinction lace surmounted by bird and crown. Cap: 1 upright bar on each side of the badge. |
| Captain | 2 rows of distinction lace surmounted by bird and crown. Cap: 2 upright bars on each side of the badge. |
| Major | $2\frac{1}{2}$ rows of distinction lace surmounted by bird and crown. Cap: 1 row of gold oak leaves on the peak. |
| Lieutenant Colonel | 3 rows of distinction lace surmounted by bird and crown. Cap as for Major. |
| Colonel | 4 rows of distinction lace surmounted by bird and crown. Cap as for Major. |
| Brigadier General | 1 broad row of $2\frac{1}{2}$ in. (63·5 mm) lace surmounted by bird and crown. Cap: 2 rows of gold oak leaves on peak |
| Major General | 1 broad row and 1 ordinary row of distinction lace surmounted by bird and crown. Cap as for Brigadier General. |
| Lieutenant General | 1 broad row and 2 ordinary rows of distinction lace surmounted by bird and crown. Cap as for Brigadier General. |
| General | 1 broad row and 3 ordinary rows of distinction lace surmounted by bird and crown. Cap as for Brigadier General. |

Other ranks wore a single-breasted khaki tunic with stand and fall collar. Immediately below the shoulder seam the ROYAL FLYING CORPS embroidered title was replaced by a bird device in red silk (changed to light blue in July). Wireless technicians wore a hand and thunderbolt device below the bird. Rank was indicated by. . . .

| | |
|---|---|
| Warrant officer 1st class | Royal Arms in light blue silk embroidery, worn on both sleeves of jacket and greatcoat below the elbow (by AMO 617) |
| Warrant officer 2nd class (quartermaster sergeant) | Crown in light blue worsted embroidery on both sleeves below the elbow |
| Flight sergeant | 3 chevrons and crown of light blue worsted embroidery |
| Sergeant | 3 chevrons of light blue worsted embroidery |
| Corporal | 2 chevrons of light blue worsted embroidery |
| 1st class mechanic | 2-bladed propeller of light blue worsted embroidery, worn immediately underneath the bird. |

King's regulations for the Royal Air Force further indicated that hair would be worn short and the upper lip would be shaved.

The officers of the new-born RAF accepted the new uniforms somewhat grudgingly as a break with precious traditions. In Italy, Norman Macmillan remembered the reaction. 'Many of them, because of past association, others from economy because they were poorly paid, continued to wear their original uniforms until the end of the war'.[2] And this reaction was certainly duplicated in France as photographs and records testify.

Because of this resistance to change the Air Ministry ordered that promotion in the new service would not permit an officer to wear the badges of an equivalent naval or army rank on naval or army uniforms. An RAF officer without the new uniform would not be able to display his new rank title—as a result the number of new RAF uniforms progressively increased. (Ratified in AMO 111 of April 24, 1918).

The light blue uniform caused much more of a stir. It was the same cut as the khaki tunic and could be bought and worn as mess dress for the duration of the war. Rank distinction lace was in gold braid, the whole to be worn with black shoes and a white wing collar and black tie. Norman Macmillan recalled its appearance in Italy, 'This uniform in a very pale sky blue gave its wearer a theatrical appearance that was quite unmilitarily startling when seen for the first time. It suited fair-haired men, but not men with black hair and a swarthy countenance. . . . Some pilots bought this light blue uniform. It was first seen in Italy when Joubert la Ferté returned from home leave and his re-entrance thus embellished, created a mild shock'.[3]

In fact the light blue uniform made only a fleeting appearance. An editorial in *Flight* in March 1918 summed up the position, 'At present any officer who is seen in its full glory, even for everyday plumage will be a *rara avis* owing to the non-existence and non-procurability of the particular cloth. Burberry's in this respect appear to have struck lucky and we doubt whether many others have any at all.' Khaki remained very much the RAF's colour until replaced in September 1919 by blue-grey.

---

[1]'The irreverent called these strips "bananas": they looked rather stupid additions and wearing them was soon ended by Air Ministry Order.'
(Norman Macmillan, *Offensive Patrol*, Jarrold's, 1975.)

[2,3]*Offensive Patrol*

1922 and Air Commodore Samson proudly displays his new rank and blue-grey RAF uniform introduced with the new rank titles in 1919. Samson's beard was strictly non-regulation. To his many wartime decorations is added the diagonally striped ribbon of the Distinguished Flying Cross introduced in December 1918

# Index